*A Microprocessor Course*

# A Microprocessor Course

*Mark E. Fohl*

PBI
a petrocelli book
new york / princeton

Printed in the United States
2 3 4 5 7 8 9 10

**Library of Congress Cataloging in Publication Data**

Fohl, Mark E
A microprocessor course.

Includes index.
1. Microprocessors. I. Title.
QA76.5.F53 001.6'4'04 79-4625
ISBN 0-89433-072-1

*affectionately dedicated to Claire, Karen and Barbara*

# *Contents*

# *Acknowledgments*

The author would like to express sincere gratitude to the Administration of Franklin University; to Ed Shaut, Judy Hoover, and the other fine people at the Worthington, Ohio office of Motorola Semiconductor Products; and to Grace Maurer for outstanding secretarial assistance.

# Preface

The microprocessor will be recognized as a major social development of the twentieth century. Electronics and manufacturing technologies have given an inexpensive computer to the world to use as it likes. Electronics designers have incorporated microprocessors into such products as automatic bank tellers and zig-zag sewing machines. But microprocessors have progressed from industry into the private home. For about the cost of a medium-quality stereo system, an individual can purchase a device which can entertain and educate, keep records and notes, monitor and control energy usage, plus do more upon command. This usage of the microprocessor naturally becomes the field of personal computing where the power and flexibility of the microprocessor is limited only by the imagination and skill of the user.

The need for understanding microprocessors is growing. Even if individuals choose not to enjoy or utilize a computer of their own, it behooves them to understand that which is becoming more popular around them and is having a great effect on their lives. The purpose of this book is to present the microprocessor, to explain its operation and application.

Although a knowledge of the binary number system and basic digital logic would be helpful as a prerequisite, both topics are covered early in the book. Much of the theory behind the microprocessor and its operation will be dealt with only briefly. Emphasis is on the hows, and the whys will be covered only enough to explain the hows. Both the hardware (electronic devices) and software (programming) aspects of microprocessors are presented. It is the opinion of the author, however, that the true power of the microprocessor lies in its programs. Software topics, therefore, are dealt with in more detail.

Chapters 1 through 3 introduce the concept of what a computer is and cover a few topics fundamental to all computers. Chapter 4 continues by presenting the microprocessor as a digital device, both as it operates internally and as it appears to the outside world. Chapters 5, 6, and 7 are a description of how data is handled internally. Chapter 7 covers concepts outside the microprocessor but essential to harnessing the power of the computer. Chapter 8 provides two examples of complete computer systems. Chapters 9 and 10 conclude by presenting related topics and trends and directions in the field of computing.

This book is based on the class notes of a highly successful two-trimester microprocessor course sequence taught by the author at Franklin University in Columbus, Ohio. The course is offered to upperclass undergraduate students, and special students from industry, many of whom already hold a bachelor's degree.

Mark Fohl

# 1 *Introduction*

The computer is a machine. It is not arcane, mystical, or sacred. It is not attended to by high priests or shamans. Like any other machine, its actions are totally dependent upon the instructions given it by its operator. By and large, computers can only add, make comparisons, and take alternate actions depending on the results. Unlike most machines, however, computers perform these simple actions very rapidly. Computers can perform hundreds of thousands, some even millions and tens of millions, of operations in a second. At these speeds, more complicated tasks take a little longer, but are still done in fractions of a second. It is perhaps because of this that computers have been accused of being able to think. This idea could never be further from the truth. Many of our thought processes, such as balancing a checkbook or playing tic-tac-toe, can be duplicated by performing a large number of simple operations. We are amazed that a computer can perform these tasks in such a seemingly short time. This amazement should be reckoned with because the thought process is a privilege that only we humans enjoy, and the thought process attributed to computers is just repetition of simple actions.

If the computer is indeed only a machine, how does it work? What is it made of? All computers, as we know them today, are electronic devices. Some have a very large number of components, and others a small number. All of them perform their operations on numbers. While some are very powerful and able to perform complex arithmetic operations on large numbers, others are very simple computers which operate on small numbers. All computers, however, have the same three basic subsystems: the *central processing unit* or CPU, *memory*, and *input/output* or I/O. The three subsystems are shown graphically in Figure 1.1.

The CPU is the most important subsystem. It is here that all the operations are performed, all the specific instructions are executed. All the additions are performed, all the comparisons and all the decisions are made in the CPU. The CPU, in addition, controls all the other devices in the computer system and is therefore the very heart of the computer.

The CPU, however, cannot act alone. Instructions executed by the

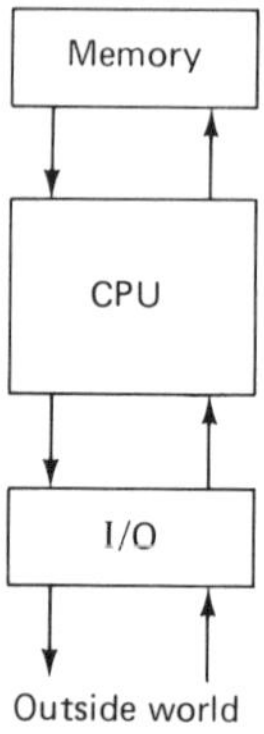


*FIGURE 1.1: Subsystems of a Computer*

CPU must come from a source outside the CPU. The instructions, taken in groups, are called *programs* and the programs reside in memory. In addition, much of the data operated upon by the CPU originates in memory and is later returned to memory following processing.

Both the CPU and memory, working together, would be ineffectual without input and output. I/O is the means by which the CPU communicates with the rest of the world. It is through the I/O that orders are given to the CPU and the results are then given by the CPU. I/O is also a means for storing and retrieving relatively large amounts of information, both programs and data.

The earliest computers were made of vacuum tubes. They required enormous amounts of power, took up a lot of space, were difficult to keep cool, and broke down often. The development of the transistor was one of a series of major breakthroughs in computer technology. Each tube was replaced by a transistor, and the computer required substantially less power and space, was easy to cool, and didn't fail nearly as often. Each of the disadvantages associated with computer circuitry was reduced by an order of magnitude or more. The next major breakthrough was the development of the integrated circuit in which several transistors and a few resistors and capacitors were all fabricated on one silicon wafer. This development again substantially reduced the disadvantages of the computer. This technology progressed rapidly to the point called large-scale integration (LSI) technology, wherein thousands of transistors could be fabricated on a single device. The natural result was to place an entire computer subsystem on one device. This is, in fact, the development of the microprocessor. The microprocessor is simply the CPU portion of a computer fabricated on one single electronic device.

Physically, a microprocessor is an integrated circuit electronic device. At fabrication, it is approximately one-quarter inch square with about 40 connections to the outside world. For simplicity and conformity with other electronic devices, the microprocessor is packaged in a dual in-line ceramic or plastic package (DIP) which measures about two inches by one-half inch, as shown in Figure 1.2. The package is called dual in-line because the connectors to the outside lie in two parallel lines at the sides of the package.

It must be emphasized that a microprocessor is only one of the three major subsystems within a computer. Even though the microprocessor by itself is an outstanding technological development, it is useless without memory and I/O. This is so much the case that the microprocessor, even though it is the most important subsystem, is physically only a very small part of a modern computer system and represents only a fraction of the total cost. Even with parallel developments in memory and I/O circuit technology, the microprocessor is still overwhelmed in many systems by the other LSI circuits in the system.

All applications for computers, large and small, can be roughly divided into three major categories: data processing, scientific computing, and monitoring and control.

Data processing applications can be characterized by relatively simple numerical operations with large volumes of input and output. Accounting, payroll, and other management information system (MIS) applications are examples. They generally involve only addition, subtraction, multiplication, and division, but they usually generate reams of paper or the equivalent. Another data processing example is an on-line reservation control system used by airlines and motel chains. Data is entered from and displayed on thousands of remote terminals, and the same data is stored and modified on large-volume mass storage devices. All of these operations require only very simple calculations.

Scientific computing is practically the direct opposite of data processing in that it involves very little input and output but tremendous amounts of internal calculation. It is sometimes referred to as "number crunching" because of all the internal operations. Examples of scientific computing include simulation of scientific and random processes, approximations to higher mathematical functions, and statistical applications.

The monitoring and control applications bear very little resemblance to the other two. These applications can be characterized by the monitoring of a particular process and taking an action accordingly. An example is a

*FIGURE 1.2: Microprocessor DIP*

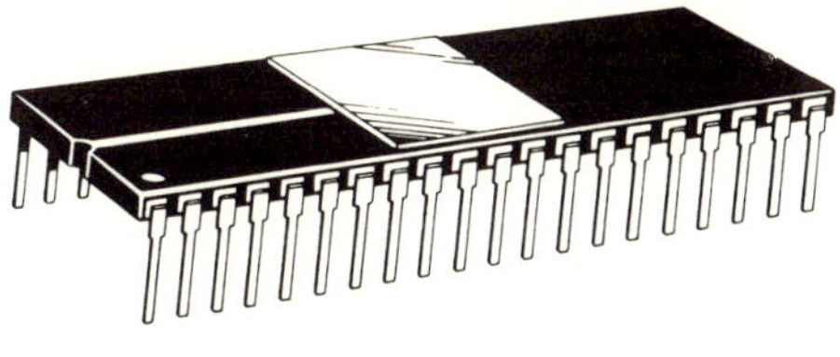

traffic control system in which the number of cars traveling through a part of a city is monitored. Depending upon the volume and direction of traffic, the frequency of traffic light changes is altered to allow the greatest flow of vehicles. Monitoring and control applications typically require very few numerical calculations and very little input and output as we know it. They do, however, require a lot of interface with the outside world and they often involve very intricate decision-making processes.

Although microprocessors have been and can be applied in all three categories of application, they have been resoundingly successful in the third category. In the past, most monitoring and control applications were implemented by random digital logic circuits. The relationship between the inputs and outputs was a function of the design of the logic circuit, which often involved large numbers of individual components. This is a very costly proposition, both in design and fabrication. It was also inflexible, since changes on the process required both design and production changes. Only very high volume products or very important products could justify the cost of this type of monitoring and control.

With the advent of the microprocessor, a powerful logical device was available. In this device, the relationship between the inputs and outputs is determined by the programs in microprocessor memory. This made the design extremely flexible, because changes in functions could be accomplished simply by changing memory contents. Because the microprocessor system involved the addition of only a few components, it represented a very cheap logical device. The small number of components meant smaller space and electrical power requirements, and also an increase in reliability.

The microprocessor system became an ideal control element. The low cost allowed microprocessors to be included in many more applications. This increased their popularity, which in turn decreased their cost. A spiral began which ended in the current microprocessor revolution. Now, many products and processes which previously had no use for electronics could employ a computer. In addition, the microprocessor, with its extremely low cost, gave rise to the personal and hobby computer phenomenon. What once cost hundreds of thousands of dollars now costs only a few hundred dollars.

From the preceding discussion, it can be seen that the microprocessor is a hardware device: it is an electronic component which possesses electrical parameters and takes its place among other electrical components. The microprocessor is also a software device: much of its power and flexibility lie in its programs.

# 2 *The Binary Number System*

The binary number system is another way to represent numbers. We know how many we have if we say we have three pigs or seventeen apples or two hundred and fifty-seven dollars. We know because we can count them, and if we want to write the number down, we can do so very easily. We write and think of numbers in the decimal number system, a number system based on ten. But in order to understand computers, we must learn binary. Binary is a number system based on two; computers use binary because their transistors have two states, on and off. Actually, binary is very important because it is the bridge between hardware and software. The machine works in binary, all the programs are ultimately given to the machine in binary, and all data is ultimately represented in binary.

If computers are to be fully comprehended, then the binary number system must first be understood. This chapter will begin with decimal numbers, then proceed to positional numbers in general and binary numbers in particular. Binary addition and subtraction will be covered next, followed by other logical and arithmetic operations in binary. Binary numbers are not nearly so difficult to grasp as they appear. Once the fundamentals are understood, the ones and zeros are not so overwhelming, and mastery comes with a little practice.

## *Decimal Numbers and Positional Number Systems*

Both decimal numbers and binary numbers are positional number systems. Positional means that the position of each digit has a specific meaning. For example, in the number 4372, the 4 refers to thousands and the 3 refers to hundreds. The number is quite different than 3472, even though both use the same digits. Actually, 4372 may be written as

$$4 \times 1000 + 3 \times 100 + 7 \times 10 + 2 \times 1$$

or

$$4 \times 10^3 + 3 \times 10^2 + 7 \times 10^1 + 2 \times 10^0$$

The number is the sum of digits multiplied by a base raised to a power. Any further digits to the left of the 4 would be multiplied by higher powers of 10. In general, a positional number system can be written as

$$\ldots + d \times b^3 + d \times b^2 + d \times b^1 + d \times b^0$$

where $b$ is the base and $d$ is any digit from zero to the base minus 1. In decimal, $b = 10$, and $d = 0,1,2,3,4,5,6,7,8,9$. In binary, $b = 2$, $d = 0$ and 1, and numbers are written the same as they are in decimal. For example, the binary number 10110 can be written as

$$1 \times 2^4 + 0 \times 2^3 + 1 \times 2^2 + 1 \times 2^1 + 0 \times 2^0$$

$$\text{or} \quad 16 + 0 + 4 + 2 + 0 = 22_{10}$$

Note the subscript 10 with the 22: 22 is the decimal number, and 10 is the base. The base will be included with all numbers when there is any ambiguity. Normally, numbers without a base usually refer to decimal numbers.

Binary contains a lot of ones and zeros. Each of these is a *binary digit*, or *bit*. (Bits will always be used to refer to binary digits.) Binary numbers are often classified by their number of bits, as in an 8-bit binary number or a 16-bit binary number.

In decimal, a 3-digit decimal number can represent $10^3$ or 1000 different values from 000 to 999. The same principle applies to binary. A 4-bit binary number can represent $2^4$ or 16 values, an 8-bit binary number can represent $2^8$ or 256 values, and a 16-bit binary number can represent $2^{16}$ or 65,536 values.

## *Conversion*

If binary and decimal are both representations of numbers, then it must be possible to convert from one representation to another. Binary to decimal conversion is quite easy since all that is involved is addition of powers of 2. For example,

$$\begin{aligned} 1001101 &= 1 \times 2^6 + 1 \times 2^3 + 1 \times 2^2 + 1 \times 2^0 \\ &= 64 + 8 + 4 + 1 \\ &= 77 \\ \text{and} \quad 10001 &= 2^4 + 2^0 \\ &= 17 \end{aligned}$$

Decimal to binary conversion is not so easy, but the procedure is quite simple. To convert decimal numbers to binary, divide the decimal number by 2 repeatedly and save the remainders. For example, to convert 23 to binary, we divide as follows:

```
2 |23  remainder 1
2 |11  remainder 1      1 0 1 1 1
2 |5   remainder 1
2 |2   remainder 0      Checking
2 |1   remainder 1      16 + 4 + 2 + 1 = 23
   0
```

10111 binary, then, is 23 decimal. Dividing 23 by 2 gives 11 with remainder 1; dividing 11 by 2 gives 5 with remainder 1, and so on. The rule to remember is that the first remainder is the rightmost, or least significant bit, and the following remainders proceed from right to left. It wasn't necessary to stop dividing when the quotient became zero, but any further divisions would only add leading zeros to the leftmost one. As another example, convert 34 to binary as follows:

```
2 |34  remainder 0
2 |17  remainder 1      1 0 0 0 1 0
2 |8   remainder 0
2 |4   remainder 0
2 |2   remainder 0
2 |1   remainder 1
   0
```

So 34 decimal is 100010 binary. The same process can be done with larger numbers, but it takes longer.

## *Binary Operations*

Now it is possible to convert decimal numbers to binary and vice versa. In general, numbers can be represented in either base. This is not good enough, however. Representing numbers in binary isn't worthwhile unless something can be done with them.

### *Addition*

The first thing that comes to mind is the most fundamental operation, addition. When considering addition in binary, one digit at a time must be considered, just as in decimal. In binary, there are four combinations of adding 1 bit:

```
a)   0     b)   0     c)   1     d)  1
   + 0        + 1        + 0        + 1
     0          1          1         10
```

Adding 0 to 0 gives 0 (as adding in any base does), adding 0 to 1 or 1 to 0 gives 1, and adding 1 to 1 gives 2. Or does it? It does, as a matter of fact, because 10 binary is the same as 2 decimal. What happens, actually, is that when 1 is added to 1 in binary, the results are a zero sum digit and a 1 carry bit to the next column on the left. Below, the process is shown in truth table format. A truth table contains all the possible input combinations and the resulting outputs for each combination.

| $I_2$ | $I_2$ | $S$ | $C$ |
|---|---|---|---|
| 0 | 0 | 0 | 0 |
| 0 | 1 | 1 | 0 |
| 1 | 0 | 1 | 0 |
| 1 | 1 | 0 | 1 |

The format shows the four input combinations, the sum digit, represented by $S$, and the carry digit, represented by $C$. Pursuing this further will show that this table is not enough because the case of a carry input from the preceding column is not considered. The truth table below shows this case in which there are now two input digits and a carry in ($C_i$), and in which there is still the sum digit and the carry out ($C_o$):

| $C_i$ | $I_1$ | $I_2$ | $S$ | $C_o$ |
|---|---|---|---|---|
| 0 | 0 | 0 | 0 | 0 |
| 0 | 0 | 1 | 1 | 0 |
| 0 | 1 | 0 | 1 | 0 |
| 0 | 1 | 1 | 0 | 1 |
| 1 | 0 | 0 | 1 | 0 |
| 1 | 0 | 1 | 0 | 1 |
| 1 | 1 | 0 | 0 | 1 |
| 1 | 1 | 1 | 1 | 1 |

All the possible cases are shown. Notice that with $C_i = 0$, this truth table is the same as the first one. Regular addition can now be performed using binary numbers:

| | | | | | | | |
|---|---|---|---|---|---|---|---|
| a) | Carry: | 1 1 0 | | b) | Carry: | 0 1 1 1 1 0 0 | |
| | Inputs: | 0 1 1 0 | 6 | | Inputs: | 0 0 1 0 0 1 0 1 | 37 |
| | | + 0 0 1 1 | + 3 | | | + 0 0 0 1 1 1 0 0 | + 28 |
| | Sum: | 1 0 0 1 | 9 | | Sum: | 0 1 0 0 0 0 0 1 | 65 |

In both examples the carry bits play an important role, without which the addition process wouldn't work. In order for binary numbers to be of any value at all, the addition process must give results identical to those of the addition process in decimal.

*Negative Numbers*

So much for addition; it works, and the binary number system is fine so far. But what about subtraction, and what about negative numbers in general? First of all, subtraction in binary is not as easy as subtraction in decimal, so another method has to be found. In decimal numbers, subtracting can be accomplished by adding negatives, as in the following example:

$$\begin{array}{r} 9 \\ -\underline{4} \\ 5 \end{array} \qquad \begin{array}{r} 9 \\ +\underline{(-4)} \\ 5 \end{array}$$

Adding negative 4 to 9 is the same as subtracting 4 from 9. This is the approach that will be taken in binary: to perform subtraction, the negative value of the subtrahend will be added. There is still a problem, though, because negative numbers have not yet been represented in binary.

There are several ways to represent negative numbers in binary. Among them are sign-magnitude, 1's complement, and 2's complement. The first thing that's necessary is to reserve one bit for sign. Sign, after all, is a two-way proposition, either positive or negative, and this can easily be accomplished by using one bit for sign. The bit that will be used will always be the leftmost bit. Now that a sign bit has been established, a representation must be adopted. The 1's complement is formed simply by changing all the ones to zeros and the zeros to ones. The 2's complement is formed by taking the 1's complement and adding 1. In this text the 2's complement representation will be used because the operations are much easier in this complement. For this reason, almost all modern computers use the 2's complement representation for their operations.

Negative numbers will be considered first. The 2's complement is formed by changing all the ones to zeros and zeros to ones and then adding 1. Look at the following examples:

$$\begin{array}{lrl} \text{a)}\ -13: & 13 = & 0\,0\,0\,0\,1\,1\,0\,1 \\ & -13 = & 1\,1\,1\,1\,0\,0\,1\,0 \\ & & \underline{\phantom{0\,0\,0\,0\,0\,0\,0\,}1} \\ & = & 1\,1\,1\,1\,0\,0\,1\,1 \end{array} \qquad \begin{array}{lrl} \text{b)}\ -87: & 87 = & 0\,1\,0\,1\,0\,1\,1\,1 \\ & -87 = & 1\,0\,1\,0\,1\,0\,0\,0 \\ & & \underline{\phantom{0\,0\,0\,0\,0\,0\,0\,}1} \\ & = & 1\,0\,1\,0\,1\,0\,0\,1 \end{array}$$

In each case, the ones and zeros are exchanged and 1 is added. In each case also, the leftmost bit is a 1. This brings up two very important rules concerning *signed* 2's complement binary numbers:

1. The leftmost bit is the sign bit; if it's zero, the number is positive, and if it's one, the number is negative.
2. If the number is negative, then *it will be in 2's complement form.*

The second rule is very important, and failure to abide by it can lead one astray very rapidly. Case (a) in the example above doesn't bear any resemblance to 13, but it is in fact −13. Consider the binary number 11111000. The assumption is that it is a signed binary number. The sign bit is negative, but the absolute value of the number is not yet known. In order to find out, the 2's complement must be determined: 00000111 + 1 = 00001000, or simply 8. Therefore, by rules of 2's complement signed binary numbers, 11111000 = −8.

Before proceeding to subtraction, there is one additional point to cover. From now on, all binary operations will involve 8 bits unless specifically stated otherwise. This is not only a convenient number to work with, but it is also the number of bits that many microprocessors work with. The use of 8 bits is so popular that the term *byte* has been adopted to indicate 8 bits. Four bits has become known as a half-byte, a "nibble" or a "nybble."

Earlier, it was shown that 8 bits represented 256 different values, 00000000 to 11111111, or from 0 to 255. With signed binary numbers, the positive numbers range from 00000000 to 01111111, or 0 to 127. The negative numbers range from 11111111 to 10000000, or from −1 to −128. The total range is from −128 to +127, which also happens to be 256 different values. There is no loss of range with signed binary numbers.

### *Subtraction*

It was shown earlier that in binary numbers subtraction was performed by adding the negative. Consider the following example:

```
  36    1 1 1
- 14      0 0 1 0 0 1 0 0        14 = 0 0 0 0 1 1 1 0
  22  +   1 1 1 1 0 0 1 0      - 14 = 1 1 1 1 0 0 0 1
          0 0 0 1 0 1 1 0                         + 1
                                      1 1 1 1 0 0 1 0
```

First, convert the decimal numbers to binary. With the −14, the absolute value is converted to binary first, then the 2's complement is determined. The two binary numbers are added in the normal fashion, with one exception—carry out of the leftmost bit. In signed binary arithmetic, all carries out of the sign bit are ignored. From this example, then, the correct sign is maintained throughout the operation. Consider another example:

```
  27          1   1 1
- 45      0 0 0 1 1 0 1 1     45 = 0 0 1 0 1 1 0 1
- 18  +   1 1 0 1 0 0 1 1          1 1 0 1 0 0 1 0
          1 1 1 0 1 1 1 0                      + 1
                                   1 1 0 1 0 0 1 1
```

```
 11101110
 00010001
      + 1
 --------
 00010010 = 18
```

In this example the result of the binary addition is negative, and that is indeed the correct answer. To find out what the answer is, the 2's complement has to be taken to find the absolute value of the answer. In this case also, the correct sign is maintained throughout the operation.

*Overflow*

There is one final point to cover in performing arithmetic operations in binary. Consider this example:

```
   74     01001010
 + 86     01010110
 ----     --------
          10100000 = -96??
```

The operation was performed according to the rules of signed 2's complement binary arithmetic, but there is an obvious error. Two positive numbers were added and the result was negative. The fallacy is that the true sum of the two numbers will exceed the range of 8-bit signed binary numbers. This condition is called overflow. The actual meaning of overflow is the attempt to exceed the range of numbers possible, but the symptoms are adding numbers of like signs and obtaining a result with a different sign.

## Logical Operations

The other major class of operations that can be done with binary numbers is called the Boolean or logical operations. The name logical operations is used because these operations are similar to those in symbolic logic. The binary numbers have no numerical significance, but may, however, represent physical data or conditions. For example, an 8-bit binary number may represent relay contacts. If the specific contact is open, the corresponding bit is 1; if the contact is closed, then the bit is 0. In this way, physical data can be represented in a computer by binary numbers. It is on this type of data that logical operations are performed.

There are two basic types of logical operations—those which operate on a pair of binary numbers, and those which operate on a single binary number. Operations which involve pairs are governed by truth tables. The three logical operations involving a pair of binary numbers are the AND, OR, and EXCLUSIVE OR operations.

In the logical AND operation, the result bit is a 1 only if both input bits are 1. This operation is sometimes called the logical product, and the truth table is as follows:

| $I_1$ | $I_2$ | $R$ |
|---|---|---|
| 0 | 0 | 0 |
| 0 | 1 | 0 |
| 1 | 0 | 0 |
| 1 | 1 | 1 |

In this truth table, the operation is given for all possible cases of two input bits. When operating on pairs of numbers more than 1-bit long, the result is determined one bit at a time. Each result bit of a logical operation depends only on the corresponding input bits. This differs from addition, because in addition a result bit may be affected by a carry from a preceding bit. Consider the following examples of the logical AND operation:

```
a)      00110011      b)      01111100
    AND 11110000          AND 01010101
        --------              --------
        00110000              01010100
```

In the logical OR operation, each result bit is a 1 if either or both of the input bits are 1. The logical OR operation is sometimes called the logical sum or the INCLUSIVE OR. The truth table and two examples follow:

| $I_1$ | $I_2$ | $R$ |
|---|---|---|
| 0 | 0 | 0 |
| 0 | 1 | 1 |
| 1 | 0 | 1 |
| 1 | 1 | 1 |

```
a)     00110011      b)     01111100
    OR 11110000          OR 01010101
       --------             --------
       11110011             01111101
```

In the logical EXCLUSIVE OR operation, the result bit is a 1 if either, but not both, input bits are 1. The logical EXCLUSIVE OR is sometimes written as XOR or EXOR. The truth table and two examples follow:

| $I_1$ | $I_2$ | $R$ |
|---|---|---|
| 0 | 0 | 0 |
| 0 | 1 | 1 |
| 1 | 0 | 1 |
| 1 | 1 | 0 |

```
a) 0 0 1 1 0 0 1 1      b) 0 1 1 1 1 1 0 0
   1 1 1 1 0 0 0 0         0 1 0 1 0 1 0 1
   ---------------         ---------------
   1 1 0 0 0 0 1 1         0 0 1 0 1 0 0 1
```

The remainder of the logical operations involve only one binary number. These are the logical *complement*, and the *shift* and *rotate* operations.

The logical complement, sometimes called the 1's complement, changes the ones to zeros and the zeros to ones. Consider the following two examples of logical complement:

```
a)          0 0 1 1 0 0 1 1     b)          0 1 1 1 1 1 0 0
   COMP            ↓               COMP            ↓
            1 1 0 0 1 1 0 0                 1 0 0 0 0 0 1 1
```

The shift and rotate operations are somewhat different from all the other operations, if only because there is more variety. Shift operations involve moving bits within the number. There are two kinds of shift, a *shift left* and a *shift right*, and either shift may involve varying numbers of bits. Below is an example of a shift left:

```
←0 0 1 1 0 0 1 1
  ↙ ↙ ↙ ↙ ↙ ↙ ↙      0
 0 1 1 0 0 1 1 0   ↙
```

This is an example of a shift left 1. Each bit is moved one position to the left. The leftmost bit is "shifted out," it is gone forever, never to be seen again. When all the bits have been shifted one bit left, there is a vacant position on the right. This position is always filled with zeros.

Now consider an example of a shift left 2, which is equivalent to two consecutive shift left 1s:

```
 ←——                          
←0 1 1 1 1 1 0 0              ←0 1 1 1 1 1 0 0
  ↙ ↙ ↙ ↙ ↙ ↙ ↙ 0 0              ↙ ↙ ↙ ↙ ↙ ↙ ↙      0
 1 1 1 1 0 0 0 0              ←1 1 1 1 1 0 0 0   ↙
                                 ↙ ↙ ↙ ↙ ↙ ↙ ↙      0
                                1 1 1 1 0 0 0 0   ↙
```

In this case, the leftmost 2 bits are shifted out, and two additional zeros are required to fill positions on the right.

The shift right operation is similar except that all the bits are moved to the right. This means that the rightmost bits are shifted out, and that zeros are required to fill in on the left. The following is an example of a shift right 4:

```
     1 1 1 1 0 0 0 0↗
      ↘ ↘ ↘ ↘ ↘ ↘ ↘
0 →  0 1 1 1 1 0 0 0↗
      ↘ ↘ ↘ ↘ ↘ ↘ ↘                or, simply  1 1 1 1 0 0 0 0
0 →  0 0 1 1 1 1 0 0↗                                 ↓
      ↘ ↘ ↘ ↘ ↘ ↘ ↘                             0 0 0 0 1 1 1 1
0 →  0 0 0 1 1 1 1 0↗
      ↘ ↘ ↘ ↘ ↘ ↘ ↘
0 →  0 0 0 0 1 1 1 1
```

As a second example, consider a shift right 3:

```
0 1 0 1 0 1 0 1
0 0 0 0 1 0 1 0
```

Rotate operations are very similar to shift operations. They can be either to the right or to the left, and can involve varying numbers of bits. The difference between the two is that in rotate operations, bits are not shifted out and zeros are not required for fill-ins. In rotate operations, the end bits are brought around to the other side to fill in the void. For example:

```
a) Rotate left 3    0 1 1 1 1 1 0 0
                    1 1 1 0 0 0 1 1

b) Rotate right 2   0 0 1 1 0 0 1 1
                    1 1 0 0 1 1 0 0
```

Rotate operations involve shifting, but the rotate preserves all data: nothing is shifted out, and zeros are not used as filler. It is important to remember that shift and rotate operations are logical operations, and this means that the binary numbers have no numerical meaning. This brings us to the final topic of binary operations, and that is the arithmetic shifts.

The *arithmetic shift* operations are special shifts designed to work with binary numbers which have a numerical significance. If a decimal number is taken and a zero added on the right, this is equivalent to multiplying the number by 10. Similarly, dropping the rightmost digit from a decimal number is roughly equivalent to dividing the number by 10. Consider the following examples:

a) 114 : 1140 = $114 \times 10$   b) 114 : 11 = $114 \div 10$

In each, the number was shifted one digit. The same principle holds in binary also. A shift left is equivalent to multiplication by 2, and a shift right is roughly equivalent to dividing by 2. When considering binary numbers with a numerical significance, the sign must be preserved in all numerical operations. For this reason, arithmetic shift operations have been designed to preserve the numerical integrity of the data.

There are two differences between the arithmetic shift and the logical shift. In the arithmetic shift left, the sign bit never changes, and the bit immediately to the right of the sign bit is shifted out. In the arithmetic shift right, the sign bit not only remains unchanged, but also propagates to the right. Consider the following:

a) Arithmetic shift right 3   0 0 1 1 0 0 0 0

```
0 0 1 1 0 0 0 0→
↓↘ ↘ ↘ ↘ ↘ ↘ ↘
0 0 0 1 1 0 0 0→
↓↘ ↘ ↘ ↘ ↘ ↘ ↘
0 0 0 0 1 1 0 0→
↓↘ ↘ ↘ ↘ ↘ ↘ ↘
0 0 0 0 0 1 1 0→            Numerically, 48 ÷ 8 = 6
```

b) Arithmetic shift left 1   0 0 0 1 0 0 0 1

```
  ↖
0 0 0 1 0 0 0 1
↓   ↙ ↙ ↙ ↙ ↙ ↙
0 0 1 0 0 0 1 0←0           Numerically, 17 × 2 = 34
```

c) Arithmetic shift right 2   1 1 1 1 1 0 1 1

```
1 1 1 1 1 0 1 1→
↓↘ ↘ ↘ ↘ ↘ ↘ ↘
1 1 1 1 1 1 0 1→
↓↘ ↘ ↘ ↘ ↘ ↘ ↘
1 1 1 1 1 1 1 0             Numerically, −5 ÷ 4 ≅ −2
```

d) Arithmetic shift left 3   1 1 1 1 1 0 0 0

```
  ↖
1 1 1 1 1 0 0 0
↕   ↙ ↙ ↙ ↙ ↙ ↙
1 1 1 1 0 0 0 0←0
↕   ↙ ↙ ↙ ↙ ↙ ↙
1 1 1 0 0 0 0 0←0
↓   ↙ ↙ ↙ ↙ ↙ ↙
1 1 0 0 0 0 0 0←0           Numerically, −8 × 8 = −64
```

Note that with positive binary numbers, the arithmetic shifts are by and large like the logical shifts. There is an overflow condition possible with the arithmetic shift left, and that condition occurs when a bit of the opposite value of the sign bit is shifted out. The following is an example of the arithmetic shift overflow:

Arithmetic shift left 2   0 1 0 0 0 0 0 1

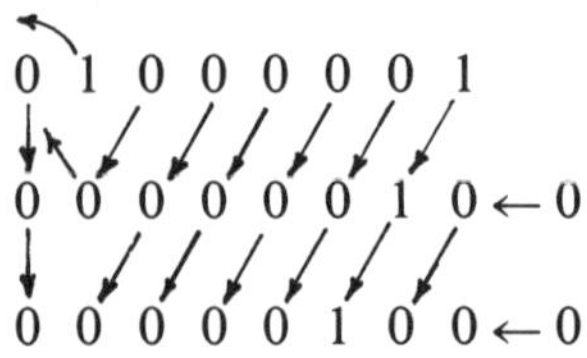

Numerically, $65 \times 4 = 4^{??}$

## *Octal and Hexadecimal Systems*

There are two other number systems of special interest. These are the octal number system, based on the number 8, and the hexadecimal number system, based on the number 16. Both are positional number systems, and both have special qualities with respect to the binary number system.

The octal system, based on the number 8, is represented as follows:

$$\ldots + d \times 8^3 + d \times 8^2 + d \times 8^1 + d \times 8^0, \quad d = 0,1,\ldots,7$$

Conversion from octal to decimal numbers and vice versa is the same as conversion between binary and decimal. For example:

$$176_8 = 1 \times 8^2 + 7 \times 8 + 6 = 126_{10}$$

and

8 |114 remainder 2
8 |14 remainder 6
8 |1 remainder 1
0

$$114_{10} = 162_8$$

The most important thing about octal, however, is that each digit is equivalent to three binary bits. The equivalence is shown in Table 2.1. This makes conversion between octal and binary quite simple. For example:

$$4251_8 = \underline{100}\,\underline{010}\,\underline{101}\,\underline{001}$$

and

$$\underline{01}\,\underline{101}\,\underline{110} = 1\,5\,6_8$$

Note that in the second example there were only 8 bits and 3 octal digits shown. In this case, the groups of 3 bits formed beginning at the right and

*TABLE 2.1: Octal-Binary Equivalents*

| *Octal* | *Binary* |
|---|---|
| 0 | 000 |
| 1 | 001 |
| 2 | 010 |
| 3 | 011 |
| 4 | 100 |
| 5 | 101 |
| 6 | 110 |
| 7 | 111 |

proceeding to the left. If there remains some number of bits fewer than 3, then zeros can be used to fill in to 3. A 16-bit binary number can be converted to octal as follows:

$$1\,1\,1\,1\,0\,1\,0\,0\,1\,1\,0\,0\,1\,0\,0\,1 = 1\,7\,2\,3\,1\,1_8$$

The hexadecimal system, based on the number 16, is represented as follows:

$$\ldots + d \times 16^3 + d \times 16^2 + d \times 16^1 + d \times 16^0, \quad d = 0,1,\ldots,13,14,15$$

Conversion between decimal and hexadecimal proceeds the same as conversion between decimal and octal or decimal and binary. The special quality about hexadecimal is that each digit is equivalent to 4 binary bits. The conversion between hexadecimal and binary proceeds like conversion between octal and binary. The problem with hexadecimal is that it has 16 digits while there are only 10 decimal numbers with which to represent them. Some letters of the alphabet must be borrowed in order to fill out the 16. The conversion among hexadecimal, decimal, and binary is shown in Table 2.2.

*TABLE 2.2: Equivalents in Decimal, Binary, and Hexadecimal*

| *Decimal* | *Binary* | *Hexadecimal* | *Decimal* | *Binary* | *Hexadecimal* |
|---|---|---|---|---|---|
| 0 | 0000 | 0 | 8 | 1000 | 8 |
| 1 | 0001 | 1 | 9 | 1001 | 9 |
| 2 | 0010 | 2 | 10 | 1010 | A |
| 3 | 0011 | 3 | 11 | 1011 | B |
| 4 | 0100 | 4 | 12 | 1100 | C |
| 5 | 0101 | 5 | 13 | 1101 | D |
| 6 | 0110 | 6 | 14 | 1110 | E |
| 7 | 0111 | 7 | 15 | 1111 | F |

Conversion between hexadecimal (sometimes called hex) and binary is as follows:

$$4A72_{16} = \underline{0100}\ \underline{1010}\ \underline{0111}\ \underline{0010}$$

and

$$0\,1\,0\,1\,1\,1\,1\,0 = *5E$$

Note that the asterisk preceding the number indicates that the number is hexadecimal.

The reason for considering octal and hexadecimal is to provide a convenient way to represent binary numbers. Binary is indeed the number system used by computers, but it is cumbersome to work with and error prone when so many bits must be used. The hex and octal number systems are used solely to provide a shorthand means for using binary.

All operations on binary numbers are also valid on both octal and hex numbers. Addition, subtraction, ANDing, ORing, EXCLUSIVE ORing, complementing, and shifting can be done using octal or hex numbers. This is so because the octal and hex are only representations of binary.

Although both octal and hex are valid representations of binary and both find wide use in academia and industry, it is the author's opinion that hexadecimal is the more attractive alternative. The primary reasons for this are that 8- and 16-bit numbers are more clearly represented by hex, and fewer digits are used with hex. Some of the logical operations in hexadecimal are as follows:

| | | | | | |
|---|---|---|---|---|---|
| | *B6 | | *B6 | | *B6 |
| AND | *7A | OR | *7A | EXOR | *7A |
| | *32 | | *FE | | *CC |

If these operations aren't immediately clear, then it may be necessary to convert the hex numbers to binary, perform the operations, then convert the results back to hex.

Some of the shifting and rotating operations in hex are as follows:

| | | |
|---|---|---|
| *D6 | Logical shift left 2 : | *58 |
| | Logical shift right 2 : | *35 |
| | Rotate left 2 : | *5B |
| | Rotate right 2 : | *B5 |
| | Arithmetic shift left 2 : | *D8 |
| | Arithmetic shift right 2 : | *F5 |

Caution should be exercised when using hexadecimal to represent binary numbers in arithmetic operations. Negative numbers are those with the most significant bit equal to 1. In hex, that means any number beginning with the digits 8, 9, A, B, C, D, E, or F is negative. For example:

$$*F6 = 1\,1\,1\,1\,0\,1\,1\,0 = -10_{10}$$

## *Binary Coded Decimal*

There is yet another representation worth considering since many microprocessors have special provisions for it. This is the binary coded decimal (BCD) scheme. In this scheme, each four bits represents one decimal digit, rather than the usual one hexadecimal character. The binary value 00100101 would represent the decimal value 25 rather than the hexadecimal value *25. In BCD, the only allowable bit combinations are 0000 through 1001. The binary values 1010 through 1111, corresponding to the hex values *A through *F, are invalid. (This is known as the 8421 code because the bits have the decimal values 8, 4, 2, and 1 from left to right.) As long as this representation is used consistently, it is a convenient way of representing decimal values. Conversion between decimal and binary is unnecessary when BCD is used, which is the major advantage in using it. The major disadvantage is that an 8-bit binary value can only represent the values 00 through 99 as opposed to 0 through 255 with straight binary.

If BCD is to be a valid representation of numbers, then numerical operations must be possible. Addition in BCD proceeds the same as binary addition, but adjustments must be made under certain conditions. Consider the following example in which 13 is added to 36:

```
   13    0001¦0011
 + 36    0011¦0110
   --    ---------
   49    0100¦1001
```

Performing binary addition in the normal manner gives the correct result, 49 in BCD. Consider the next example in which 27 is added to 16:

```
   27    0010¦0111
 + 16    0001¦0110
   --    ---------
   43    0011¦1101
              \__/
               |
          invalid digit
```

In this case, the normal addition yields *3D, which is invalid as a BCD value. Consider also the example in which 29 is added to 37:

```
   29      0010¦1001
 + 37      0011¦0111
   --      ---------
   66      0110¦0000   ??
```

The result is certainly valid in BCD, but 29 + 37 is not equal to 60. A special rule must be adopted if binary addition is to be applied to BCD numbers. The rule is this: a binary 6 must be added to any sum which yields an invalid digit or to any sum in which a carry is propagated out of the fourth bit of the digit. If this rule is applied to the preceding two examples, the results will be correct in both cases:

```
  27        0010¦0111
+ 16      + 0001¦0110
            ---------
            0011¦1101   invalid digit,
          +     ¦0110      add 6
  --        ---------
  43        0100¦0011

  29        0010¦1001
+ 37      + 0011¦0111
            ---------
            0110¦0000   carry out of fourth bit,
          +     ¦0110      add 6
  --        ---------
  66        0110¦0110
```

A carry out of the fourth bit is permissible, as shown in the first of the two examples.

Subtraction of BCD numbers is another matter. One method is to perform straight binary subtraction, making adjustments for invalid BCD digits. But straight binary subtraction has not been introduced in this book, so the second method must be relied upon. Just as in binary subtraction, the 2's complement of the subtrahend is added, in BCD subtraction the 10's complement of the subtrahend is added. For two-digit BCD numbers, the 10's complement is formed by subtracting the number from 100. Following addition of the complemented subtrahend, correction of invalid digits proceeds as in normal BCD addition. Also, a carry out of the more significant digit indicates a positive result, while no carry out of the more significant digit indicates a negative result in 10's complement form. Consider the following examples:

```
  27      10's complement of 16 = 84     0010 0111       27
- 16                                   + 1000 0100    +(-16)
----                                     ---------
  11                                     1010 1011
                                       + 0110 0110    ------
                                         ---------
                                         0001 0001       11
                          Carry indicates positive result

  44      10's complement of 63 = 37     0100¦0100       44
- 63                                   + 0011¦0111    +(-63)
----                                     ---------
- 19                                     0111¦1011
                                       +     ¦0110    ------
                                         ---------
                                         1000¦0001      -19
               No carry indicates negative result, 100 - 81 = 19
```

The examples show that both addition and subtraction are possible in BCD.

## *Summary*

In this chapter, the equivalence between decimal numbers and binary numbers was shown. Decimal number operations were performed in binary, and logical operations in binary were introduced. This provides a foundation for microprocessor operation, as all such operations are indeed performed in binary.

Among the binary operations not covered were fractions, multiplication, division, and square root. Although these operations are deserving of further study, they were not discussed because most microprocessors don't have equivalent operations in hardware. For reference, consult, for example, *Digital Computer Design Fundamentals* by Y. Chu (Addison-Wesley).

### *EXERCISES*

*1.* Convert the following decimal numbers to binary using 8-bit numbers:

a) 53  b) 7  c) 72  d) 99

*2.* Convert the following decimal numbers to binary using 8-bit signed 2's complement representation:

a) −6  b) −32  c) −77  d) −106

*3.* Convert the following signed 2's complement representation binary numbers to decimal:

a) 00100101  b) 01101101  c) 11110110
d) 10000001  e) 11100101  f) 01110000

*4.* Perform the following operations using 8-bit signed 2's complement representation binary numbers:

| a) | b) | c) |
|---|---|---|
| 37 | 45 | 67 |
| + 19 | + 63 | − 34 |

| d) | e) | f) |
|---|---|---|
| 25 | − 20 | − 35 |
| − 79 | + 125 | − 11 |

*5.* On each of the following pairs of binary numbers, perform the operations AND, OR, and EXOR:

| a) | b) |
|---|---|
| 11000110 | 01011100 |
| 11101110 | 01001011 |

| c) | d) |
|---|---|
| 00101111 | 00010011 |
| 10111000 | 10011010 |

**6.** On each of the binary numbers 00001110, 01101010, and 11000101, perform the following operations:

a) Logical shift left 4
b) Arithmetic shift right 2
c) Logical shift right 3
d) Arithmetic shift left 1
e) Logical complement

**7.** What is the value of any binary number EXCLUSIVE ORed with itself?

**8.** Fill in the blanks of the following table using 8- or 16-bit binary numbers:

| | *Binary* | *Octal* | *Hexadecimal* |
|---|---|---|---|
| a) | 01001110 | | |
| b) | | | A5 |
| c) | | 174 | |
| d) | | 046501 | |
| e) | | | C049 |
| f) | 1000100101111011 | | |

**9.** On each of the following pairs of hexadecimal numbers, perform the operations AND, OR, and EXOR. Express the answer in hexadecimal.

| a) | b) | c) |
|---|---|---|
| C6 | 45 | 991A |
| B8 | 7D | 3102 |

**10.** How many values are possible with 10-bit binary numbers? How many positive values are possible using 10-bit signed binary numbers?

# 3 Hardware

Now that the binary number system, the foundation of all computers and computer science, has been covered in detail, it is necessary to introduce the machinery which implements the binary operations. This machinery performs addition, subtraction, and all the other arithmetic and logical operations.

The logical structure of the machinery will be studied. The logical structure is the functional elements and the way they are connected, rather than the circuitry which implements these elements. The elements are all binary in nature, that is, both the inputs and the outputs can have only two values. Because binary and binary digits are involved, the elements are often referred to as digital logic elements. The logic elements will be discussed because they have been roughly the same since the first computers, while the circuitry has changed and is changing with ever increasing frequency.

The discussion begins with logic gates, the most basic component of digital logic. The gates and their interconnections will be studied in the development of simple combinational logic circuits. More detailed circuits will be studied until a full arithmetic/logic unit (ALU) is developed. Sequential logic, flip-flops, and registers will then be discussed.

## Gates

Combinational logic is so called because the output of a combinational logic circuit depends only on the current inputs and not on any previous conditions. The fundamental building block of combinational logic is the gate. A gate is an electronic device which usually has between two and eight inputs and one output. The inputs and output of a gate can either be zero volts or the power supply voltage of the circuit which very often is +5 volts. Because the inputs and output can have only two values, its operation can be viewed as binary. Its inputs and output, then, can be represented by zeros and ones. A "logic 0," referred to as "low," is equivalent to zero volts;

a "logic 1," referred to as "high," is equivalent to +5 volts. In this and subsequent chapters, gate inputs and output can only be 0 or 1. Because a gate is a physical device, there is a definite delay between the time the inputs change and the output changes. This time is called the gate delay time, and the amount of time differs among the different types of circuitry used to implement the gate. For the purposes of this discussion, however, delay items will not be considered, and the gate output will change as the inputs change. This is indeed a simplistic discussion of digital logic, but it will suffice for us.

There are several types of gates, and the operation of each type is governed by a truth table. The most simple gate types are AND, OR, and EXCLUSIVE OR. Figure 3.1 shows the diagrammatic representation and the truth table for a 2-input AND gate. The AND gate performs a function identical to the logical AND operation: the output *R* will be logic 1 (=5 volts) if both inputs are logic 1. The OR and EXCLUSIVE OR gates also behave similar to the logical operations OR and EXOR. Figures 3.2 and 3.3 show the diagrammatic representations and truth tables for the OR and EXCLUSIVE OR gates, respectively.

There is one final simple gate type called an *inverter*. The inverter, as its name implies, changes the input value to the opposite state (see Figure 3.4).

AND and OR gates can have more than two inputs. The most popular options of AND and OR gates are 2-input, 3-input, and 4-input, and 8-input. It is not necessary to draw the truth tables for all these, but it is important to remember that in an AND gate, all inputs must be 1 in order

*FIGURE 3.1: Two-input AND Gate: Diagrammatic Representation, and Truth Table*

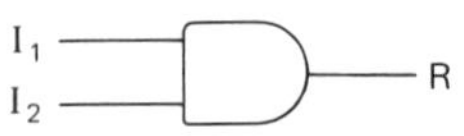


| $I_1$ | $I_2$ | R |
|---|---|---|
| 0 | 0 | 0 |
| 0 | 1 | 0 |
| 1 | 0 | 0 |
| 1 | 1 | 1 |

*FIGURE 3.2: Two-input OR Gate: Diagrammatic Representation, and Truth Table*

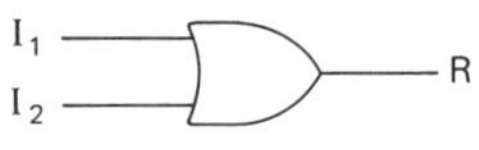


| $I_1$ | $I_2$ | R |
|---|---|---|
| 0 | 0 | 0 |
| 0 | 1 | 1 |
| 1 | 0 | 1 |
| 1 | 1 | 1 |

*FIGURE 3.3: EXCLUSIVE OR Gate: Diagrammatic Representation, and Truth Table*

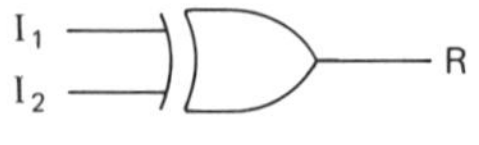


| $I_1$ | $I_2$ | R |
|---|---|---|
| 0 | 0 | 0 |
| 0 | 1 | 1 |
| 1 | 0 | 1 |
| 1 | 1 | 0 |

*FIGURE 3.4: Inverter: Diagrammatic Representation, and Truth Table*

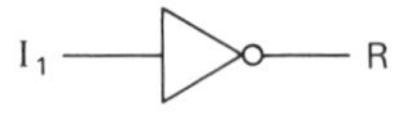


| $I_1$ | R |
|---|---|
| 0 | 1 |
| 1 | 0 |

for the output to be 1, and in an OR gate, the output will be 1 if any input is 1. While the AND and OR gates may have a variable number of inputs, the EXCLUSIVE OR gate may only have two inputs, and an inverter may only have one input.

There is another class of gates which include an inverter on the output. These gates are called NAND and NOR, short for NOT AND and NOT OR, respectively. These gates can have two or more than two inputs. There is no equivalent gate for EXCLUSIVE OR. Figures 3.5 and 3.6 show the NAND and NOR gates. The bubble on the output signifies inversion. Care should be exercised when speaking about gates because an AND gate sounds almost like a NAND gate.

Now that the basic gate types have been introduced, what can be done with them? Many of the applications for digital logic lie in the nonelectronics world. These applications by and large recognize an input condition and cause something to happen in response to certain specific conditions. A rather trivial but nonetheless valid example of this type of application is the seat belt buzzer that has become so familiar on many automobiles built in the 1970s. The general idea is to activate a buzzer if the occupants of the front seat have not fastened their seat belts. The buzzer can be controlled by a simple logic circuit. In order to do this, physical conditions must be translated into logic-level voltages. Once this is done, the logic can be used as an effective monitor and control device. Figure 3.7 shows the logic circuit and legend for the seat belt buzzer. The buzzer will buzz if the driver or a front seat passenger have not fastened their belts. Note also that the ignition key must be engaged in order for the buzzer to sound.

*FIGURE 3.5: Two-input NAND Gate: Diagrammatic Representation of Equivalent Circuit, and Truth Table*

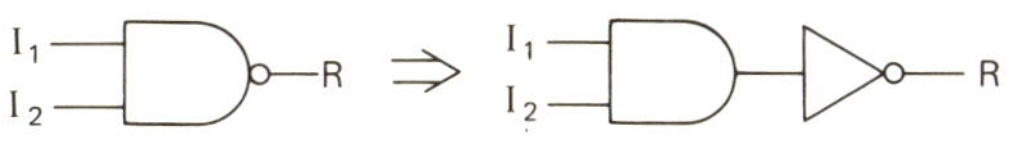


| $I_1$ | $I_2$ | R |
|---|---|---|
| 0 | 0 | 1 |
| 0 | 1 | 1 |
| 1 | 0 | 1 |
| 1 | 1 | 0 |

*FIGURE 3.6: Two-input NOR Gate: Diagrammatic Representation of Equivalent Circuit, and Truth Table*

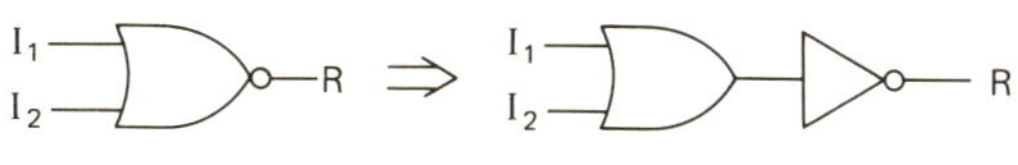


| $I_1$ | $I_2$ | R |
|---|---|---|
| 0 | 0 | 1 |
| 0 | 1 | 0 |
| 1 | 0 | 0 |
| 1 | 1 | 0 |

*FIGURE 3.7: Logic Circuit for Seat Belt Buzzer Example*

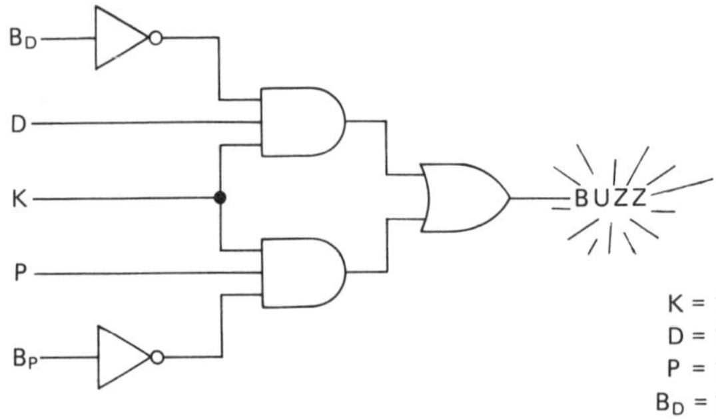


Legend:

K = 1 if key is in ignition
D = 1 if driver is in his seat
P = 1 if passenger is in his seat (front seat)
$B_D$ = 1 if driver's seat belt is buckled
$B_P$ = 1 if passenger's seat belt is buckled

There are literally millions of uses like this in which the final application is nonelectronic in nature. Among the applications which are digital or electronic in nature, many are specifically useful in the design of computers. Two of these are the decoder and the multiplexer. The *decoder* is a circuit which has a few inputs and several outputs. Only one of the outputs is high, corresponding to a specific value of the inputs. A 1-of-4 decoder, for example, has two inputs and four outputs. There are four possible input values. One and only one of the outputs will be high for each of the input combinations. The circuit for a 1-of-4 decoder is shown in Figure 3.8. Other common decoder circuits are 1-of-8 (three inputs) and 1-of-16 (4 inputs).

A second circuit used primarily in electronics and computer applications is called a *multiplexer*. The multiplexer, shown in Figure 3.9, allows use of one output line by many input lines. The four input lines are gated through the AND gates. The other input on each AND gate is the output of the decoder. Three of the decoder outputs will be low, forcing the AND

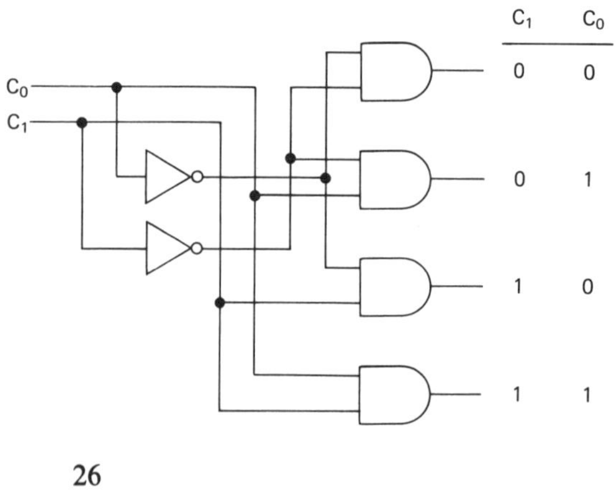


*FIGURE 3.8: Logic Circuit for 1-of-4 Decoder*

*FIGURE 3.9:*
*Multiplexer*

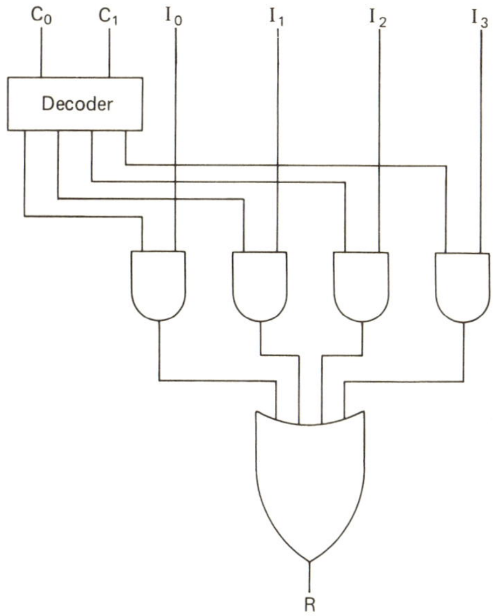


gate outputs to zero. Only the input line on the AND gate with the high decoder output will propagate to the output $R$. The inputs to the decoder, $C_0$ and $C_1$, select which of the four input lines will be gated through to R. The decoder is an essential part of the circuit because it guarantees that only one of the inputs can be gated to the output at a time. Figure 3.9 is a 4-to-1 multiplexer. There are also 8-to-1 and 16-to-1 multiplexers.

The decoder and multiplexer circuits are very important, as will be shown later. The most important logic circuits will now be discussed.

## The Adder and ALU

Chapter 1 developed the concept of binary numbers. Numerical operations were developed for binary which allowed the same addition and subtraction capability in binary as we are familiar with in decimal. Now that gates are available that operate with binary signals, the gates will be connected so that the addition process can be performed. If this can be done, we will then have an electronic device that can perform arithmetic.

Recall the truth table for binary addition on page 8. There are two input bits and two results, the sum and the carry. The truth table for the sum output is identical to that of an EXCLUSIVE OR gate, and the truth table for the carry is identical to that of an AND gate. Figure 3.10 shows the logic diagram for a 1-bit adder. It is called a half-adder because it implements only half the truth table. Bear in mind that this circuit will

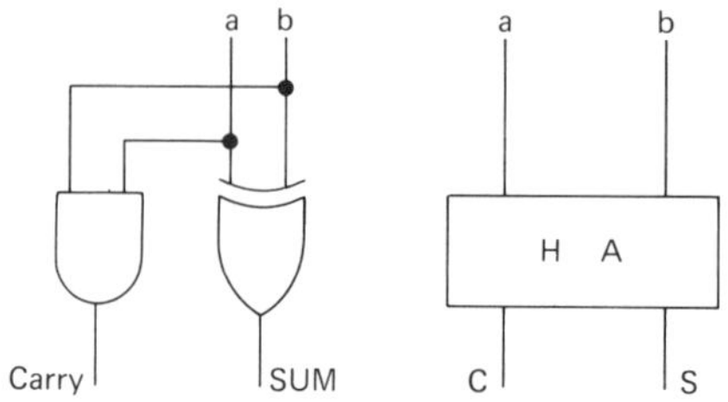


*FIGURE 3.10:*
*Half-adder with Equivalent*

perform additions on only one pair of bits, *a* and *b*. In order to extend the addition to several bits, it is first necessary to include a carry in to the addition. Figure 3.11 shows the logic diagram for a full adder. This circuit implements the truth table for full addition as shown on page 8. The equivalent full adder using two half-adders is also shown. This 1-bit full adder can now be combined with other identical circuits so that there is an electronic circuit that can perform 8-bit binary additions. This is the first step on the way to a computer.

In chapter 2, all the binary arithmetic operations plus several logical operations were covered. The AND, OR and EXCLUSIVE OR operations were presented. If the computer is to perform these operations, as well as the arithmetic operations, then there must be circuitry to implement the operation. Close inspection of the logic diagram in Figure 3.11 shows that the input bits go directly to an AND gate and an EXCLUSIVE OR gate. If the outputs of these gates can be extended beyond the full adder, then two of the three logical operations will be available. It is only necessary to add an OR gate to provide the last logical operation. Figure 3.12 shows the circuitry for a 1-bit arithmetic/logic unit (ALU).

If a multiplexer is added to the outputs of the ALU of Figure 3.12, the circuit will have only one output. The specific output will be determined by

*FIGURE 3.11: One-bit Full Adder with Equivalents*

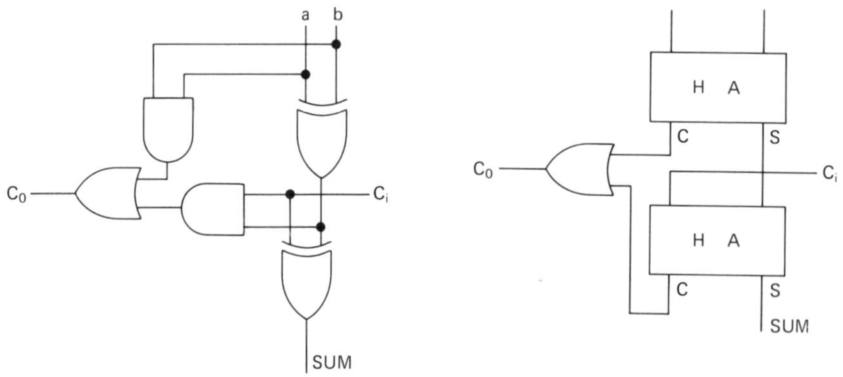

*FIGURE 3.12:*
*One-bit Arithmetic/Logic Unit (ALU)*

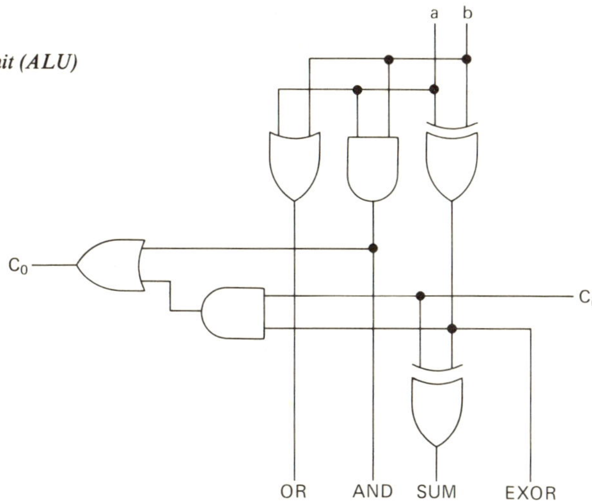


the control inputs. If the ALU circuits are combined sideways so that the carry out of one bit becomes the carry in of the next bit, an 8-bit ALU can easily be constructed. Figure 3.13 shows two bits of arithmetic/logic unit with common control inputs. Of course, the control inputs must be the same, otherwise in an 8-bit operation some of the bits may be EXCLUSIVE ORed, while others may be added, and still others may be ANDed.

Careful construction of the 8-bit ALU brings us one step closer to a full central processing unit.

## Sequential Logic

All the circuits of the previous section were combinational logical circuits, that is, the outputs of the circuits depended only on the current inputs. Consider the circuit of Figure 3.14. It is called an RS flip-flop, and it is the simplest of the sequential circuits. The two outputs of the circuit are called $Q$ and $\overline{Q}$. When the rules are followed, these outputs will always be complementary, that is, when one is high, the other will be low. If $S$ is logic 1 and $R$ is logic 0, the $S$ inverter will be low, and that forces the Q NAND gate high; in this case, both inputs on the $\bar{Q}$ NAND gate will be high, which makes the output 0. If $S$ changes to 0 (both inputs are now 0), $Q$ stays high because $\overline{Q}$ is low; in this case, if both inputs are 0, $Q$ will be high and $\overline{Q}$ will be low. If $R$ now goes high, the $R$ inverter will go low, and $\overline{Q}$ will go high; both inputs on the Q NAND gate are high, so $Q$ goes low. If $R$ goes low (both inputs again low), $\overline{Q}$ stays high because $Q$ is low; in this case, if both inputs are low, $Q$ will be low and $\overline{Q}$ will be high. This seems to contradict

*FIGURE 3.13: Two Bits of 8-bit ALU*

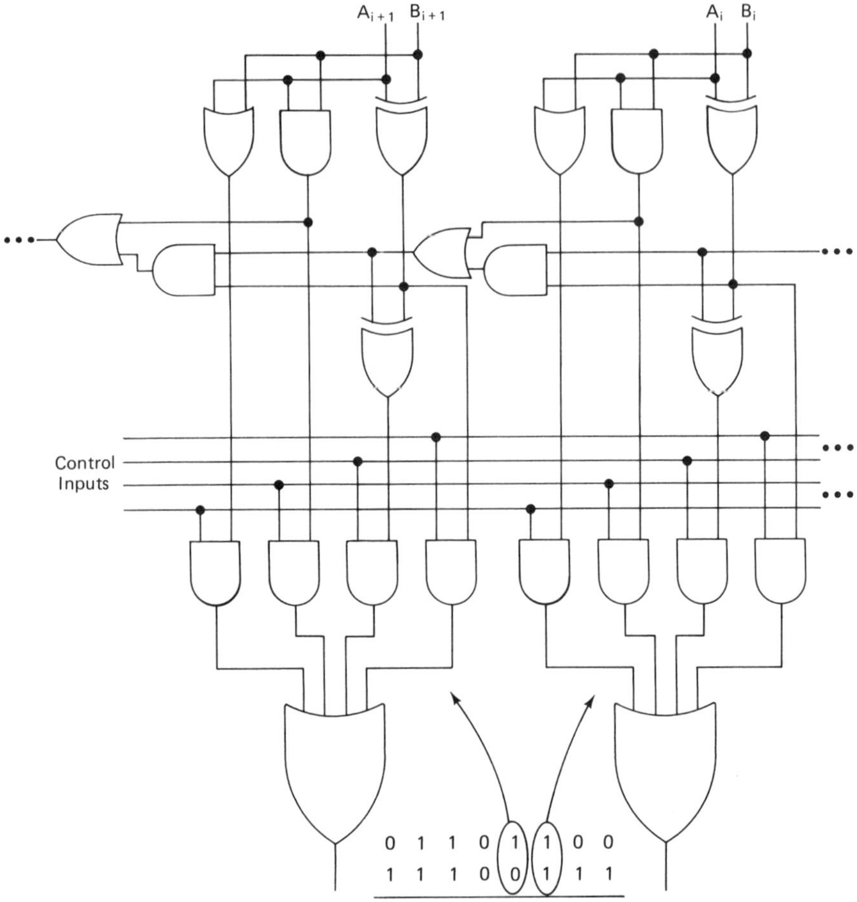


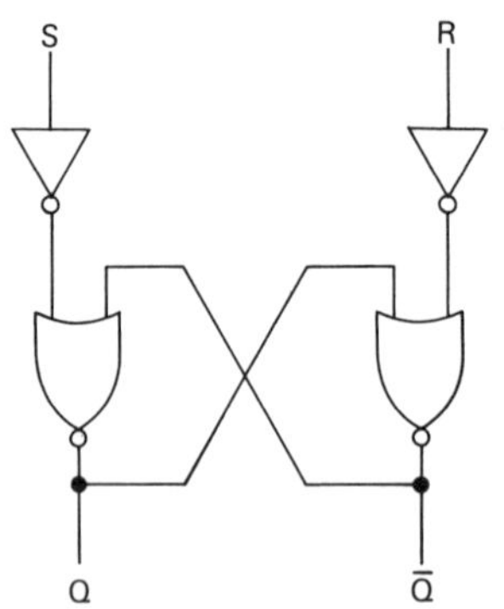


| S | R | $Q_n$ |
|---|---|---|
| 0 | 0 | $Q_{n-1}$ |
| 0 | 1 | 0 |
| 1 | 0 | 1 |
| 1 | 1 | X (illegal) |

*FIGURE 3.14: RS Flip-flop and Truth Table*

the previous condition when both low inputs caused the opposite output state. The contradiction is resolved because the output of the circuit depends not only on the current inputs, but also on the previous state of the output. This is the nature of sequential logic. This condition is indicated in the truth table. The output is stated as a function of time: $Qn$ indicates $Q$ at time $n$. The $Q$ output is specific if either $S$ is 1 and $R$ is 0, or $S$ is 0 and $R$ is 1. But if both inputs are 0, the output $Q$ at time $n$ is the same as the output at the preceding time, $Q_{n-1}$. Both inputs being 1 at the same time constitutes an illegal condition because both $Q$ and $\overline{Q}$ will be 1, and not complementary.

The circuit is called a flip-flop because the output "flip-flops" back and forth between two possible conditions. It is called an *RS flip-flop*, or set-reset flip-flop, because the output tends to follow the input: if $S$ is high, the $Q$ output is set to 1; and if $S$ is low, the $Q$ output is reset to 0. The circuit is important because information can be retained in the flip-flop even though the input changes. The flip-flop, then, can be a short-term storage element.

The RS flip-flop is called an *asynchronous* sequential circuit because the inputs and, consequently, the outputs can change at any time. The *RST flip-flop*, shown in Figure 3.15, is quite similar to the RS flip-flop, except that changes in $R$ and $S$ are only effective when $T$ is 1. The $T$ input is called the clock input. The RST is a *synchronous* flip-flop because the outputs can change only at certain times.

There are specific things which can be done with RS flip-flops which alter their operation and create new flip-flops. One example is the *D flip-flop*, sometimes called the D latch. The circuit, shown in Figure 3.16, is called a latch because the logical value on the D input will be "latched" in when $T$ goes high, that is, the value on $D$ will be retained until $T$ goes high

*FIGURE 3.15: RST Flip-flop*

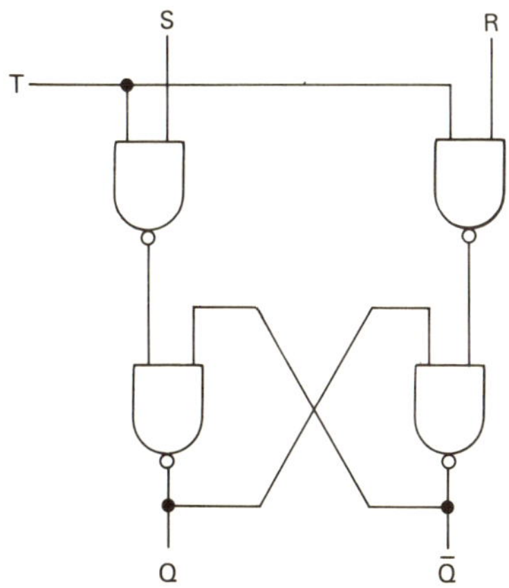

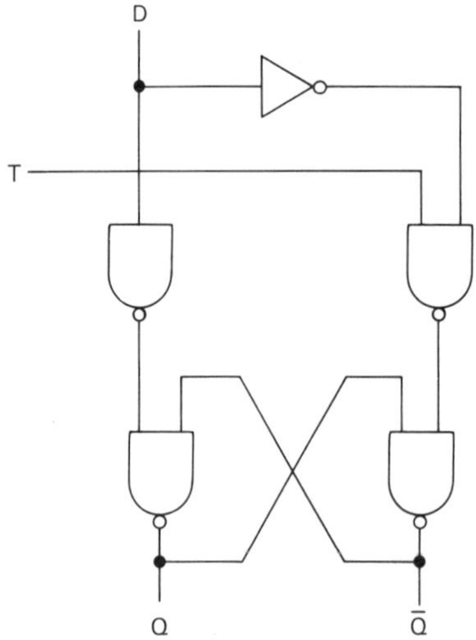


*FIGURE 3.16:*
*D Latch*

again. This occurs because what are normally the *S* and *R* inputs of the flip-flop are complementary. The D latch is synchronous because of the clock input.

Another variation of the flip-flop is called the *master-slave flip-flop* (Figure 3.17). It is actually two flip-flops with complementary clock inputs. The top flip-flop is the master flip-flop because it can take any value from the input lines. The bottom flip-flop, the slave, can take only the value of the master. The *T* input, when low, disables the master and enables the slave. Even though the slave is enabled, its output doesn't change because the master can't change. When *T* is high, the master can change, but the slave is disabled. The slave output, and consequently the flip-flop output, changes again when *T* goes low. The master-slave flip-flop is also a synchronous flip-flop.

Just as the gates are the primary building blocks of combinational logic, so are flip-flops the building blocks of sequential logic. Flip-flops can be combined to provide still another element of a central processing unit.

## Registers

Flip-flops are logic circuits built from gates, but their primary importance has little to do with the gates. They are important in their own right, and for this reason have their own symbols. The symbols for RS, RST, and D flip-flops are shown in Figure 3.18.

The most important function of a flip-flop is temporary storage of data. Each can store one bit of data. If several flip-flops are combined, then

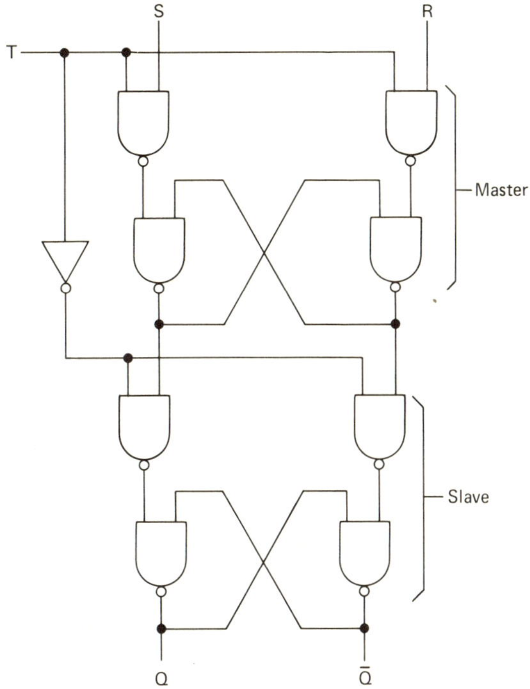


*FIGURE 3.17: Master-slave Flip-flop*

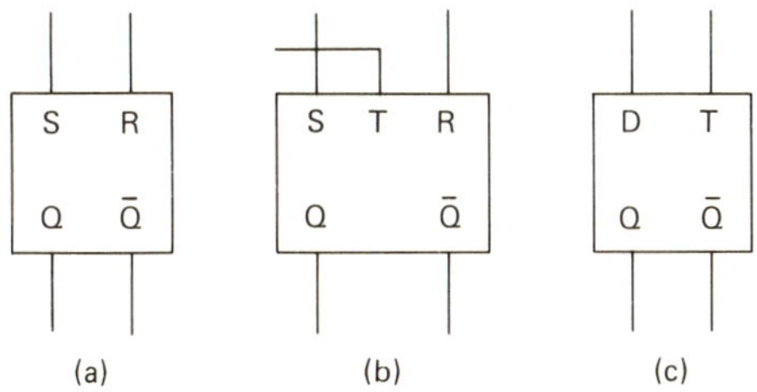


*FIGURE 3.18: Symbols for (a) RS, (b) RST, and (c) D Flip-flops*

several bits of data can be stored. If the several flip-flops have a common clock, then the group of flip-flops can be collectively called a register. A simple register made with D flip-flops is shown in Figure 3.19. Each of the flip-flops is independent of the others except for the common clock.

Registers have several important applications, one of which is a *counter*. A counter is a register whose outputs follow a counting sequence. The simplest sequence is just a binary count sequence. The circuit in Figure 3.20 is a 3-bit binary up counter. Note that this particular counter has no other inputs except the flip-flop outputs. This need not be the case with all counters. If all the flip-flops start out low, a series of 8 clock pulses will produce the output sequence 001, 010, 011, 100, 101, 110, 111, and 000.

A second important application of a register is called a *shift* register. It

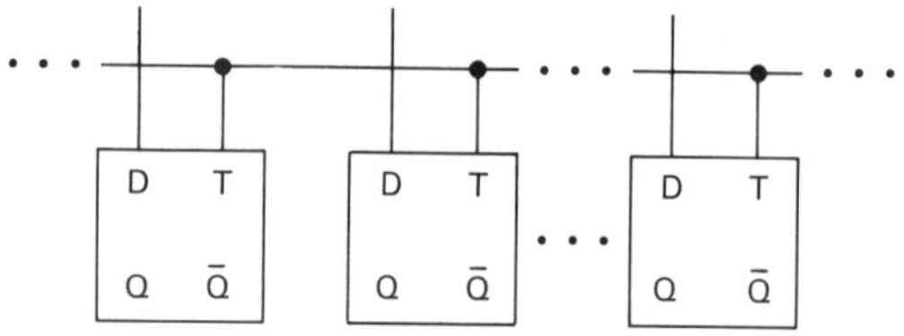


*FIGURE 3.19: n-bit Register*

*FIGURE 3.20: 3-bit Binary Up Counter*

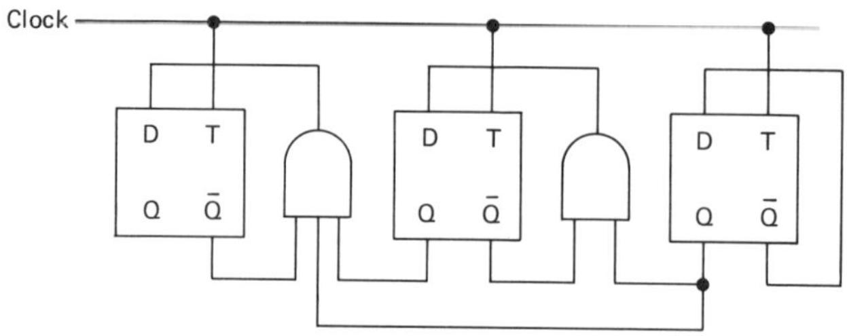


is so called because information is shifted from one bit to another in one direction. Figure 3.21 shows a 4-bit shift register. In this case, the shift register is a serial-entry shift register, that is, information can only enter the register one bit at a time. Note that the register shifts information to the right. Assuming that the register initially contains 1101 and that all incoming bits are zeros, the register contents at the next clock pulses will be 0110, 0011, 0001, 0000. This operation is identical to the logical shift operation discussed in chapter 2.

The introduction of the shift register represents another step toward the development of a central processing unit.

## *Register and Arithmetic/Logic Unit*

Earlier in the chapter, the arithmetic/logic unit was developed. The ALU provides the capability of performing both logical and arithmetic operations on binary numbers. Now that the register has been introduced, there

*FIGURE 3.21: 4-bit Serial-right Shift Register*

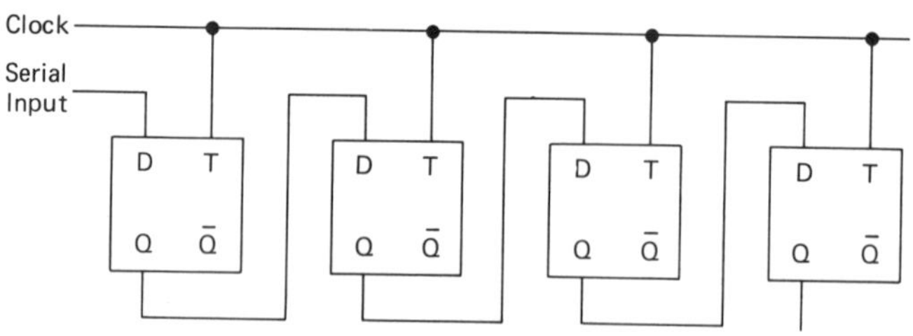

is a means not only of storing the results of the operations, but also of performing some of the operations not possible in the arithmetic/logic unit. The combination of a register and an arithmetic/logic unit (RALU) provides the nearest thing to a central processing unit except the unit itself. Careful design of the total unit allows several operations to be performed

*FIGURE 3.22: Two Least Significant Bits of RALU*

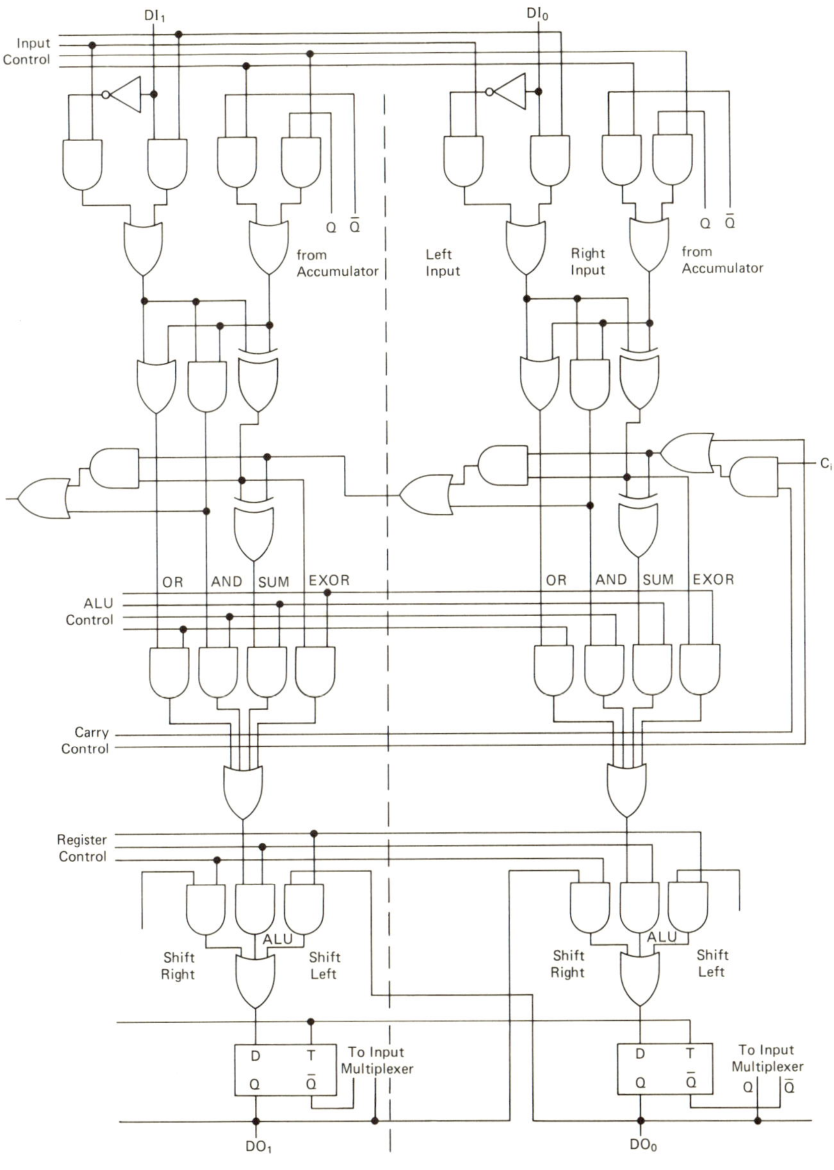

with the cumulative results of each operation available in the register. Since the cumulative results of each operation are available, the register with an ALU is sometimes called an *accumulator.*

Figure 3.22 shows the two least significant bits of a RALU. Note that there are a few features which are shown on the original ALU or register. These features include the two multiplexers at the ALU inputs at the top, the carry control inputs, and the register control inputs. These features allow the orderly execution of operations. The register control inputs allow the results of either a shift operation or an ALU operation to be stored in the accumulator. The input multiplexers are extremely important, as they select not only the input but also the input function. The *data input* (DI), which is data from some external source, can be added to the contents of the accumulator by proper manipulation of the control inputs. DI can also be deposited directly into the accumulator by selecting DI, not selecting either $Q$ or $\overline{Q}$ on the other input, then selecting the sum function at the ALU and the ALU function at the register. DI can be subtracted from the accumulator by selecting the negative DI (i.e., the 1's complement of DI) and the $Q$ input, and by forcing the $C_i$ to 1. This is equivalent to adding the 2's complement of DI to the accumulator.

There are some additional features which could be added to Figure 3.22. For example, there could be multiplexers and selection logic on the shift inputs. Arithmetic shifts and rotates can be implemented by manipulation of the least and most significant shift inputs.

## Summary

The basic elements of digital logic design and the operation and a few applications of gates and flip-flops have been considered. For further study of digital logic, consult, for example, *The Design of Digital Systems* by J. Peatman (McGraw-Hill).

Two important points must be made about the coverage in chapter 3. The first is that the chapter was intended to be a review for those already familiar with logic design and an introduction for those not familiar. The design examples were very simple and not necessarily the best way to implement the function. The coverage was by no means complete. The second point is that the major intention was to show that there is a basis for computer operations; that the operations are indeed performed by machine and not by magic or with mirrors. It is not necessary to fully understand the hardware operation in order to pursue the study or use of microprocessors. This is not to say that the material is unimportant. Many devices external to the microprocessor are logical devices. In addition, understanding of microprogramming and bit slice processors is totally dependent on understanding the logical operation of the central processing unit.

### *EXERCISES*

*1.* Draw the circuit for an EXCLUSIVE OR function using only AND and OR gates and inverters.

*2.* Using AND, OR, and EXCLUSIVE OR gates, draw the logic circuit for a full adder which will add two 2-bit binary numbers.

*3.* Draw the logic diagram for a 4-bit down counter (i.e., one which counts down: 0000, 1111, 1110, etc.).

# 4 The Microprocessor

The microprocessor, as it was originally designed, is simply a miniaturized version of the central processing unit of a computer. It is a register and arithmetic/logic unit along with the necessary control and timing logic for the orderly execution of instructions.

## Registers

Recalling some of the discussion of chapter 1, the computer is composed of a central processing unit, memory, and input/output. Instructions which are executed by the central processing unit must first be fetched from memory. Much of the data processed in the CPU also resides in memory. When data is in fact gotten from memory, it is not taken from just anywhere, but from specific addresses. The logical structure of the CPU will be discussed in terms of the instructions, data internal to the CPU, and how the data is stored and retrieved from memory.

A discussion of the logical structure of a central processing unit necessarily includes registers. Registers are involved in instruction execution, data storage, and address generation. Collectively, registers are called the *programmers' model* of the computer, because the programmer controls the computer via control of the registers.

The first register under consideration is the accumulator. The accumulator, as shown in chapter 3, can store the cumulative results of arithmetic and logical operations. The number of bits in the accumulator is referred to as the data word size, data word length, or, simply, word size. Computers in general and microprocessors in particular are classified by word size. Typical larger-scale computer word sizes are 12 bits, 16 bits, and 32 bits. Most microprocessor word sizes are 4, 8, 12, and 16 bits.

In chapter 3, a detailed analysis of the arithmetic/logic unit was presented. The logic circuits which actually perform the operations were covered. Control signals were shown which, among other things, selected one operation from among many to be gated to the accumulator. These control signals originate from a register called the *instruction* register. This register contains the microprocessor instruction currently being executed. The instruction register usually contains the same number of bits as the accumulator. (This allows both data and instructions to reside in the same memory.) Each microprocessor instruction is unique, and each usually causes several different actions within the microprocessor. These actions are implemented by decoders which allow certain instruction register values to be recognized. Figure 4.1 depicts the instruction register and decoders. Although only one decoder is shown, there are generally several decoders on the output of the instruction register.

All microprocessor instructions are fetched from memory. A register called the *program counter* contains the address in memory from which each instruction is fetched. Generally, instructions are executed sequentially from successive memory locations. It is for this reason that the program counter is called a counter, because it normally counts up by some small number after execution of each instruction. The program counter must contain enough bits to address all of system memory. Total system memory is determined by the number of address lines emanating from the microprocessor chip, and the program counter must contain this number of bits.

There may be one or more registers in a microprocessor which aid in addressing data, as the program counter addresses instructions. Among these registers are the *index register* and the *stack pointer*. In order to provide full addressing capability, both of these must contain the same number of bits as there are address lines emanating from the microprocessor. In general, a microprocessor has only one stack pointer, but many microprocessors have more than one index register.

In addition to all the aforementioned special-purpose registers, there

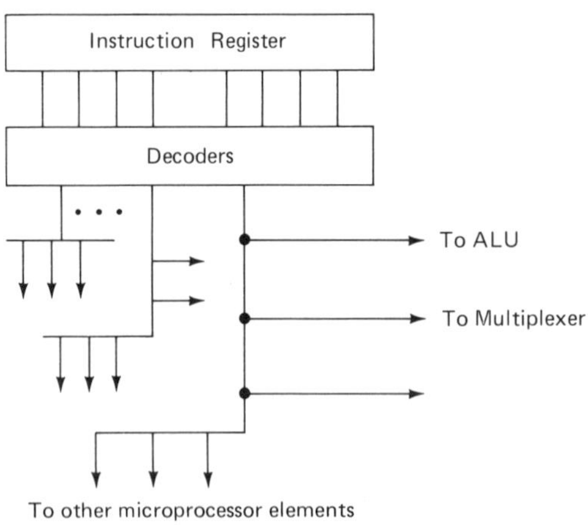


*FIGURE 4.1: Instruction Register and Decoder*

may be additional general-purpose registers used for temporary data storage or for addressing. Sometimes these registers are labeled by letters, such as the B, C, and D registers, and sometimes by numbers, such as register 1, 2, and 3.

There is another class of register employed in many microprocessors. This class is called *buffers*. A buffer is generally used for temporary storage of data which is in transit from one device or subsystem to another. Buffers are under hardware control only and are not available to the programmer.

It is advantageous for microprocessors to have as many registers as hardware considerations allow. One of the reasons for this is that operations among registers are faster than operations involving only memory or operations involving registers and memory. Another reason is that instructions which refer only to registers occupy fewer memory locations than those which involve both register and memory reference.

## Programmers' Model of the MC6800

Figure 4.2 shows the expanded block diagram of the internal structure of the MC6800 microprocessor chip. The internal structure contains all the functional elements which comprise the microprocessor. These elements are the individual registers, the arithmetic/logic unit, the instruction decoding and control unit, the output or address buffers, and the data buffers. Data flows from register to register and to the data and output buffers along an internal data bus. The bus is shown connecting all the elements. Also shown are the logical signals which connect the microprocessor to the outside world. The registers and signal pins are what the programmer uses to direct the microprocessor to perform the task at hand.

All the registers shown are 8 bits. The MC6800 has two accumulators, accumulator A and accumulator B. Both can contain the cumulative results of arithmetic and logical operations, and both accumulators can be involved in data transfers to and from memory and other external devices. The accumulators are almost identical; there are only two minor functions possible with the accumulator A that are not possible with accumulator B.

Note that the program counter, stack pointer, and index register have two components each, namely, the H and L components. Since these registers are used for addressing memory, they each must contain 16 bits. The 16 bits are treated as two 8-bit segments. The H segment is the higher order or more significant 8 bits, and the L segment is the lower order or less significant 8 bits. These registers are shown in 8-bit segments because sometimes data is transferred directly between these registers and memory, and because data can only be transferred internally 8 bits at a time.

The condition code register actually contains only 6 bits, but when

*FIGURE 4.2: Expanded Block Diagram of the MC6800 Microprocessor* (Courtesy of Motorola Semiconductor Products, Inc.

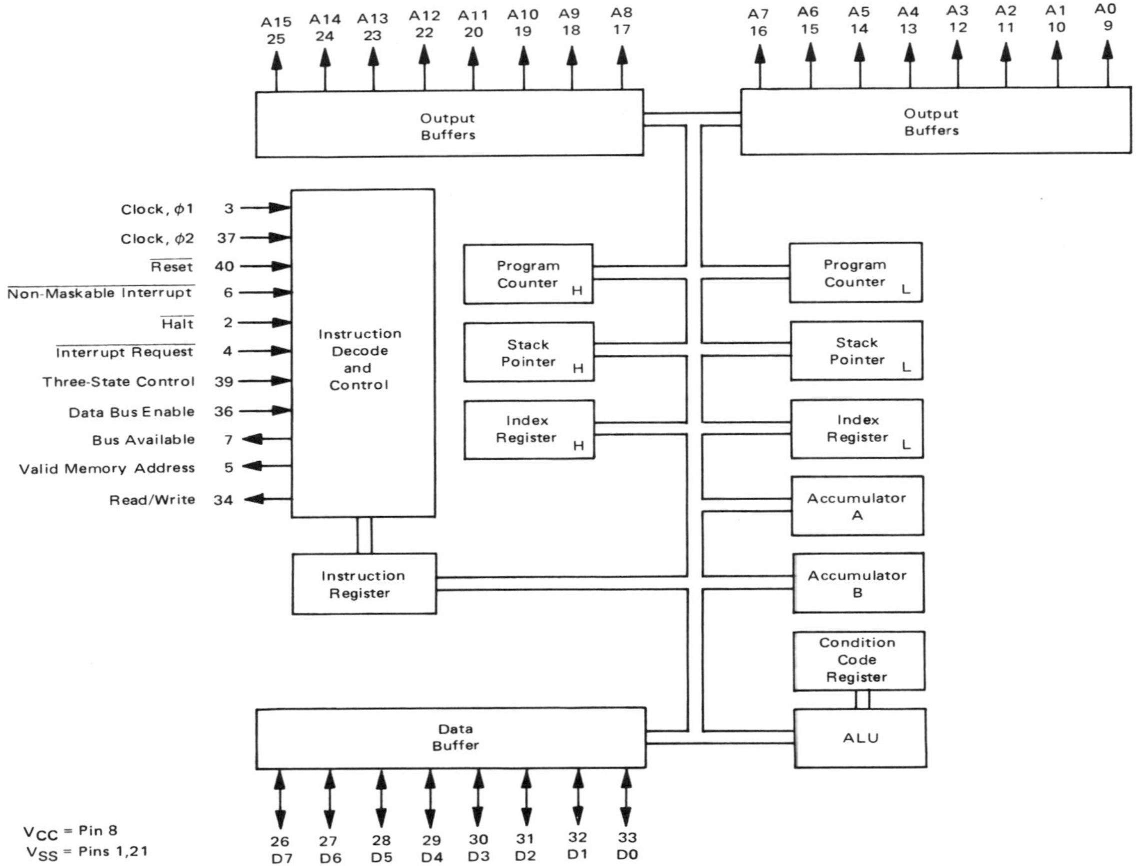

this register is treated as data, two 1s are inserted into the high-order two bits, thus making the transfers 8-bit transfers. There are six conditions represented by single bits in the condition code register. Five of these indicate the results of data transfers or arithmetic or logical operations. The sixth bit is an interrupt mask bit which inhibits or allows the normal action of the microprocessor to be interrupted. (More will be said about interrupts and the interrupt mask bit later.) The condition code register bits, from most significant to least significant, are as follows: the H bit, or half-carry bit, indicates a carry from bit 3 to bit 4 during an add operation; the I bit, or interrupt mask bit; the N bit, or negative bit, is identical to bit 7 of an accumulator after an arithmetic or logical operation; the Z bit, or zero bit, is set to indicate a zero arithmetic or logical result, and is reset otherwise; the V bit, or overflow bit, indicates a signed overflow result of an arithmetic operation; and the C bit, or carry bit, is set to indicate a carry out of bit 7 during an add operation or a borrow into bit 7 during a subtract operation. These bits are affected by many instructions, and detailed descriptions of each instruction show how the individual bits are affected.

The processor control signals shown on the left side of Figure 4.2 are used mostly for hardware control of the microprocessor and for hardware interaction between the microprocessor and external devices. The programmer, however, should be aware of the functions of each of these signals. The two clock signals, $\phi 1$ and $\phi 2$, provide the timing signals necessary for orderly operation internal to the microprocessor. The reset signal is used to start the microprocessor in a predetermined fashion. Reset is used either when power is first applied to the microprocessor or to rescue the microprocessor from an unknown state (usually the result of program errors). The bar over the reset indicates that the mechanism is triggered by a logic low level (i.e., zero volts) applied to this signal pin. The nonmaskable interrupt signal (NMI), when low, will trigger the internal interrupt mechanism, and cannot be disabled or masked out by the programmer. The interrupt request signal (IRQ) triggers an almost identical mechanism, but can be inhibited by the programmer by setting the I bit of the condition code register. The halt signal, when low, stops all internal microprocessor operations and gives control of all busses to an external device. The *three-state control* signal, or TSC, allows other devices to use the address bus and read/write signal. The data bus enable, when low, allows another device to control the data bus. (More will be said about three-state operation in the next section.) The bus available signal, when high, indicates that the microprocessor has stopped as the result of a halt signal, and that all busses are available to an external device. The valid memory address signal, VMA, indicates that the logical states of the address bus are stable and no longer fluctuating. The read/write signal indicates to other devices that the microprocessor is either reading data from another device (R/W is logic 1) or is writing data to another device (R/W is logic 0). The meanings and uses of these signals will become clearer when a system design is considered in chapter 8.

The programmers' model is a brief description of all the elements of a microprocessor which are under control of the programmer or which affect the logical operation of the microprocessor. Similar descriptions exist for all microprocessors and are usually included in promotional literature or system design literature.

## The Physical Device

The Motorola MC6800 microprocessor chip is an N-channel silicon gate metal oxide semiconductor (MOS) device. It is approximately 2 inches long by .6 inches wide. It has 40 signal pins, and the chip is in standard dual in-line package (DIP) form. The package is available in either plastic or ceramic.

The chip is powered by one 5-volt power supply. There is one power supply (Vcc) input and two ground (Vss) inputs. The MC6800 is designed to operate at temperatures between 0 and 70°C. Power dissipation is typically 600 milliwatts, but can be as high as 1.2 watts, depending on operating temperature and clock frequency.

Two clocks, $\phi 1$ and $\phi 2$, are required for internal timing and synchronization. As shown in Figure 4.3, the clocks are nonoverlapping with a 50% duty cycle. The maximum frequency at which the clocks can operate is 1 megahertz, or 1 million cycles per second. The MC6800 is a dynamic device. This means that if power is removed or if the clocks run too slowly, internal data is lost. For this reason, the minimum frequency at which the clocks can operate is .1 megahertz, or 100,000 cycles per second.

Many of the MC6800 signals are three state, that is, they can be in the

*FIGURE 4.3: MC6800 Two-phase Clocks*

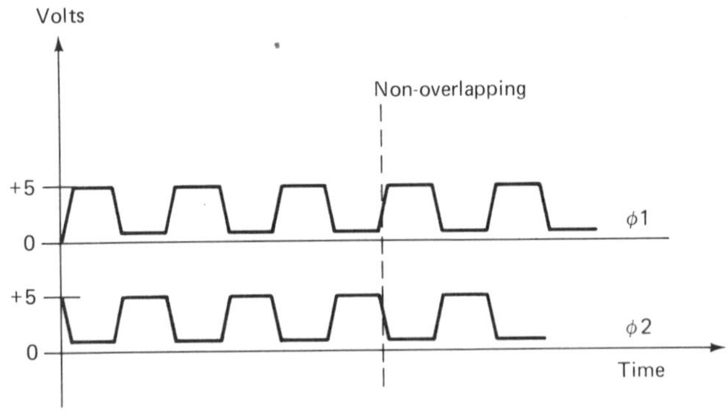

logic 0 state (0 volts), the logic 1 state (+5 volts), or in the high impedance state. The high impedance state has the electrical characteristic of not being connected at all. This feature, which most microprocessors possess, allows the bus concept of operation. Bus operation involves many signal pins being connected together, any one of which is capable of specifying the logical state of the line. Figure 4.4 shows data bus bit 0 of the MC6800 and two memory chips. When storing information to memory, the MC6800 puts a logical level (0 volts or +5 volts) on the bus. If the memory chips were also to put logic levels on the bus at the same time, physical damage to the chips might result. But when the memory chips are in the third or high impedance state, the logic level specified by the MC6800 remains without interference. Similarly, when the MC6800 is reading information from memory, its data bus goes into the high impedance state, and the logic level of one of the memory chips governs the level of the bus. In the MC6800, the 8 data signals, 16 address signals, and the read/write signal are all capable of three-state operation.

Most of the MC6800 output lines are TTL compatible. That means that they can drive one standard transistor-transistor logic (TTL) load in addition to a few MOS device loads. Maximum loading of MOS device outputs is determined by the input capacitance of the devices being driven. Thus the MC6800 literature states that each data bus output can drive one standard TTL load and 130 picofarads (pF).

Figure 4.5 shows the disposition of the 40 signal pins of the MC6800. Note the small dot or hump near pin 1. This is used for location of pin 1 so the chip is inserted correctly. Note also that pin numbers 35 and 38 are marked N.C. for "not connected."

It is interesting to note that the MC6800, as well as most large-scale integration semiconductor devices, is actually a small wafer about a quarter of an inch square. This square is packed very densely with transistors and other semiconductor elements which are connected so as to form the functional equivalents of gates, flip-flops, and other logical devices. This small square also has connectors so that the internal elements can be connected to the outside world. These connectors are in fact the 40 signal

*FIGURE 4.4:*
*Bus Concept*

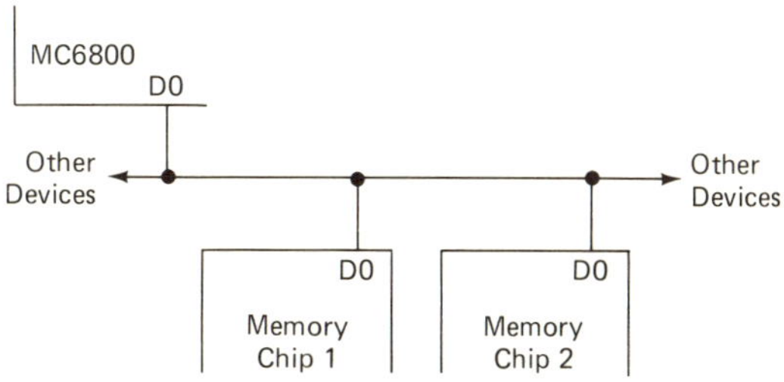

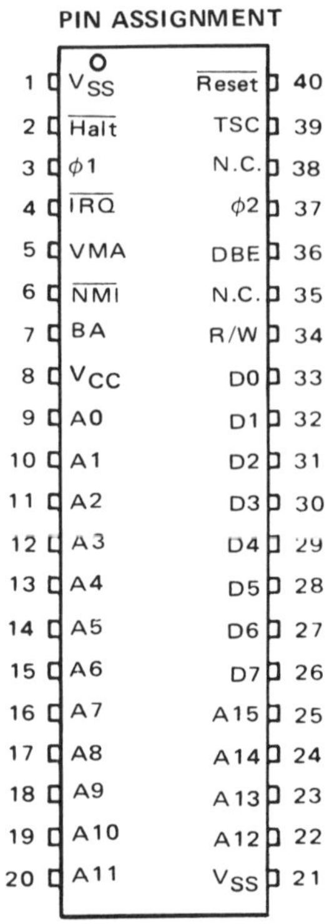


*FIGURE 4.5:*
*Pin Disposition of the MC6800* (Courtesy of Motorola Semiconductor Products Inc.)

pins of the MC6800 dual in-line package. The small chip is put in the relatively larger DIP for protection and overall more rugged operation, as well as to offer a somewhat standard package.

## Summary

All major microprocessors contain by and large the same functional elements. There is an arithmetic/logic unit, several registers, and the control logic necessary for instruction execution. All this is put in a package in such a way that the internal elements can interface with devices on the outside world. The microprocessor is more than a logic diagram, more than a collection of gates and registers; it is a physical electronic device which has distinct circuit parameters and which consumes power.

The Motorola MC6800 microprocessor was not chosen for consideration because it is the best microprocessor available. There are many microprocessors available, all of which have distinct advantages and disadvantages. The "best" microprocessor is determined largely by how its advantages can be applied to a specific application. Many nontechnical considerations also apply to selection of a specific microprocessor. The MC6800 does possess several extremely fine qualities. The architecture and instruction set of the MC6800 are simple and straightforward. This provides computing power in many applications without being narrow or special purpose. A fine family of compatible memory and I/O interface devices is also available.

# 5 Memories

Memory refers to the storage and subsequent recall of information. Just as we humans remember or memorize things, so does electronic memory keep information for computer systems. In earlier chapters it was stated that memory is one of the major subsystems of the computer and that both programs and data reside in memory. It is now appropriate to discuss memory and the part that it plays in the overall computer system. The discussion of memory precedes that of instructions and programming because a knowledge of memories may add perspective to instruction addressing and addressing modes.

## Memory Organization

Computer memory may be viewed as a series of storage cells or registers where binary information is kept. In chapter 3, a hardware register was described as a device for the temporary storage of binary data. Memory serves the same purpose, but memory is not made of flip-flops, and is not one but a collection of individual data storage elements. Each element is sometimes called a location, and it has associated with it a unique address by which it alone can be accessed. Each memory location contains a specific number of bits. The exact number of bits varies among computer systems, but within a given computer system, the number of bits is the same as data word size and/or instruction word size. Generally, within a given computer system, data word size, instruction word size, and memory word size are all the same.

The number of words in memory not only varies among computer systems, but also varies with the application within a single computer system. Normally, the maximum number of memory locations available to a given computer system is specified by the number of address lines on the microprocessor. If the microprocessor has 16 address lines, then the maximum number of memory locations is $2^{16}$ or 65,536. An actual computer system may contain anywhere from some small number to the maximum number of memory locations depending on how much is needed to store the programs and data required for the specific application. Figure 5.1 shows the logical organization of a typical memory system. The memory locations are labeled by their addresses, beginning with *0000 at the top and continuing to the highest numbered location in the system. In many cases the memory need not be contiguous; several blocks of memory beginning at various addresses may comprise a system's total memory. In this particular memory, each location contains 8 bits, and the bits are numbered from 0 on the right to 7 on the left just as the Motorola registers are numbered. Each of these locations may contain an instruction or data for the M6800 system.

## *Memory Characteristics*

Computer memory is available as an electronic device, just as the CPU is available as a microprocessor. Each memory device type has certain characteristics which distinguish it from other memory device types. Among these characteristics are number of bits, how the bits are organized, what kind of memory it is logically and physically, and certain other electronic characteristics such as access time and power requirements.

The number of bits is usually expressed in powers of 2 rounded to thousands, the thousands being denoted by the letter k. Sometimes the k is capitalized to indicate 1024; for example, a 1K memory contains 1024 bits, and an 8K memory contains 8192 bits. How these bits are arranged is also important. A 1K memory can be arranged as 128 unique addresses of 8 bits each, or 1024 addresses of 1 bit each, or any other combination of locations and bits. If memory devices with one bit per location are used in a system,

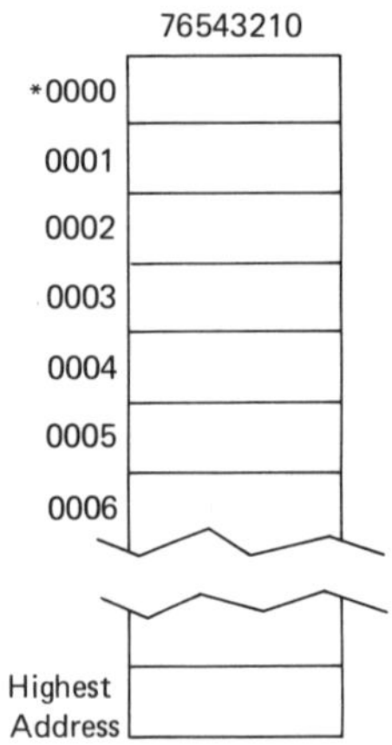


*FIGURE 5.1:*
*Typical Memory Organization*

then 8 of them must be used in order to provide storage for bytes of data. There are no advantages or disadvantages inherent in any particular organization, except possibly that those organizations with 8 bits per location are convenient.

There is one type of memory called *read-only memory*, or ROM. As the name implies, data can only be read from the device; the contents cannot be altered once they are written. ROMs are usually used for storing programs or for storing data that is intended to be permanent. The contents of these memories cannot be destroyed accidentally. When ROMs are purchased, the contents are known by the producer at manufacturing time and are inserted by the vendor. This puts a severe requirement on the purchaser, namely, the purchaser must be absolutely certain that the contents specified are indeed correct, otherwise, the purchase price of the ROMs is wasted.

There is another class of memory which is read-only under most conditions, but the contents of which can be inserted by the purchaser. It is called *programmable read-only memory*, or PROM. This differs from ROMs in that the purchaser deposits the contents rather than the manufacturer. The contents of the memories are still permanent, however.

Still another memory is that called the erasable, programmable read-only memory, or EPROM. In these, the contents of the memories can be deposited by applying abnormal voltages to certain chip inputs. The difference is that the contents can be erased and new contents can subsequently be deposited. One of the more popular types of erasing is by ultraviolet light. Each memory chip of this type has a window through which can be seen the semiconductor device. When this device is exposed to large doses of ultraviolet light, the contents fade away and the chip can be reprogrammed. During normal operation, these memories are read-only in nature. The obvious advantage with this type of device is that contents are alterable while the device retains its read-only characteristic. This means that a program can be put into an EPROM and tested, and if the program doesn't work or if new features are to be added to the program, the memory contents can be changed and the program can be retested. The disadvantages are that they are more expensive and they tend to have more signal pins than other memories of similar storage capacities. Other names for memories of this type are erasable read-only memory, or EROM, and electrically alterable read-only memory, or EAROM. Caution should be exercised because some of these acronyms are used incorrectly, and one should be sure that there is agreement on memory type.

Another type of memory is *random access memory*, or RAM. This is actually a misnomer because the phrase random access implies that all memory addresses are accessible in the same amount or nearly the same amount of time. All varieties of ROM certainly possess this characteristic.

The phrase has come to mean that the memory can both be read and written during normal operation. This means that data, operated upon by the microprocessor, can be stored into the memory chip for later reference.

There are two notable characteristics of read/write memories. The first characteristic deals with what happens when electrical power is removed from the memory subsystem. If the memory is volatile, the contents of the memory locations will be lost when power is lost. A nonvolatile memory retains its contents while power is off. Almost all semiconductor RAMs are volatile. A semiconductor memory is one which is fabricated in basically the same manner and with the same material as the microprocessor chip. ROMs, of course, are nonvolatile. Magnetic type memories, such as magnetic core and magnetic bubble memories, are nonvolatile. The advantage associated with nonvolatile memories is obvious. The disadvantage is that additional circuitry is required to interface the magnetic storage medium with the semiconductor devices in the system. Also, magnetic memories tend to be slower and bulkier than their semiconductor counterparts.

A characteristic of semiconductor devices in general, and memories in particular, is that involving static or dynamic operation. Static operation means that memory contents remain intact until power is removed from the device or until contents are altered by program operation. A dynamic memory is one in which the contents just fade away after a certain amount of time. Recall that the MC6800 is also dynamic. When dynamic memories are used, memory contents must be read and rewritten once every few milliseconds. Obviously, a microprocessor would not be very effective if it had the added burden of reading and rewriting memory. Special logic subsystems can be designed which do nothing but continuously read and write memory contents. The only impact on the microprocessor is that it cannot access memory while the dynamic memory subsystem is accessing it. The advantage of dynamic memories is that they are cheaper and more densely packed than static memories. In general, memories involving 8K bytes or more can be designed more cheaply using dynamic memories.

Another characteristic of all memories is access time. This is the time necessary for data to be fetched from memory and available to the microprocessor on a read operation, and the time necessary for data to be stored in the memory during a write operation. Access time is important when very fast microprocessors are used, because the memory must be able to keep up with the microprocessor. All other parameters being equal, faster memories are more expensive.

Certain other parameters to consider when discussing memories are TTL compatibility, number of signal pins, number of power supplies required, and whether or not the data leads are bidirectional. In the next section, two specific memory chips will be considered.

## The MCM6830 ROM

The Motorola MCM6830 is an 8K ROM which is organized as 1024 8-bit locations. It is a mask programmable ROM, that is, the ones and zeros are specified by placing a mask over the wafer in one of the last stages of production. This is, of course, done by the manufacturer. The chip is fabricated with N-channel MOS circuitry. Its data outputs are three state and are both TTL and DTL compatible. The chip requires only a +5 volt power supply, and the maximum access time is 500 nanoseconds. The MCM6830 is available in a 24-pin package. A portion of the MCM6830 product specification sheet is shown in Figure 5.2.

Consider the pin assignment of the portion of the product spec. The eight data outputs are pins D0 though D7. The 10 address inputs are pins A0 through A9. These address inputs allow addressing of each of 1024 bytes. How is it that a memory chip with only 10 address inputs is compatible with a microprocessor with 16 address outputs? How can 2 MCM6830 chips be used in the same system if each only has 10 address inputs? The answer to both these questions is a class of inputs known as *chip selects*. The chip selects aid in system addressing and their function is to select one chip in the system exclusive of all others. Each chip select on a memory chip can be either active low or active high. For a given memory chip, all the chip select inputs must be at their proper polarities in order for the data in the chip to be accessed. If one or more of the chip selects is not at the proper polarities, then the data outputs are in the high impedance state. The MCM6830 has four chip selects, CS0 through CS3. The active levels of the chip selects are programmable and must be specified by the purchaser along with the memory contents.

## The MCM6810 RAM

The MCM6810 is a 1K static RAM fabricated with N-channel MOS circuitry. It is organized as 128 bytes. The data leads are bidirectional as well as three state, and are TTL compatible. The MCM6810 also requires only a single +5 volt power supply. There are two maximum access times available, 450 nanoseconds and 350 nanoseconds. There are six chip select inputs, two of which are active high and the others active low. The MCM6810 as well as all RAMs have a read/write (R/W) input. This signal, which is normally connected to the R/W output of the microprocessor, specifies whether data is to be read from the memory chip or written to the memory chip. Read is indicated by a logic one on R/W, and write is indicated by a zero on R/W. The data leads on the MCM6810 are in the

*FIGURE 5.2: MCM6830 Product Specification Sheet* (Courtesy of Motorola Semiconductor Products Inc.)

### 1024 X 8-BIT READ ONLY MEMORY

The MCM6830A is a mask-programmable byte-organized memory designed for use in bus-organized systems. It is fabricated with N-channel silicon-gate technology. For ease of use, the device operates from a single power supply, has compatibility with TTL and DTL, and needs no clocks or refreshing because of static operation.

The memory is compatible with the M6800 Microcomputer Family, providing read only storage in byte increments. Memory expansion is provided through multiple Chip Select inputs. The active level of the Chip Select inputs and the memory content are defined by the customer.

- Organized as 1024 Bytes of 8 Bits
- Static Operation
- Three-State Data Output
- Four Chip Select Inputs (Programmable)
- Single 5-Volt Power Supply
- TTL Compatible
- Maximum Access Time = 500 ns

**ABSOLUTE MAXIMUM RATINGS** (See Note 1)

| Rating | Symbol | Value | Unit |
|---|---|---|---|
| Supply Voltage | $V_{CC}$ | -0.3 to +7.0 | Vdc |
| Input Voltage | $V_{in}$ | -0.3 to +7.0 | Vdc |
| Operating Temperature Range | $T_A$ | 0 to +70 | °C |
| Storage Temperature Range | $T_{stg}$ | -65 to +150 | °C |

NOTE 1: Permanent device damage may occur if ABSOLUTE MAXIMUM RATINGS are exceeded. Functional operation should be restricted to RECOMMENDED OPERATING CONDITIONS. Exposure to higher than recommended voltages for extended periods of time could affect device reliability.

## MOS

**(N-CHANNEL, SILICON-GATE)**

**1024 X 8-BIT**
**READ ONLY MEMORY**

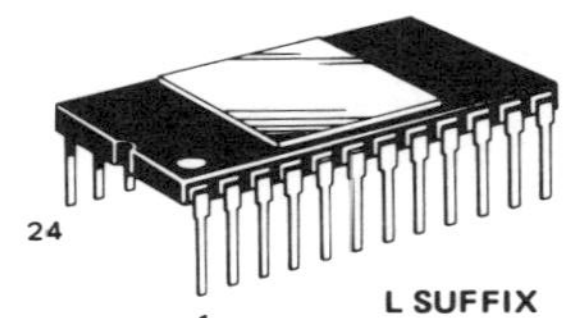


**L SUFFIX**
CERAMIC PACKAGE
CASE 716

NOT SHOWN: **P SUFFIX**
PLASTIC PACKAGE
CASE 709

**PIN ASSIGNMENT**

| Pin | Name | Name | Pin |
|---|---|---|---|
| 1 | Gnd | A0 | 24 |
| 2 | D0 | A1 | 23 |
| 3 | D1 | A2 | 22 |
| 4 | D2 | A3 | 21 |
| 5 | D3 | A4 | 20 |
| 6 | D4 | A5 | 19 |
| 7 | D5 | A6 | 18 |
| 8 | D6 | A7 | 17 |
| 9 | D7 | A8 | 16 |
| 10 | CS0 | A9 | 15 |
| 11 | CS1 | CS3 | 14 |
| 12 | $V_{CC}$ | CS2 | 13 |

*FIGURE 5.3: MCM6810 Product Specification Sheet* (Courtesy of Motorola Semiconductor Products Inc.)

## 128 X 8-BIT STATIC RANDOM ACCESS MEMORY

The MCM6810 is a byte-organized memory designed for use in bus-organized systems. It is fabricated with N-channel silicon-gate technology. For ease of use, the device operates from a single power supply, has compatibility with TTL and DTL, and needs no clocks or refreshing because of static operation.

The memory is compatible with the M6800 Microcomputer Family, providing random storage in byte increments. Memory expansion is provided through multiple Chip Select inputs.

- Organized as 128 Bytes of 8 Bits
- Static Operation
- Bi-Directional Three-State Data Input/Output
- Six Chip Select Inputs (Four Active Low, Two Active High)
- Single 5-Volt Power Supply
- TTL Compatible
- Maximum Access Time = 350 ns – MCM6810AL1
  450 ns – MCM6810AL

**ABSOLUTE MAXIMUM RATINGS** (See Note 1)

| Rating | Symbol | Value | Unit |
|---|---|---|---|
| Supply Voltage | $V_{CC}$ | -0.3 to +7.0 | Vdc |
| Input Voltage | $V_{in}$ | -0.3 to +7.0 | Vdc |
| Operating Temperature Range | $T_A$ | 0 to +70 | °C |
| Storage Temperature Range | $T_{stg}$ | -65 to +150 | °C |

NOTE 1: Permanent device damage may occur if ABSOLUTE MAXIMUM RATINGS are exceeded. Functional operation should be restricted to RECOMMENDED OPERATING CONDITIONS. Exposure to higher than recommended voltages for extended periods of time could affect device reliability.

**MOS**

(N-CHANNEL, SILICON-GATE)

**128 X 8-BIT STATIC RANDOM ACCESS MEMORY**

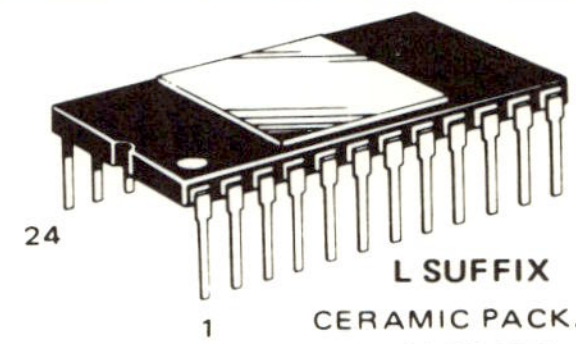


**L SUFFIX**
CERAMIC PACKAGE
CASE 716

NOT SHOWN: **P SUFFIX**
PLASTIC PACKAGE
CASE 709

**PIN ASSIGNMENT**

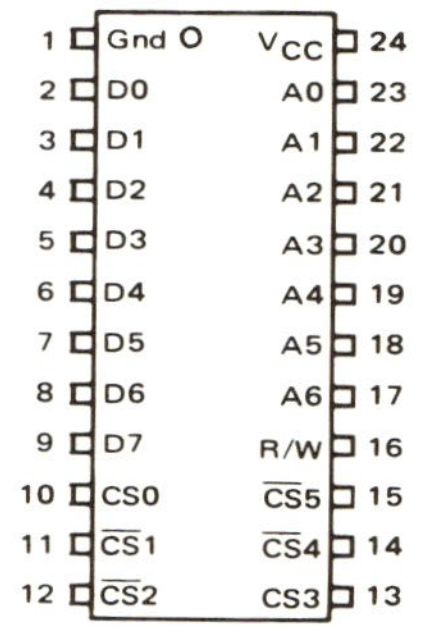

high impedance state unless all the chip selects are at their active levels and R/W is in the read state. A portion of the MCM6810 product specification sheet is shown in Figure 5.3.

## Summary

Memory is that part of the computer where programs and data are stored. The memory itself is constructed with specific devices, each of which may possess different architectural and electrical properties. Specific information for each device can be found in the product specification sheet for that device.

### EXERCISES

*1.* Explain briefly the difference between volatile and nonvolatile memory.

*2.* Explain briefly the difference between static and dynamic memory.

*3.* Explain briefly the difference between ROM, PROM, and EPROM.

*4.* If a 1K byte memory is to be constructed (i.e., 1024 locations of 8 bits each), how many memory chips would be required if the following chip types are used:

a) $128 \times 8$
b) $256 \times 8$
c) $256 \times 4$
d) $1024 \times 1$
e) $4096 \times 1$

In which of the above cases would expansion to 2K bytes be easiest? Why?

# 6 Instructions and Related Topics

It was stated earlier that all functions performed by a computer were accomplished by the execution of specific instructions. It is now appropriate to consider these instructions carefully. Before covering the specific instructions of the Motorola MC6800, some general properties of instructions will be considered.

Instructions are related to programs as gates are related to logic circuits. Instructions are the lowest and most detailed level of control available to the programmer. The programmer builds programs with instructions. Just as logic circuits can be built incorrectly or inefficiently, so also can programs be written incorrectly or inefficiently by using the wrong instructions or by using the instructions in incorrect combinations. Because instructions are the primary building blocks of software, a thorough knowledge of instructions is necessary for a thorough understanding of microprocessors.

Each instruction is a unique entity within a computer which combines a specific operation with none, one, or more than one operand. The operation specifies an action, and the operands specify those items which are acted upon. The specific actions can be divided into several classes which will be discussed later. The operands, in general, are either CPU registers, specific memory locations, or input/output devices.

There are three phases in the execution of each instruction:

1. The instruction is fetched from memory
2. The instruction is executed
3. The next instruction is prepared for

The instruction is first fetched from memory. Specifically, the contents in the memory location, whose address is in the program counter, are fetched. These contents will be a binary entity called the *opcode*. The opcode, which is always the same number of bits as the instruction register, uniquely identifies the instruction. The opcode is deposited in the instruction register where it is decoded. The decoding of the opcode causes the specific instruction to occur within the CPU. The last of these actions is adjusting the program counter so that another instruction can be fetched from memory and executed.

## *Instruction Types*

Instructions are divided into classes based on the kind of operation they perform. They can be divided loosely into the following groups:

1. *Data movement*—In these instructions, data is moved from one location to another. Data can be moved from memory to a CPU register, from a CPU register to another CPU register, from a CPU register to memory, or possibly from one memory location to another.
2. *Data alter*—In this group, data is altered in specific ways. These instructions may alter either a CPU register or a memory location. The data involved may be altered by clearing (setting to all zeros), incrementing, decrementing, or complementing, either logically or 2's complement. This group is intended to be distinct from the next group.
3. *Arithmetic/logic*—These instructions include all the arithmetic and logic operations discussed in chapter 2: addition, subtraction, possibly multiplication and division, ANDing, ORing, and EXCLUSIVE ORing. In these instructions, a specific operation is performed and the results are maintained, generally in an accumulator. In addition, properties of the results are maintained by the appropriate setting or resetting of condition code bits.
4. *Shift/rotate*—This group may be considered an extension of the preceding group. It includes both the arithmetic and logical shifts and the rotates. An accumulator, or a memory location, may be involved. Condition code bits are also affected by these instructions.
5. *Comparison/test*—This is a special group of instructions designed to determine certain properties of data without destroying it. For example, it can be determined whether a particular register contains a value larger than 7 by subtracting 7 from the register and checking the result. But the subtraction destroys the original contents of the register. The comparison and test instructions generally perform an operation and affect the condition code bits, but do not store the results of the operation.
6. *Branch and control*—After an instruction is executed, the instruction in the next memory location is usually executed after it. This causes instructions to be executed in sequence. The branch and

control instructions alter the flow of instructions so that one sequence may follow another, or a sequence may be repeated. Altering the flow can be unconditional, or can depend on a specific result of an operation or compare.

7. *Input/output*—These instructions deal specifically with operations involving I/O peripherals. They include data transfer operations and control of I/O devices.
8. *Special-purpose instructions*—This final category is included to cover any instructions which don't fall into the other categories. For any given computer, there are always a few special-purpose instructions.

## Addressing Modes

Each instruction specifies both an operation and an operand. The operand is not necessarily changed by the instruction, but it is always involved. More often than not, the operand resides in memory. The operand must be fetched from memory just as the opcode is fetched from memory. While the opcode is fetched from the address specified by the program counter register, there may be several methods of specifying the address of the operand. These methods are collectively referred to as addressing modes. In most microprocessors, several addressing modes are available so that either memory or processing time can be conserved. The ways in which memory and time are conserved will become more apparent as the specific modes are discussed.

There are six popular modes of addressing among microprocessors. These are immediate, direct, indexed, indirect, relative, and implied. There may be other addressing modes in specific microprocessors, but they tend to be special-purpose modes and are often combinations of the six basic modes. The following descriptions of these six modes assume 8-bit instruction and data words, and 16-bit addresses.

The *immediate* addressing mode is one in which the operand resides in the byte immediately following the opcode. Immediate mode instructions occupy two bytes of memory, one for the opcode and one for the data byte.

In the *direct* mode, the address of the operand immediately follows the opcode. In most cases, these instructions occupy three bytes of memory, one for the 8-bit opcode, and two for the 16-bit address.

The *indexed* mode of addressing relies on an index register to aid in addressing. Index registers are generally 16-bit registers, so the index register itself is capable of generating an address. What is often the case, though, is that the byte following the opcode is also used in indexed addressing. The offset, as it is sometimes called, is added to the index register and the sum is used as an effective address. The offset may be a signed or unsigned value. The index register itself is generally unaffected after execution of an indexed instruction, even though an offset is involved. Indexed instructions generally occupy two bytes of memory, one for the opcode and one for the offset.

The *indirect* mode of addressing relies on some other source to generate an address. There are two kinds of indirect addressing, register and memory. In register indirect addressing, the contents of a register are used as the operand address. The register used is usually a general-purpose one. This addressing differs from indexed addressing in that there can be no offset involved in register indirect addressing. In memory indirect addressing, the operand address is specified by the contents of one or two memory locations. Indirect addressing instructions may occupy one, two, or three bytes depending upon the type of indirect addressing used.

The *relative* mode of addressing, which is generally used in branch instructions, relies on the program counter for operand addressing. Relative addressing is similar to indexed addressing, except that the program counter is used instead of the index register. The offset or relative value, which follows the opcode, is usually a signed value.

The *implied* mode of addressing is one in which the operand is implicit in the opcode. For example, in an instruction which increments an accumulator, the operand, which is the accumulator, is specified as part of the instruction. Implicit operand instructions are usually 1-byte instructions.

Before describing specific instructions, it is appropriate to discuss mnemonics. While each instruction is represented by a unique opcode, which is decoded in the instruction register, the opcode does not lend itself to human usage. A *mnemonic* is a convenient way of representing instructions. Mnemonics are unique three- or four-letter representations of instructions which give some indication of the function of the specific instructions. In the following descriptions, the instructions will be identified primarily by mnemonics.

In the descriptions that follow, the operation of each instruction will be explained verbally and there may be a graphic example. There will be a logic equation which represents the operation of the instruction. This equation will indicate the operation involved and the operands, but will not show the effect on the condition code register unless it is one of the operands.

## *MC6800 Instructions*

Recall that the registers within the MC6800 include the accumulators A and B, the index register, the stack pointer, the program counter, and the condition code register. In this environment are 72 instructions with seven addressing modes. The instructions occupy one, two, or three bytes of memory, and require variable amounts of time for execution.

The addressing modes of the MC6800 include the immediate mode and the indexed mode which occupy two bytes of memory each. The MC6800 has two modes of direct addressing called the direct mode and the extended mode. The direct mode allows addressing of only the first 256 bytes of memory and occupies two bytes, while the extended mode allows addressing of anywhere in 65K of memory and occupies three bytes. The relative mode is employed for branch instructions. There is an implied mode of addressing, and there is also an accumulator addressing mode in which one of the accumulators is the operand. Both the implied and accumulator instructions occupy one byte each.

## Data Transfer Instructions

Data transfer instructions in the MC6800 are load and store instructions. The load and store accumulator instructions will be covered first. Other loads, stores, and transfer instructions will be postponed until pointer register instructions are discussed.

The most fundamental instruction of any computer is the load accumulator instruction. This instruction transfers a byte of data from memory to an accumulator. The MC6800 has two such instructions, load accumulator A, denoted by the mnemonic LDA A, and load accumulator B, denoted by LDA B. Each of these instructions has four addressing modes, immediate (IMM), direct (DIR), indexed (IND), and extended (EXT). The distinction among the addressing modes lies in the opcodes. The logic equation for load accumulator is Acc $\leftarrow$ M, or the accumulator is replaced by the contents of the addressed memory location. The opcodes for the LDA A instruction are *86, *96, *A6, and *B6, which use the immediate, direct, indexed, and extended addressing modes, respectively. Similarly, the opcodes for load accumulator B are *C6, *D6, *E6, and *F6, which use immediate, direct, indexed, and extended addressing, respectively. Operation of the four modes of the load accumulator instruction are shown graphically in Figure 6.1.

In order for the instructions to be executed, the program counter must contain the address of the opcode. Following execution of each instruction, the program counter will be adjusted to contain the address of the first byte following the last byte of the preceding instruction.

Figure 6.1a shows the immediate addressing mode. In this case, the byte immediately following the opcode is transferred to accumulator A. This instruction is used when a specific value is to be loaded into an accumulator. The total instruction occupies two bytes.

Figure 6.1b shows the direct addressing mode. The byte following the opcode is used as the less significant 8 bits of the address of the byte to be loaded. The more significant 8 bits are zeros in this particular case. This instruction occupies only two bytes of memory, and only the locations *0000 through *00FF are accessible using this instruction.

In Figure 6.1c, the byte immediately following the opcode is added to the contents of the index register (IX), and the sum is the address of the operand. The value in the index register must previously have been loaded, and the contents of the index register prior to execution of the instruction remain after execution, that is, the contents remain constant through an indexed instruction. Indexed instructions allow access to all of memory while occupying only two bytes.

Figure 6.1d shows the extended addressing mode. In this case, the byte immediately following the opcode is the more significant 8 bits of the

*FIGURE 6.1: Load Accumulator Instructions*

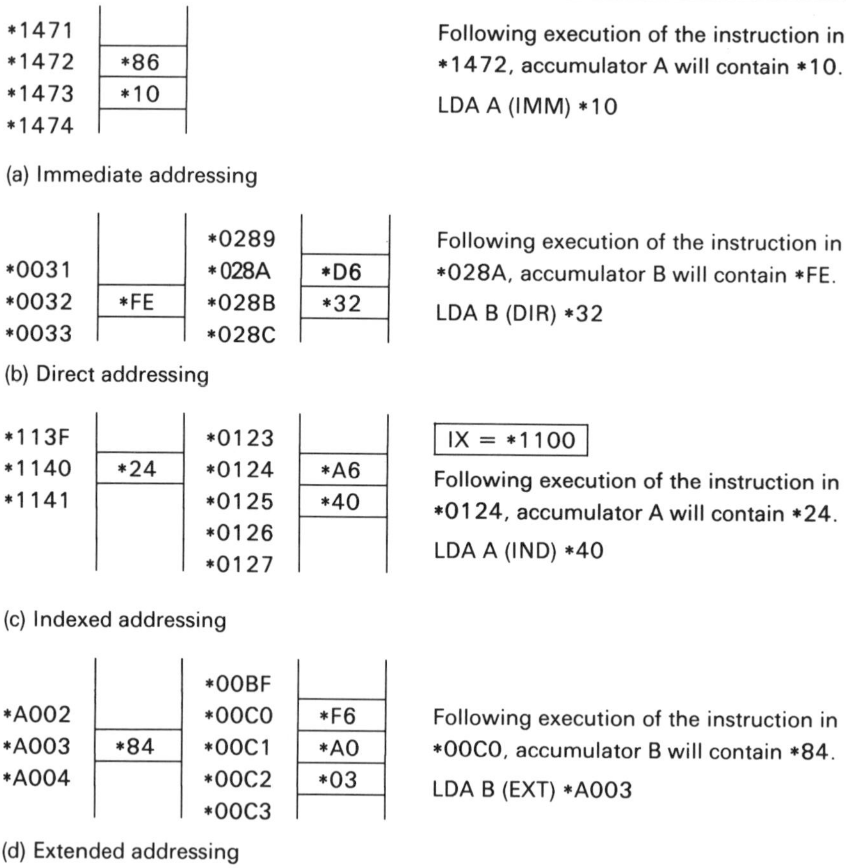

effective address, and the second byte after the opcode is the less significant 8 bits of the effective address. The extended addressing mode allows access to anywhere in memory.

The load accumulator instruction affects only the Z, N, and V bits of the condition code register. If the loaded byte is zero, then Z will be set. If bit 7 of the loaded byte is set, then N will be set. The overflow bit is always reset after a load accumulator instruction.

Remember that the addressed memory location is not affected by the load accumulator instruction. The contents of the location remain the same after execution of the instruction. A copy of the contents of the memory location is transferred to the accumulator.

The addressing modes of the remaining instructions will not be covered in similar detail unless it is the first time the mode is discussed or unless there is something unusual about the instruction.

The store accumulator is exactly the opposite of the load accumulator. In it the contents of the accumulator are transferred to the addressed memory location. The logic equation for the store accumulator instruction is M ← Acc, or the addressed memory location is replaced by the contents of the accumulator. The MC6800 has two store accumulator instructions, store accumulator A (STA A) and store accumulator B (STA B). Each of these is available in the direct, indexed, and extended addressing modes. The immediate mode is not used in store accumulator instructions because a store immediate does not store data in a specific location. Data must be stored in a specific location so it can be recalled later on. The opcodes for the store accumulator A are *97, *A7, and *B7 for the direct, indexed, and extended modes. The corresponding opcodes for store accumulator B are *D7, *E7, and *F7. Figure 6.2 shows two examples of the store accumulator instruction.

After execution of the store accumulator instruction, the contents of the accumulator are unaffected. A copy of the contents of the accumulator is transferred to the addressed memory location.

The store accumulator instruction affects only the Z, N, and V bits of the condition code register. If the stored number is zero, then Z will be set, and if bit 7 of the stored number is set, then N will be set. The V bit is reset by the store accumulator instruction.

## *Data Alter Instructions*

The data alter instruction group is one in which the contents of registers and memory locations are affected in specific ways. This group includes CLR (clear), INC (increment), DEC (decrement), COM (1's complement),

*FIGURE 6.2: Store Accumulator Instructions*

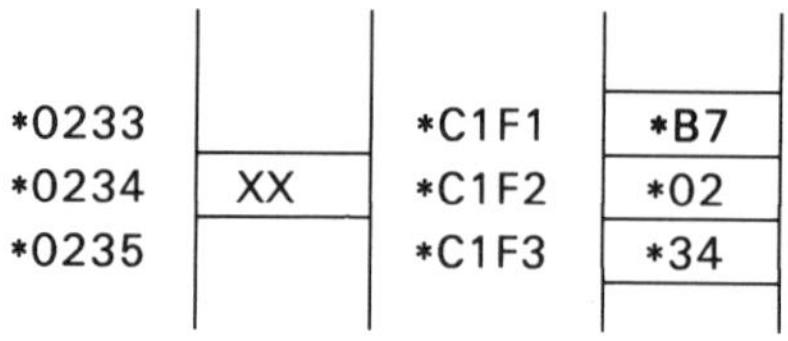


ACC A = *15

Following execution of the instruction in *C1F1, memory location *0234 will contain *15.

STA A (EXT) *0234

(a) Extended addressing

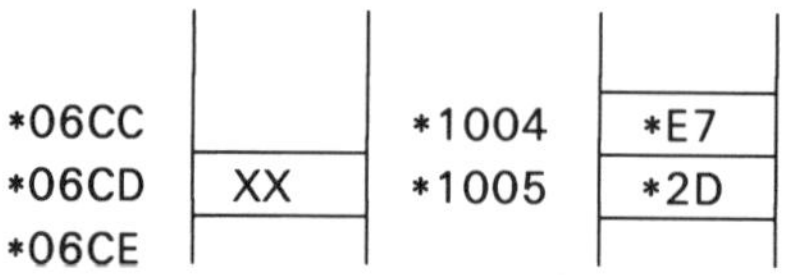


IX = *06A0 ACC B = *FF

Following execution of the instruction in *1004, memory location *06CD will contain *FF.

STA B (IND) *2D

(b) Indexed addressing

and NEG (2's complement). In each of these instructions, only one register or memory location is involved.

The *clear* instruction simply changes the contents of the operand to *00. There are two register clear instructions, CLR A and CLR B, the opcodes of which are *4F and *5F, respectively. The two memory clear instructions use the indexed and extended addressing modes, and the opcodes are *6F and *7F, respectively. The operation of two clear instructions is shown in Figure 6.3. The register clear instructions occupy one byte each, the indexed clear occupies two bytes, and the extended mode clear occupies three bytes. Following any clear instruction, the Z bit is set, and the N, C, and V bits are all reset. The logic equations for CLR are M ← 00 and Acc ← 00.

The *increment* instruction adds one to the contents of the operand. There are register increment instructions, INC A and INC B, represented by the opcodes *4C and *5C, respectively, and there are two memory increment instructions, the indexed increment, represented by *6C, and the extended increment, represented by *7C. Like the clear instruction, the accumulator increments occupy one byte each, the indexed increment occupies two bytes, and the extended increment occupies three bytes. Figure 6.4 shows an example of an increment instruction. Following execution of an increment instruction, the N bit and Z bit are set or reset, depending on the results of the increment. The V bit is set only if an increment is attempted on the binary value 01111111. The rationale behind this is that a negative number can change to a positive number via an increment, but a positive number cannot change to a negative number. The

*FIGURE 6.3: Clear Instructions*

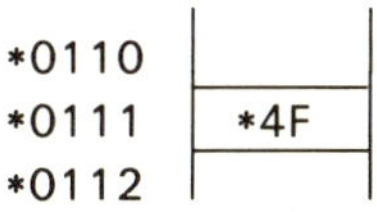


Following execution of the instruction in *0111, accumulator A will contain *00.

CLR A

(a) Accumulator addressing

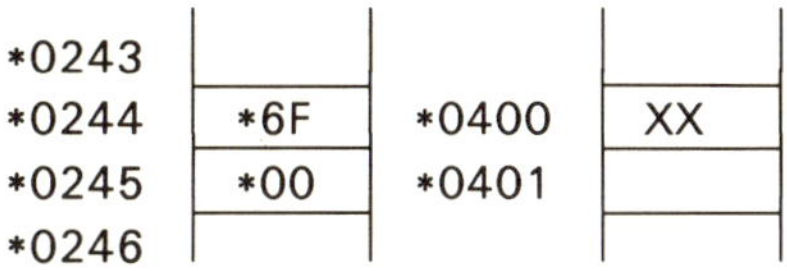


IX = *0400

Following execution of the instruction in *0244, memory location *0400 will contain *00.

CLR (IND) *00

(b) Indexed addressing

*FIGURE 6.4: Increment Instruction*

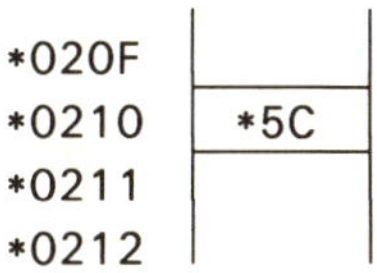


B = *FF

Following execution of the instruction in *0210, accumulator B will contain *00.

INC B

carry bit is not affected by increment. The logic equations for increment are M ← M − 1 and Acc ← Acc − 1.

The *decrement* instruction is identical to the increment instruction except that one is subtracted from the operand. The opcodes for decrement are *4A, *5A, *6A, and *7A, corresponding to the DEC A, DEC B, indexed mode, and extended mode, respectively. Figure 6.5 shows an example of a decrement instruction. The decrement instruction sets or resets the N and Z bits according to the results of the operation. The overflow bit (bit V) is set only if a decrement is attempted on the binary value 10000000. This guards against changing a negative number to a positive number via a decrement. The carry bit as well as the remaining condition code bits are not affected by DEC. Decrement is represented by the equations M ← M − 1, and Acc ← Acc − 1.

The next instruction in the series of data alter instructions is the *complement* instruction. COM logically complements, or 1's complements, the operand. The logical complement is available as COM A, COM B, an indexed mode complement, and an extended mode complement, repre-

*FIGURE 6.5: Decrement Instruction*

| Address | Contents | Address | Contents |
|---|---|---|---|
| | | *00C4 | |
| *000F | | *00C5 | *7A |
| *0010 | *26 | *00C6 | *00 |
| *0011 | | *00C7 | *10 |
| | | *00C8 | |

Following execution of the instruction in *00C5, memory location *0010 will contain *25.

DEC (EXT) *0010

sented by the opcodes *43, *53, *63, and *73, respectively. Figure 6.6 shows an example of the complement instruction. COM affects the N and Z bits according to the results of the operation. In addition, the V bit is reset and the C bit is set unconditionally. COM is represented by the equations $M \leftarrow \overline{M}$ and $Acc \leftarrow \overline{Acc}$.

The last of the data alter instructions is the *negate* or 2's complement instruction. NEG converts the operand to its arithmetic 2's complement form. The opcodes for NEG A, NEG B, indexed mode NEG, and extended mode NEG are *40, *50, *60, and *70, respectively. Figure 6.7 shows the operation of a negate instruction. NEG affects the N and Z bits according to the results of the operation. The V bit is set only if a negate is attempted on the binary value 10000000. This would be the only case where negating a negative value yields a negative result. The C bit is set only when the value 00000000 is negated. The other condition code register bits are not affected. The logic equations for NEG are $M \leftarrow 00 - M$ and $Acc \leftarrow 00 - Acc$.

*FIGURE 6.6: Complement Instruction*

| Address | Contents |
|---|---|
| *012A | |
| *012B | *43 |
| *012C | |

A = *70

Following execution of the instruction in *012B, accumulator A will contain *8F.

COM A

*FIGURE 6.7: Negate Instruction*

| Address | Contents | Address | Contents |
|---|---|---|---|
| *0143 | | | |
| *0144 | *70 | *0304 | |
| *0145 | *03 | *0305 | *10 |
| *0146 | *05 | *0306 | |
| *0147 | | | |

Following execution of the instruction in *0144, memory location *0305 will contain *F0.

NEG (EXT) *0305

## *Arithmetic and Logic Instructions*

Arithmetic and logic instructions are probably the most important and most powerful instructions within a microprocessor. These specific instructions are what distinguishes a computer from a collection of random electronic logic elements. These instructions indeed give the computer its ability to compute. The arithmetic and logic instructions within the MC6800 can be loosely divided into two groups: those with two operands and those with one operand. The first group includes the add, subtract, INCLUSIVE OR, EXCLUSIVE OR, and AND; the second group includes the shift and rotate operations. Each instruction in the first group employs the four memory addressing modes: immediate, direct, indexed, and extended. Also, each instruction in the first group is available using accumulator A or accumulator B. The second group of instructions is available in either accumulator mode as well as the indexed and extended memory modes.

The most fundamental arithmetic operation is addition. In the MC6800, this operation is the add accumulator instruction, represented by the logic equation Acc $\leftarrow$ Acc + M. The memory operand can be addressed by the immediate, direct, indexed, and extended addressing modes. The four opcodes for ADD A are *8B, *9B, *AB, and *BB, representing the immediate, direct, indexed, and extended memory addressing modes, respectively. The corresponding opcodes for ADD B are *CB, *DB, *EB, and *FB, respectively. An example of the add accumulator instruction is shown in Figure 6.8. The sign bit (N), zero bit (Z), overflow bit (V), and carry bit (C) are all affected by the add accumulator instructions, and each is affected according to the result of the operation. The half-carry bit H is also affected, but discussion of this bit will be deferred until later in the chapter.

The subtract accumulator instruction is another of the fundamental arithmetic operations. In this case, the contents of the addressed memory location are subtracted from the accumulator, as indicated by the equation Acc $\leftarrow$ Acc − M. The subtract operation is available with both accumulators and in the four memory addressing modes. The corresponding

*FIGURE 6.8: Add Accumulator Instruction*

| Address | Contents |
|---|---|
| *0362 | |
| *0363 | *8B |
| *0364 | *15 |
| *0365 | |

A = *27

Following execution of the instruction in *0363, accumulator A will contain *3C.

ADD A (IMM) *15

opcodes for SUB A are *80, *90, *A0, and *B0, and the opcodes for SUB B are *C0, *D0, *E0, and *F0, respectively. The condition code bits N, Z, and V are affected in the usual way according to the results of the operation. The carry bit is also affected by subtract, but in this special case, the carry bit is set to indicate a borrow, that is, C is set whenever a larger number is subtracted from a smaller number. Figure 6.9 shows the operation of a subtract instruction.

The add accumulator instruction discussed earlier performs an 8-bit signed addition operation. This allows operations on integers ranging in value from −128 to +127, however, few real world applications work with numbers so restricted. Many microprocessors avoid this restriction by the use of an instruction which allows the addition and subtraction of numbers larger than 8 bits. The addition instructions are the add with carry, ADC A and ADC B, represented by the equation $Acc \leftarrow Acc + M + C$. The accumulator is replaced by the sum of the accumulator plus the contents of the addressed memory location plus the carry bit. Consider the addition of two 16-bit numbers. The two less significant bytes are added first, and the carry bit is set or reset according to the result. The two more significant bytes are then added, with the previous carry included in the sum. The ADC A opcodes for the four memory addressing modes are *89, *99, *A9, and *B9, respectively. The corresponding opcodes for the ADC B are *C9, *D9, *E9, and *F9, respectively. An example of the ADC instruction is shown in Figure 6.10. The condition code register bits are affected the same as they are after a normal add instruction. Following an add with carry instruction, the carry bit will reflect the carry from the latest add, that is, the add with carry.

*FIGURE 6.9: Subtract Accumulator Instruction*

| Address | Contents | Address | Contents |
|---|---|---|---|
| *00E4 | | *02AF | |
| *00E5 | *6F | *02B0 | *D0 |
| *00E6 | | *02B1 | *E5 |
| *00E7 | | *02B2 | |

B = *60

Following execution of the instruction in *02B0, accumulator B will contain *F1.

SUB B (DIR) *E5

*FIGURE 6.10: Add with Carry Instruction*

| Address | Contents | Address | Contents |
|---|---|---|---|
| *004F | | *0140 | |
| *0050 | *20 | *0141 | *D9 |
| *0051 | | *0142 | *50 |
| | | *0143 | |

B = *07   C = 1

Following execution of the instruction in *0141, accumulator B will contain *28.

ADC B (DIR) *50

The subtract with borrow instruction, SBC A, and SBC B, is the subtraction counterpart of the add with carry. The accumulator is replaced by the result of the accumulator minus the contents of the addressed memory location minus the carry bit. Recall that the carry bit is set to indicate a borrow in the subtract instructions. The logic equation for the SBC instruction is Acc ← Acc − M − C. An example of the subtract with borrow instruction is shown in Figure 6.11. The opcodes for the four addressing modes of SBC A are *82, *92, *A2, and *B2, and the corresponding opcodes for the SBC B are *C2, *D2, *E2, and *F2, respectively. This instruction allows the subtraction of binary integers of 16 bits or more. All the condition code bits are set to reflect the result of the subtract with borrow.

The MC6800 has three logic instructions which implement the operations OR, AND, and EXCLUSIVE OR. Each of these instructions is available with both accumulators and with all four memory addressing modes. The OR instruction is represented by the mnemonic ORA A and ORA B. The logic equation for the OR accumulator is Acc ← Acc + M, where the + sign indicates logical OR. The four opcodes for ORA A are *8A, *9A, *AA, and *BA, corresponding to the immediate, direct, indexed, and extended addressing modes, respectively. The four opcodes for ORA B are *CA, *DA, *EA, and *FA, respectively. The AND accumulator instruction is represented by the mnemonics AND A and AND B, and by the logic equation Acc ← Acc • M. The four opcodes for AND A are *84, *94, *A4, and *B4, and the opcodes for the AND B are *C4, *D4, *E4, and *F4, respectively. The EXCLUSIVE OR accumulator instruction is represented by the mnemonics EOR A and EOR B, and the logic equation is Acc ← Acc ⊕ M. The four opcodes for EOR A are *88, *98, *A8, and *B8, and the opcodes for the EOR B are *C8, *D8, *E8, and *F8, respectively.

Each of the logical instructions involve no arithmetic significance in the binary numbers operated upon. The condition code register bits Z and N are set or reset by the logical operations, indicating a zero result or the state of bit 7 of the accumulator. The carry bit is not affected by the logical instructions, and the overflow bit is unconditionally reset.

*FIGURE 6.11: Subtract with Borrow Instruction*

| Address | Contents | Address | Contents |
|---|---|---|---|
| *0020 | | *0126 | |
| *0021 | | *0127 | *92 |
| *0022 | *16 | *0128 | *22 |
| *0023 | | *0129 | |

A = *2A    C = 1

Following execution of the instruction in *0127, accumulator A will contain *13

SBC A (DIR) *22

## *Shift and Rotate Instructions*

The shift and rotate instructions are an extension of the arithmetic and logic capability provided by the MC6800. They implement the logical shift, arithmetic shift, and rotate binary operations. Five shift and rotate instructions are provided. The addressing modes are identical to the addressing modes of the CLR instructions: either accumulator A or B is involved, or memory is involved via the indexed or extended addressing mode. The shifts and rotates affect the condition code register bits, and they also use the carry bit actively in execution of the instructions. In order to show the specific operation of each instruction, a diagram will be included in the descriptions.

The *logical shift right* instruction, LSR, obviously implements the binary logical shift right operation. The four opcodes for LSR are *44 for LSR A, *54 for LSR B, *64 for LSR indexed, and *74 for LSR extended. In the binary logical shift right operation, each bit of the operand is moved one position to the right, with a zero bit filling in on the left and the original rightmost bit being dropped. This is indeed how the operation proceeds in the MC6800, except that the original rightmost bit is shifted into the carry bit. This operation is shown in Figure 6.12a. The LSR instruction and the remaining shift and rotate instructions involve 9 bits: 8 bits of the operand plus the carry bit. The N bit is always reset by this instruction, as a zero is always shifted into the sign bit. The Z bit is set or reset according to the results in the 8 bits of the operand, and the carry bit is set according to the original rightmost bit. Even though LSR is not a signed arithmetic operation, the V bit is nevertheless set if C is one and N is zero or C is zero and N is one, and V is reset otherwise. An example of LSR is shown in Figure 6.12b.

*FIGURE 6.12: LSR Instruction*

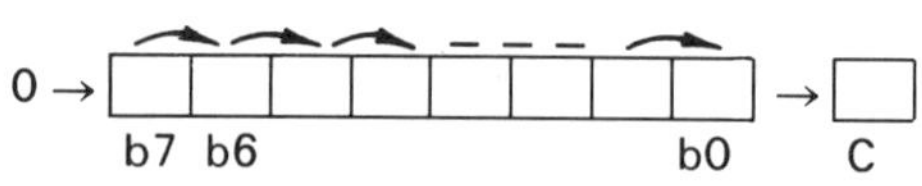


(a) Operation of LSR

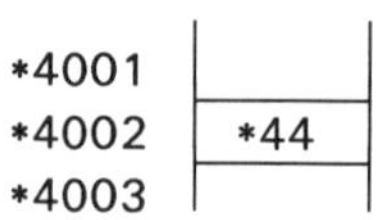


A = *97

Following execution of the instruction in *4002, accumulator A will contain *4B and the carry bit will be 1.

LSR A

(b) Example of LSR

The *arithmetic shift right* instruction, ASR, is similar in operation to LSR, except that the sign bit remains unchanged. This is exactly the same as the binary arithmetic shift right operation. The four opcodes for ASR are *47, *57, *67, and *77, corresponding to ASR A, ASR B, ASR indexed, and ASR extended, respectively. In this instruction, the N bit remains unchanged, the Z bit is set or reset according to the results in the 8 bits of the operand, and the carry bit becomes the original contents of the rightmost bit. Even though an overflow is not significant since the sign bit does not change, V will be set if $C \oplus N = 1$ and is reset otherwise. The operation of ASR and an example are shown in Figure 6.13.

In the MC6800, both the logical shift left and the arithmetic shift left operations are implemented by one instruction, arithmetic shift left. Represented by the mnemonic ASL, arithmetic shift left has four opcodes, *48, *58, *68, and *78, corresponding to ASL A, ASL B, ASL indexed, and ASL extended, respectively. In ASL, each bit of the operand is shifted one position left with a zero filling in the rightmost bit, and with the original leftmost bit moving to the carry bit. This is in fact the binary logical shift left operation. The binary arithmetic shift left operation is identical except that the sign bit is not changed. In this case, an overflow condition occurs if a bit opposite the sign bit is shifted out of the position next to the sign. In the MC6800 ASL, an overflow condition can be detected by the V bit. V will be set if $C \oplus N = 1$, that is, if a bit opposite the original sign bit is shifted into the sign bit while the sign bit is shifted into the carry bit. So the ASL instruction can implement both logical and arithmetic shifts left. When an arithmetic shift is executed, an overflow condition can be detected by the V bit. Following execution of ASL, the carry bit (C), sign bit (N, bit 7 of the operand), zero bit (Z), and the overflow bit (V) are all set or reset according to the results of the operation. The operation of ASL and an example are shown in Figure 6.14.

*FIGURE 6.13: ASR Instruction*

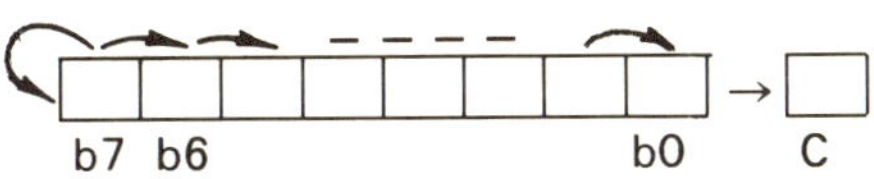


(a) Operation of ASR

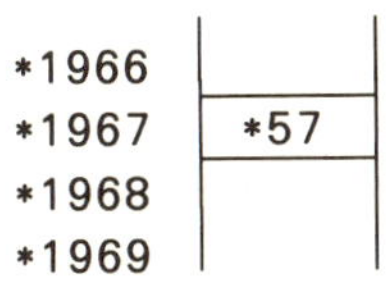


B = *97

Following execution of the instruction in *1967, accumulator B will contain *CB and C will be 1.

ASR B

(b) Example of ASR

*FIGURE 6.14: ASL Instruction*

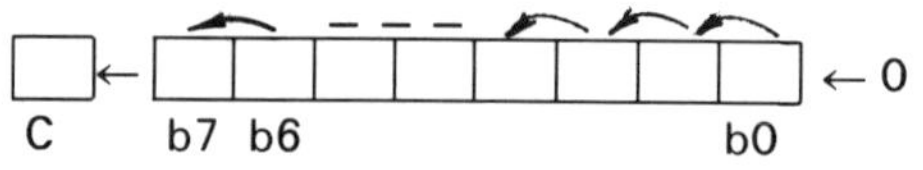


(a) Operation of ASL

Following execution of the instruction in *0150, memory location *0124 will contain *C2, C will be 1, and V will be 0.

ASL (EXT) *0124

(b) Example of ASL

Logical rotation in the MC6800 is implemented by the instructions *rotate right* (ROR) and *rotate left* (ROL). The opcodes for ROR are *46, *56, *66, and *76 for accumulator A, accumulator B, indexed mode, and extended mode, respectively. The corresponding opcodes for ROL are *49, *59, *69, and *79. Like shift instructions, rotate instructions each involve 9 bits. In ROR, each bit of the operand is moved one position right. The original rightmost bit is shifted into the carry bit, while the original carry bit is shifted into the leftmost bit. In ROL, each bit is moved one position left, the original leftmost bit is shifted into the carry which is shifted into the rightmost bit. In each case, the N and Z bits are set or reset according to the results in the 8-bit operand. While an overflow condition is not significant

*FIGURE 6.15: ROR Instruction*

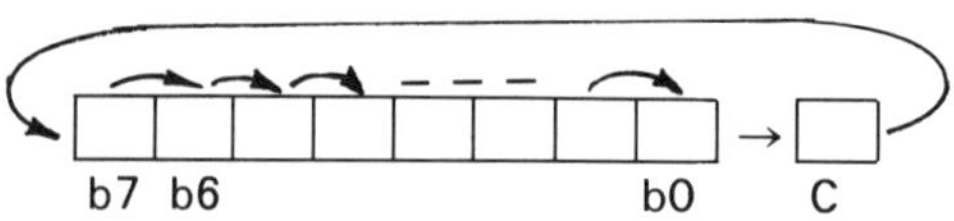


(a) Operation of ROR

IX = *0200 C = 0

Following execution of the instruction in *1021, memory location *0237 will contain *79, and C will be 1.

ROR (IND) *37

(b) Example of ROR

in a rotate operation, V is affected as it is in the shift instruction. The ROR instruction is shown in Figure 6.15, and ROL is shown in Figure 6.16.

The reason that the shift and rotate operations in the MC6800 involve the carry bit is so that multiple byte operations are possible. A 16-bit logical shift right can be accomplished by first logically shifting the more significant byte right, then rotating the less significant byte right. The shift propagates from one byte to the other via the carry bit. Similarly, a 16-bit arithmetic shift left can be accomplished by first arithmetically shifting the less significant byte left, then rotating the more significant byte left. The rotate will suffice for the arithmetic shift left because an overflow condition can be checked with the rotate. Multiple byte rotates are also possible, but they are tricky since the carry bit from the last byte rotated must be included in the first byte rotated.

## Program Control Instructions

Each of the instructions described so far not only affects the operands of the instructions, but also affects the program counter. Specifically, each instruction changes the program counter so that the instruction located in the byte following the instruction will be executed. This allows instructions to be executed in sequence one after the other, beginning at some starting point and proceeding indefinitely. It is possible, however, to alter the flow of instruction execution so that certain sequences are skipped or repeated. The altering is done by the program control instructions. Some of the program control instructions are unconditional, and some depend on the status of one or more of the condition code register bits. The two program control instructions in the MC6800 are the jump instruction and the branch instruction.

*FIGURE 6.16: ROL Instructions*

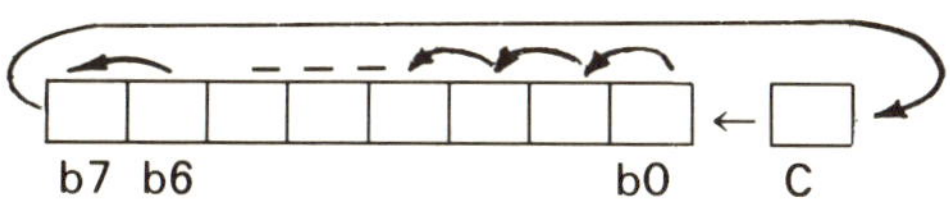


(a) Operation of ROL

| Address | Contents |
|---|---|
| *00A8 | |
| *00A9 | *59 |
| *00AA | |

B = *C4　C = 1

Following execution of the instruction in *00A9, accumulator B will contain *89 and C will be 1.

ROL B

(b) Example of ROL

The *jump* instruction simply replaces the contents of the program counter with the effective address in the instruction. Represented by the mnemonic JMP, it is available in the extended and indexed addressing modes. The logic equation for JMP is PC ← effective address. The opcodes for JMP are *6E and *7E, corresponding to the indexed and extended addressing modes. Examples of JMP are shown in Figure 6.17. Note that both the indexed and the extended JMP allow a jump to anywhere in memory because the effective address in both cases is 16 bits. The indexed jump occupies one less byte of memory but requires the index register to be preloaded. None of the condition code register bits are affected by the jump instructions.

The *branch* instruction is similar to the jump instruction in that the contents of the program counter are replaced. The new value in the program counter will be the effective address. The branch instruction employs the relative addressing mode. This mode implies that the new value in the program counter will depend on the current or old value. Relative addressing mode instructions always occupy two bytes and always involve the program counter. The first byte is the opcode, and the second byte is called the relative value. The logic equation for the branch instruction is PC ← PC + 2 + relative value. The program counter is replaced by the value in the program counter (where the branch opcode is) plus 2 plus the relative value in the second byte. The relative value in the second byte is an 8-bit *signed* value. This means that the program counter can increase in value (a forward branch) or decrease in value (a backward branch). The direction of the branch is indicated by the sign of the relative value: positive

***FIGURE 6.17: JMP Instructions***

| Address | Contents |
|---|---|
| *0161 | |
| *0162 | *7E |
| *0163 | *00 |
| *0164 | *54 |
| *0165 | |

Following execution of the instruction in *0162, the instruction in location *0054 will be executed.

JMP (EXT) *0054

(a) Extended mode

| Address | Contents |
|---|---|
| *044A | |
| *044B | *6E |
| *044C | *76 |
| *044D | |

IX = *0280

Following execution of the instruction in *044B, the instruction in *02F6 will be executed.

JMP (IND) *76

(b) Indexed mode

indicates a forward branch and negative indicates a backward branch.

The simplest branch instruction is the branch always, represented by the mnemonic BRA and by the opcode *20. Figure 6.18 shows two examples of the BRA instruction. A forward branch is shown in part (a). The address from which the next instruction will be executed is determined by adding the program counter plus 2 to the relative value. Figure 6.18b shows a backward branch. In this case, adding *0212, 2, and *E8 indicates that the next instruction should be executed from *02FC. This is incorrect since a backward branch is indicated, but *02FC is greater than *0212. The error lies in the fact that an attempt is made to add an 8-bit signed quantity with a 16-bit quantity. This cannot be done, so the 8-bit value must be changed to 16 bits, and this is done by repeating the sign bit 8 times. In part (a) the sign bit zero is automatically repeated, and in part (b) the (FF) represents the repeated sign bit. Once the sign bit is repeated, the normal hexadecimal addition process will yield the address of the next instruction. Note that the carry out of the most significant hex character is ignored. Remember that a backward branch will occur when the relative value is negative, that is, when the more significant hex character is 8, 9, A, B, C, D, E, or F. Figure 6.19 shows the addressing range of the branch instructions.

The BRA instruction is functionally identical to the JMP instruction. It is an unconditional transfer of control from one location in memory to another. The range of BRA is restricted, but it occupies two bytes of memory and does not require any other registers to be loaded. The power of branch instructions is not that they are short jump instructions, but that they can be conditional.

*FIGURE 6.18: BRA Instruction and Relative Addressing*

| Address | Contents | Calculation | |
|---|---|---|---|
| *0341 | | | Following execution of the instruction in *0342, the instruction in *0358 will be executed. |
| *0342 | *20 | * 0342 | |
| *0343 | *14 | + * 2 | |
| *0344 | | + * 14 | BRA *14 |
| | | * 0358 | |

(a) Forward branch

| Address | Contents | Calculation | |
|---|---|---|---|
| *0211 | | * 0212 | Following execution of the instruction in *0212, the instruction in *01FC will be executed. |
| *0212 | *20 | + * 2 | |
| *0213 | *E8 | *(FF) E8 | |
| *0214 | | * 01FC | BRA *E8 or BRA - *18 |

(b) Backward branch

*FIGURE 6.19: Addressing Range of Branch Instructions*

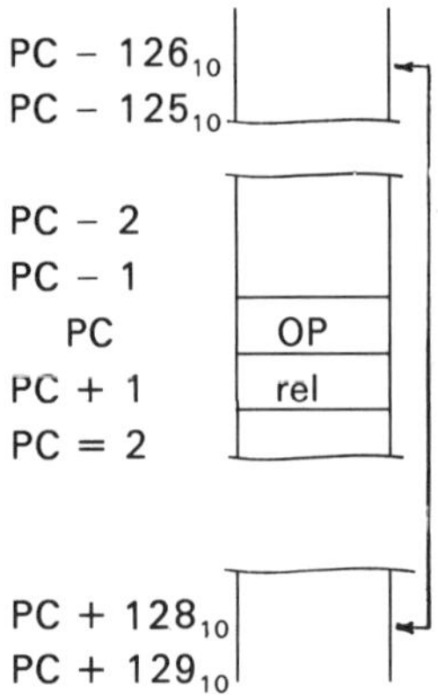


Given a branch instruction anywhere in memory, the instruction can branch anywhere forward up to $129_{10}$ bytes ahead (relative value = *7F) or anywhere backward up to $126_{10}$ back (relative value = *80).

The conditional branch instructions allow decisions to be made based on the results of operations. The results of operations are manifested in the condition code register bits, and the conditional branch instructions take alternate actions depending upon the status of those bits. There are 14 conditional branch instructions, and the alternatives available in each are either a branch or no branch. If the condition is satisfied, then the branch occurs; otherwise the next instruction in sequence is executed.

Consider the instruction *branch if equal* to zero, which is represented by the mnemonic BEQ and by the opcode *27. BEQ tests the Z bit. The logic equations are

$$PC \leftarrow \begin{cases} PC + 2 + rel & \text{if } Z = 1 \\ PC + 2 & \text{if } Z = 0 \end{cases}$$

which implies that the branch occurs if the Z bit is set, and the instruction following the branch instruction is executed if Z is not set.

A second instruction which tests the Z bit is the *branch if not equal* to zero, or BNE. The BNE instruction, represented by the opcode *26, is the direct opposite of BEQ. With BNE, the branch occurs when Z = 0, and no branch occurs when Z = 1. The logic equation for BNE is identical to that of BEQ, except for the states of the Z bit. An example of the BEQ instruction is shown in Figure 6.20.

There are six additional branch instructions in which the branch depends on only one bit. *Branch if carry set*, BCS, and *branch if carry clear*, BCC, test the status of the carry bit. The opcodes for BCS and BCC are *25, and *24, respectively, and the logic equations are similar to those for the BEQ and BNE instructions. Likewise, *branch if overflow set*, BVS, and *branch if overflow clear*, BVC, test the overflow, or V bit. BVS and BVC are

*FIGURE 6.20: Branch if Equal to Zero Instruction*

| Address | Contents | Calculation |
|---|---|---|
| *12C6 | | *12C7 |
| *12C7 | *27 | + 2 |
| *12C8 | *10 | + 10 |
| *12C9 | | *12D9 |

Following execution of the instruction in *12C7, the instruction in either *12D9 or *12C9 will be executed, depending on whether Z is set or reset.

BEQ + *10

represented by the opcodes *29 and *28, respectively. The sign of an operation can be tested by the *branch if plus*, BPL, and *branch if minus*, BMI instruction. These instructions, represented by the opcodes *2A and *2B, respectively, test the state of the N bit.

The preceding eight conditional branch instructions test the status of individual bits in the condition coder register. The remaining six conditional branch instructions involve multiple bits. Explanation of these six instructions will follow discussion of the next group of instructions.

## Comparison and Test Instructions

The condition code register bits allow characteristics of the results of arithmetic and logical operations to be recorded for further examination. It is often desirable to determine characteristics of specific quantities without performing any operations. For example, it may be desirable to know whether or not the contents of an accumulator are equal to or greater than a specific value. A method of determining this would be to subtract the value from the accumulator and then to check the Z and N bits. It may also be desirable to know if bits 2 and 5 of an accumulator are set. This could be done by ANDing the accumulator with *24 and checking the Z bit. The problem with each of these methods is that the contents of the accumulator are destroyed. Further operations on the quantity would require storing and loading of the value. The MC6800, along with most popular microprocessors, provides a method of nondestructive testing of accumulator contents. This method involves the comparison and test instructions. In the MC6800, these instructions include the compare, test, and bit instructions.

### *Compare Instruction*

The *compare accumulator instruction*, represented by the mnemonic CMP, is provided so that the contents of the accumulators can be compared numerically to specific values or to the contents of memory locations. The logic equation for compare accumulator is Acc − M. Note that the operand is subtracted from the accumulator, but the results of the operation aren't retained anywhere. In regard to hardware, this can be accomplished by gating the accumulator and the operand through the arithmetic/logic unit, but not gating the result into the accumulator. The only item affected by this operation is the condition code register. The compare instruction is available with both accumulators A and B. In addition, for each accumulator the instruction is available in the immediate, direct, indexed, and extended modes. The equivalent opcodes for CMP A are *81, *91, *A1, and *B1, respectively, while the opcodes for CMP B are *C1, *D1, *E1, and *F1, respectively.

Results of the comparisons can be checked using the conditional branch instructions. Equality or nonequality can be verified using the BEQ and BNE instructions. The nonequality relationship of the accumulator to the operand can be checked using the six remaining conditional branch instructions. Four of these instructions are available for use with signed binary numbers, and the other two are intended for use with unsigned values. The branch instructions for the signed quantities are the *branch if greater than* (BGT), *branch if greater than or equal to* (BGE), *branch if less than* (BLT), and *branch if less than or equal to* (BLE). When working with these instructions, the accumulator is mentioned first and the operand second. For example, following a comparison instruction with a BGE, the branch will occur if the accumulator is greater than or equal to the operand.

The logic equations for the BGE instruction are

$$\mathrm{PC} \leftarrow \begin{cases} \mathrm{PC} + 2 + \mathrm{rel}, & \text{if } \mathrm{N} \oplus \mathrm{V} = 0 \\ \mathrm{PC} + 2, & \text{otherwise} \end{cases}$$

The branch will occur if both the N and V bits are zero or if both are one. Figure 6.21 shows an example of the comparison instruction with the BGE instruction. Accumulator A is compared to the value 7. Three of the four combinations of N and V are possible. The example is provided only to show the relationships between the condition code register bits and the conditional branch instructions. It is not necessary to be thoroughly familiar with these relationships, only to remember that the accumulator is being compared to the operand.

The branch if greater than instruction, which tests the condition $Z + (N \oplus V) = 0$, will branch if the accumulator is greater than, but not equal to, the operand. BGT is represented by the opcode *2E.

The branch if less than is the opposite of the BGE instruction. Consequently, BLT tests the condition: $N \oplus V = 1$. In BLT, the branch occurs if the accumulator is less than the operand.

The final signed arithmetic branch instruction, branch if less than or equal to (BLE), tests the condition $Z + (N \oplus V) = 1$, which will branch if the accumulator is less than or equal to the operand.

The MC6800 provides two conditional branch instructions which

*FIGURE 6.21: Examples of the BGE Instruction*

| Address | Contents |
|---|---|
| *00FF | |
| *0100 | *81 |
| *0101 | *07 |
| *0102 | *2C |
| *0103 | *10 |
| *0104 | |

Following execution of the instructions in locations *0100 and *0102, the instruction in either *0104 or *0114 will be executed.

(a) Accumulator A contains *80 = $-128_{10}$

Subtract 7 from −128,

```
  10000000          V = 1, N = 0; V⊕N = 1, so no branch.
+ 11111001
  01111001 = OVF    −128 is not greater than or equal to 7.
```

(b) Accumulator A contains *F8 = $-8_{10}$

Subtract 7 from −8

```
  11111000          V = 0, N = 1; V⊕N = 1, so no branch.
+ 11111001
  11110001          −8 is not greater than or equal to 7.
```

(c) Accumulator A contains *11 = 17

Subtract 7 from 17

```
  00010001          V = 0, N = 0; V⊕N = 0 so branch.
+ 11111001
  00001010          17 is greater than or equal to 7.
```

operate in an unsigned manner. The first of these, *branch if higher*, or BHI, tests the condition C + Z = 0. The branch will occur if the accumulator has a higher value than the operand. For example, if accumulator A contained *FF, its value would be higher than any other operand value up to *FE. The *branch if lower or same*, BLS, is the reverse of BHI. With BLS, the branch occurs if the accumulator is lower in absolute value, or the same as the operand. BLS tests the condition C + Z = 1. BHI is represented by the opcode *22, and BLS is represented by *23.

### *Test Instruction*

Another numerical comparison instruction available in the MC6800 is *test instruction*, represented by the mnemonic TST. It can determine whether the operand is positive, negative, or zero, and can interrogate either accumulator or memory via the indexed and extended addressing modes. The four opcodes for TST are *4D, *5D, *6D, and *7D, corresponding to accumulator A, accumulator B, indexed mode, and extended mode, respectively. The logic equation is Operand – 00, or, simply, zero is subtracted from the operand. The operand is unaffected, but the Z and N bits are set or reset according to the contents of the operand. The overflow and carry bits are unconditionally reset. The primary purpose of TST is not to determine arithmetic properties of the accumulators. Properties of accumulators are recorded in the condition code bits, both when values are loaded and stored, and as the result of arithmetic and logic instruction. The primary purpose of TST is to interrogate memory locations without disturbing the accumulators.

### *Bit Instruction*

Logical testing in the MC6800 is accomplished by the *bit test instruction*. This instruction, represented by the mnemonic BIT, logically ANDs the accumulator with the operand, but does not maintain the result of the operation. BIT is available with both accumulators A and B, and both BIT A and BIT B are available in the four memory addressing modes immediate, direct, indexed, and extended. The four opcodes for BIT A are *85, *95, *A5, and *B5, and the opcodes for BIT B are *C5, *D5, *E5, and *F5, respectively. The BIT operation affects the Z and N bits, so that results of BIT can be tested using the BEQ or BNE, and possibly BPL and BMI. Figure 6.22 shows an example of BIT A. This particular instruction tests whether bit 7 or bit 4 of accumulator A is set. If either or both is a logic 1, the Z bit would be reset as a result of the instruction. In this particular case, the N bit will be set or reset according to bit 7 of the accumulator. In any event, the contents of accumulator A are not altered.

In summary then, the comparison and test instructions are what give the microprocessor the ability to perform comparisons and take alternate actions depending on the results.

Before moving on to the next major topic, it is appropriate to consider a small group of instructions which deals specifically with the condition code register bits. These instructions either set or reset specific bits. The *set carry*

*FIGURE 6.22: Example of BIT Test Instruction*

| Address | Contents |
|---|---|
| *0185 | |
| *0186 | *85 |
| *0187 | *90 |
| *0188 | |

A = *1E

Following execution of the instruction in *0186, the Z and N bits will be reset and accumulator A will be unchanged.

BIT A (IMM) *90

*instruction* (SEC) forces the carry bit to 1, and *clear carry* (CLC) forces C to 0. SEC is represented by the opcode *0D, and CLC is represented by *0C. *Set overflow* (SEV), represented by *0B, sets the V bit, and *clear overflow* (CLV), represented by *0A, resets V. The interrupt mask bit, I, is set by the *set interrupt mask instruction* (SEI) and is reset by the *clear interrupt mask instruction* (CLI). SEI is represented by *0F, and CLI is represented by *0D. More will be said about the I bit later in the chapter. There are no specific set and reset instructions for the H, N, and Z bits.

## *Stack Operations*

One of the more important concepts in microprocessors and certain other large-scale computers is the *push down stack* or simply the *stack*. The stack is an area of data storage in which items are stored and subsequently retrieved on a last-in-first-out (LIFO) basis. The stack is so named because of its similarity to a stack of plates in which only the top plate is accessible. If several plates are put on top, the last one put on will be the first one available. Similarly, those inserted most recently will be available first, and the very first one inserted will be the last one available. In microprocessors, the stack allows convenient storage of both data and addresses.

In the MC6800, the stack is an area of memory addressed by the stack pointer register. Since the stack pointer is a 16-bit register, the stack can be anywhere in memory. It must be read/write memory since data is stored on the stack. The stack can be as large as is necessary, provided sufficient memory is left over for program and data storage. The two primary instructions involved in stack operations are push and pull. The *push* operation represented by the mnemonic PSH, stores a byte of data on the stack. *Pull*, represented by PUL, retrieves a byte from the stack. Both push and pull are available with both accumulators A and B. PSH A, PSH B, PUL A, and PUL B occupy one byte each. The opcodes are *36, *37, *32, and *33, respectively.

Since memory locations cannot be stacked on top of one another like plates, all stack operations occur relative to the stack pointer. The logic equations for PSH are $Msp \leftarrow Acc$, and $SP \leftarrow SP - 1$. The memory location pointed to by the stack pointer is replaced by the contents of the accumulator (the accumulator remains unchanged, of course). The stack pointer is then decremented so that it points to the next lower numbered memory location. In this way, successive PSH instructions will store bytes of data into successively lower numbered memory locations. An example of PSH is shown in Figure 6.23.

The PUL instruction is used for retrieving data from the stack. Its logic equations are $SP \leftarrow SP + 1$, and $Acc \leftarrow Msp$. The stack pointer is first incremented, then the contents of the memory location pointed to by the

*FIGURE 6.23: PSH Instruction*

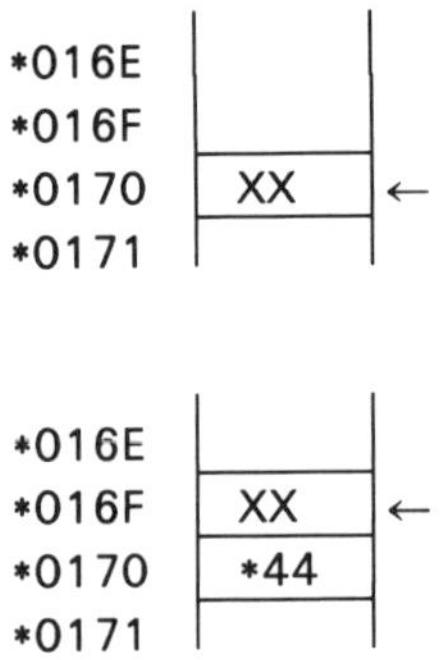


SP = *0170   A = *44

Prior to execution of a PSH A instruction, the pointer points to the top of the stack.

SP = *016F   A = *44

Following execution of the PSH A, the contents of A have been stored, and the stack pointer has been decremented. The top of the stack has moved, as indicated by the pointer.

stack pointer are transferred to the accumulator. If a PUL immediately follows a PSH, the same memory location will be accessed both times because of the decrementing then incrementing of the stack pointer. An example of PUL is shown in Figure 6.24. Note that the byte of data remains in the memory location, but is not accessible by another PUL instruction. Subsequent PUL instructions would fetch bytes from successively higher numbered memory locations. If several bytes of data are pushed onto the stack, they would be pulled from the stack in exactly the reverse order—hence the phrase "last-in-first-out."

The stack provides a convenient way of temporarily storing data. If care is exercised in the order of pushes and pulls, data can be stored without reserving specific locations. In the MC6800, the stack can be any size, provided enough read/write memory is available. The major reason for the

*FIGURE 6.24: PUL Instruction*

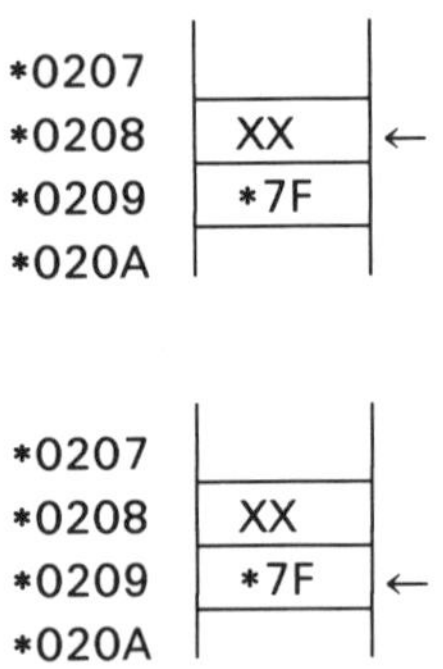


SP = *0208   B = XX

Prior to execution of a PUL B instruction, the pointer points to the current top of the stack.

SP = *0209   B = *7F

Following execution of PSH B, the stack pointer has been incremented, and the contents of the new top of the stack have been loaded into B.

stack, however, is not temporary storage of accumulator contents. The stack and the stack pointer are included in microprocessor architecture to provide subroutine capability.

## *Subroutines*

A subroutine is a function within a program which is executed several times and at several different places. Consider the example in Figure 6.25, where a specific function to be performed involves 12 instructions which in turn occupy 23 bytes of memory. If this function is required twice in the program, once beginning at location X and again at location Y, 46 bytes would be required. If the same function is required again, each occurrence would occupy another 23 bytes. An alternative method to replicating the function each time it is required is to insert the function once in a separate location, then jump to the function each time it is required. If this is done, there must be a means of returning to the point from which each jump was made. The means for implementing this alternative are the *jump to*

*FIGURE 6.25: Example Subroutine*

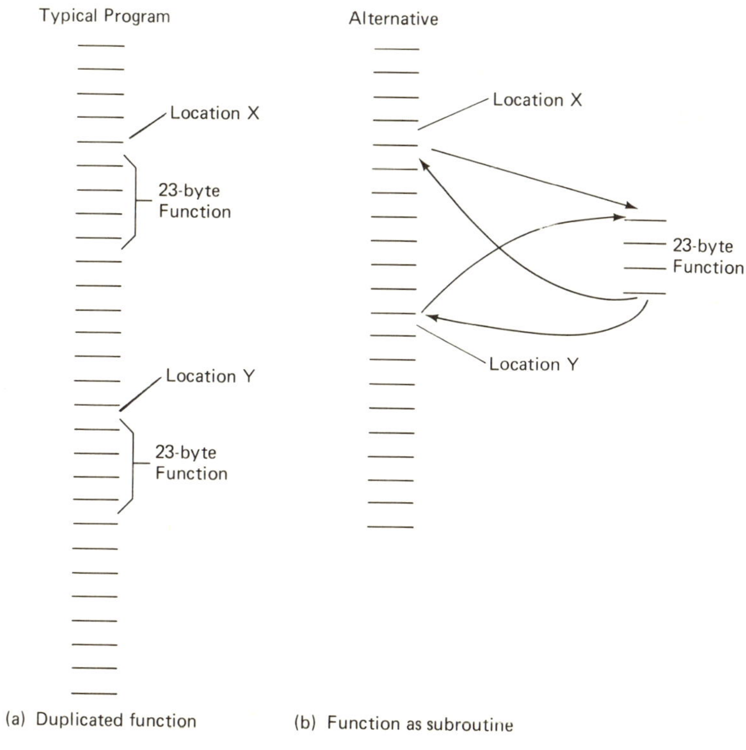

*subroutine* (JSR) and *return from subroutine* (RTS) instructions. What JSR does, in effect, is perform a jump in the normal fashion, but at the same time saves the address of the instruction immediately following the jump. This address, called the *return address*, is pushed onto the stack. The RTS instruction pulls the address from the stack.

The JSR instruction is available in both the extended and indexed addressing modes. JSR extended, represented by the opcode *BD, occupies 3 bytes, while JSR indexed, represented by *AD, occupies 2 bytes. The logic equations for the extended version are as follows:

$$
\begin{aligned}
&PC \leftarrow PC + 3\\
&M_{sp} \leftarrow PC_L\\
&SP \leftarrow SP - 1\\
&M_{sp} \leftarrow PC_H\\
&SP \leftarrow SP - 1\\
&PC \leftarrow \text{extended address}
\end{aligned}
$$

The program counter (where the opcode *BD resides) is first incremented by 3, thus pointing to the next instruction. The low-order byte of the program counter is pushed onto the top of the stack, the stack pointer being decremented as usual. The high-order byte of PC is then pushed onto the stack and the stack pointer is again decremented. Finally, the program counter is replaced with the 2-byte extended address following the opcode, allowing execution of the subroutine to begin. Note that the original program counter is pushed onto the stack with the higher-order byte occupying a lower-numbered memory location than the lower-order byte. This is consistent with the MC6800's method of storing addresses. An example of JSR extended is shown in Figure 6.26. The logic equation for JSR indexed is similar to the JSR extended, except that the original value of PC is incremented by 2, and the address is calculated by the indexed method. In addition to the JSR instructions, there is a *branch to subroutine* (BSR) instruction. Branch to subroutine is similar to jump to subroutine, except that the address of the subroutine is calculated using the relative addressing method. BSR is represented by opcode *8D.

The *return from subroutine* instruction (RTS) facilitates a return from the subroutine function to the location from which it was called. RTS, represented by the opcode *39, pulls the return address from the top of the stack. It is a 1-byte instruction, and its operands, which are implied, are the top of the stack and the program counter. The logic equations for RTS are:

$$
\begin{aligned}
&SP \leftarrow SP + 1\\
&PC_H \leftarrow M_{sp}\\
&SP \leftarrow SP + 1\\
&PC_L \leftarrow M_{sp}
\end{aligned}
$$

*FIGURE 6.26: The Jump to Subroutine Instruction*

| Address | Stack | Address | Memory |
|---|---|---|---|
| *0110 | | *0309 | |
| *0111 | XX | *030A | *BD |
| *0112 | XX | *030B | *E1 |
| *0113 | | *030C | *AC |
| | | *030D | |

SP = *0112

Prior to execution of the instruction in *030A, the stack pointer contains *0112.

| Address | Stack | |
|---|---|---|
| *0110 | | ← |
| *0111 | *03 | |
| *0112 | *0D | |
| *0113 | | |

SP = *0110

Following execution of the JSR, the return address, *030D, has been pushed onto the stack, the stack pointer has been decremented, and execution continues at *E1AC.

The program counter is replaced by the two bytes at the top of the stack, allowing instruction execution to proceed at the instruction following the JSR or BSR. All subroutines must end with an RTS instruction.

Care must be exercised with subroutines, just as with PSHs and PULs. There must always be the same number of RTSs as there are JSRs and BSRs. PSH and PUL instructions may be used within subroutines, provided the stack pointer contains the proper value when the RTS is encountered. A second subroutine may be called from within a subroutine. This is a phenomenon known as *nesting*, or nested subroutines. If this is the case, the return address of the first subroutine is pushed onto the stack, then the return address of the second, or inner, subroutine is pushed on top of that. In other words, the return addresses are stored on the stack in a last-in-first-out basis. The RTS for the inner subroutine must be encountered before the RTS for the first subroutine. The number of subroutines called within each other is known as the level of nesting. An example of three-deep nesting is when a subroutine is called, which in turn calls a second subroutine, which in turn calls a third subroutine. A return is made from the third subroutine into the second, then from the second into the first, then from the first to the main calling area. Subroutines may be nested to any level provided there is enough stack to store all the return addresses.

Subroutines are a very powerful tool in programming. Efficient use of them allows a large problem to be divided into a set of smaller problems. In addition, subroutines permit easier documentation and understanding of large programs.

## *Index Register and Stack Pointer Instructions*

Throughout the discussion of instructions so far, two registers have aided in instruction execution and memory addressing. These are the index register and the stack pointer. During the execution of specific instructions, it was assumed that these registers contained specific values. When giving examples of the indexed mode of addressing, the index register was shown as already containing a specific value; a similar situation existed with the stack pointer in discussing PSHs and PULs. These registers got their values by execution of specific instructions, instructions which are the topic of this section.

### *Index Register*

The index register and stack pointer are both 16-bit registers and, as such, must be loaded with two bytes of data. Consider the index register first. It gets its value via the *load index register* instructions, represented by the mnemonic LDX. LDX is available in the four addressing modes, immediate, direct, indexed, and extended. The operation of these modes with index register instructions is slightly different from that with accumulator instructions. The logic equations for LDX are $X_H \leftarrow M$, and $X_L \leftarrow (M + 1)$; the higher-order byte of the index register is replaced by the contents of the addressed memory location, and the lower-order byte is replaced by the contents of the next memory location. The LDX immediate occupies three bytes, the first of which is the opcode *CE; the second and third bytes are the 16-bit value which is loaded into the index register. The more significant byte is stored first (in the lower-numbered memory location) and the less significant byte is stored second. This instruction loads a specific value into the index register. The LDX direct, represented by the opcode *DE, occupies two bytes; the second byte is the lower-order byte of the address of the operand, the higher-order byte being *00. This operand is a 16-bit operand, the more significant byte of which is stored in the byte indicated by the direct address, and the less significant byte of which occupies the next byte in memory. The LDX indexed, a 2-byte instruction, works in a similar fashion: the first byte is the opcode *EE, and the second is the offset. The offset is added to the current contents of the index register, and the sum points to the first byte of a 2-byte operand. Following execution of an LDX indexed, the index register contains the new value as specified by the 2-byte operand. (This is the only indexed addressing mode instruction in which the original contents of the index register are altered.) The LDX extended instruction is represented by the opcode *FE. In this case, the 2-byte address following the opcode points to the more significant byte of a 2-byte operand, the less significant of which occupies the next higher-numbered memory location. An example of each of the four addressing modes of LDX is shown in Figure 6.27. Three of the condition code register bits are affected by the LDX instruction. The overflow bit is unconditionally reset, and the zero and negative bits are set or reset according to the value being loaded. The Z bit will be set only if both bytes being loaded are zero. N will be set if the most significant of the 16 bits, the leftmost bit, is set.

*FIGURE 6.27: Load Index Register Instruction*

| Address | Contents |
|---|---|
| *094D | |
| *094E | *CE |
| *094F | *01 |
| *0950 | *20 |
| *0951 | |

Following execution of the instruction on *094E, the index register will contain *0120.

LDX (IMM) *0120

(a) Immediate addressing

| Address | Contents | Address | Contents |
|---|---|---|---|
| *004A | | *0186 | |
| *004B | *22 | *0187 | *DE |
| *004C | *07 | *0188 | *4B |
| *004D | | *0189 | |

Following execution of the instruction in *0187, the index register will contain *2207. The 1-byte address causes the 2-byte value to be loaded.

LDX (DIR) *4B

(b) Direct addressing

| Address | Contents | Address | Contents |
|---|---|---|---|
| *1124 | | *1213 | |
| *1125 | *EE | *1214 | *04 |
| *1126 | *14 | *1215 | *62 |
| *1127 | | *1216 | |

IX = *1200

Following execution of the instruction in *1125, the index register will contain *0462. The offset *14 is added to the original contents of the index register, and the 2 bytes at the addressed location are loaded.

LDX (IND) *14

(c) Indexed addressing

| Address | Contents | Address | Contents |
|---|---|---|---|
| *04A0 | | *0626 | |
| *04A1 | *F6 | *0627 | *11 |
| *04A2 | *06 | *0628 | *10 |
| *04A3 | *27 | *0629 | |

Following execution of the instruction in *04A1, the index register will contain *1110.

LDX (EXT) *0627

(d) Extended addressing

Just as the index register is loaded, it may also be stored. The *store index register* instruction, STX, is available in the direct, indexed, and extended addressing modes. Each of these instructions stores the 16-bit contents of the index register into two bytes of memory. The higher-order byte is stored in the addressed memory location, and the lower-order byte is stored in the next higher-numbered memory location. The opcodes for STX direct, indexed, and extended, are *DF, *EF, and *FF, respectively, and those instructions occupy 2, 2, and 3 bytes of memory, respectively. The logic equations for STX are $M \leftarrow X_H$, $(M + 1) \leftarrow X_L$. The condition code register bits are affected by STX in the same way that they are affected by LDX.

The index register can be incremented and decremented as the accumulators are. The INX instruction, represented by the opcode *08, increments the index register by 1. Similarly, DEX, represented by *09, decrements the index register by 1. Both instructions occupy one byte in memory, and both instructions will set the Z bit if the resulting index register value is zero, and will reset Z otherwise.

The *compare index register* instruction, CPX, performs comparisons with the index register as the other compare instructions operate on the accumulators. The 16-bit operand is subtracted from the index register, but the difference is not retained; only the condition code register bits are affected. CPX is available in the immediate, direct, indexed, and extended modes, represented by the opcodes *8C, *9C, *AC, and *BC, respectively. The condition code register bits are affected as follows: Z is set if the index register and the operand are equal, and is reset otherwise; N is set if bit 15 of the result is set (this occurs when the operand is greater than the index register); and V is set when there is a 2's complement overflow from the less significant bytes only. The comparisons are performed treating the index register and its operand as unsigned 16-bit values. Care should be exercised when using the conditional branch instructions following CPX.

### *Stack Pointer*

The stack pointer may be loaded and stored as the index register is. The *load stack pointer* instruction, LDS, transfers a 2-byte value from memory to the stack pointer. LDS is available in the immediate, direct, indexed, and extended modes, with the opcodes *8E, *9E, *AE, and *BE, respectively. The operation of the addressing modes and the effect on the condition code register bits are the same for LDS as for LDX.

Similarly, the stack pointer may be stored away in memory by the *store stack pointer* instruction, STS. STS is available in the direct, indexed, and extended modes, represented by the opcodes *9F, *AF, and *BF, respectively. The operation of STS is identical to STX.

The stack pointer may be incremented and decremented by the INS, *increment stack pointer*, and the DES, *decrement stack pointer*, instructions. These instructions are similar to the INX and DEX instructions, but none of the condition code register bits are affected by INS or DES. INS and DES are represented by the opcodes *31 and *34, respectively.

There are two special instructions which involve the index register and stack pointer. These are the *transfer stack pointer to index register* instruction (TSX) and the *transfer index register to stack pointer* instruction (TXS). In the TSX instruction, the stack pointer is first incremented by one and then transferred to the index register. What this does, in effect, is to make data which has previously been PSHed onto the stack available via indexed instructions. If a TSX is executed, the last data item PSHed would be available to an indexed instruction with an offset of zero. In the TXS instruction, the index register is decremented by one and then transferred to the stack pointer. This is the direct opposite of TSX, and maintains consistency in case a TSX should be followed immediately by a TXS. TSX is represented by the opcode *30, and TXS is represented by *35. Each instruction occupies one byte of memory, and neither instruction affects any of the condition code register bits.

Extreme caution should be exercised when using any of the stack pointer instructions. Data or return addresses stored on the stack may become inaccessible due to misuse of the stack pointer. Much debugging time has been spent due to careless treatment of stack-related operations.

## Accumulator Instructions

There is a small group of instructions within the MC6800 which are available specifically for operations involving one or both of the accumulators. The effect of these instructions is that memory is conserved (each instruction occupies only one byte), and sometimes execution time can be conserved.

The first two instructions of this type are the transfer accumulator instructions. The *transfer A to B* instruction (TAB) replaces accumulator B with the contents of A (A remains unchanged, of course), and the *transfer B to A* instruction (TBA) replaces accumulator A with the contents of B. TAB is represented by the opcode *16, and TBA is represented by *17. Following execution of either transfer instruction, the Z and N bits will be set or reset according to the byte transferred. The overflow and carry bits are unconditionally reset after either transfer instruction.

There are two arithmetic instructions in the accumulator group. These are the *add B to A* instruction (ABA) and the *subtract B from A* instruction (SBA). ABA, represented by the opcode *1B, adds the contents of the accumulators and deposits the sum into accumulator A. SBA, represented by *10, subtracts the contents of accumulator B from accumulator A and deposits the difference into A. The condition code register bits are affected by ABA and SBA exactly as they are affected by the add accumulator and the subtract accumulator instructions which involve memory operands.

Another pair of instructions involving the accumulator deals with the condition code register. The primary use of the condition code register is to record the results of arithmetic and logical operations, and, as such, the bits are usually treated one at a time or in specific combinations. The *transfer A to CCR* (TAP) and *transfer CCR to A* (TPA) treat the bits as an actual register. (The "P" in TAP and TPA is probably derived from the expression "processor status.") The bits H, I, N, Z, V, and C occupy bits 5 through 0, respectively, of the condition code register. In TAP, the 6 least-significant bits of accumulator A are transferred in order to the condition code register. Bits 7 and 6 of A are ignored. In TPA, the condition code register bits are transferred to the least-significant 6 bits of accumulator A. TPA will also set bits 7 and 6 of the accumulator to one. TAP is represented by the opcode *06, and TPA is represented by *07. These two instructions provide a means for storing and subsequently retrieving the condition code register.

There are two other instructions which will also be included here. The first of these is an instruction which does nothing. It is called *no operation*, or no-op, for short. It is represented by the mnemonic NOP and is implemented by the opcode *01. NOP does not affect any of the registers or condition code register bits, and does not change memory. It is a 1-byte instruction, and all it does is advance the program counter by 1 so that the next instruction may be implemented.

The second instruction is the *decimal adjust accumulator* instruction, DAA. DAA, implemented by the opcode *19, is used for implementation of BCD additions within the MC6800. This instruction works in conjunction with the carry and half-carry bits of the condition code register, and operates on accumulator A only. DAA will add 6 to either half or both halves of the accumulator if an invalid BCD digit occupies that half or if a carry has propagated out of that half. It will also set the carry bit if the result is greater than 99 decimal. The primary purpose of DAA is correction of binary addition to BCD, so DAA should be executed immediately following any add instruction. Figure 6.28 shows an example of the decimal addition procedure. Accumulator A contains *68, which is 68 in binary coded decimal. The add instruction performs straight binary addition of *68 and *48, which yield *B0. The half-carry bit is set by this operation. The DAA instruction adds 6 to the less-significant 4 bits because of the half-carry bit. It also adds 6 to the more-significant 4 bits because *B is not a valid BCD digit. The final result is *16 in accumulator A with the carry bit set. This is consistent with the decimal addition process 48 + 68 = 116. It should be emphasized that DAA only works with instructions which affect the half-carry bit. Only additions in the MC6800 do this.

*FIGURE 6.28: BCD Addition Using the DAA Instruction*

| Address | Contents |
|---|---|
| *0303 | |
| *0304 | *8B |
| *0305 | *48 |
| *0306 | *19 |
| *0307 | |

A = *68

Following execution of the addition instruction in *0304, accumulator A will contain *B0, C will be 0 and H will be 1. Following execution of the DAA instruction, accumulator A will contain *16 and C will be 1.

ADD A (IMM) *48
DAA

## *Initialization and Interrupts*

Throughout chapter 6, instruction execution has been discussed. Each instruction is executed by virtue of the fact that the memory address of that instruction is in the program counter. As each instruction is executed, the program counter is modified so that another instruction can be fetched from memory and executed. The procession continues, one instruction after another. The matter of how it all gets started has not been covered yet. Getting started is a predefined procedure within the MC6800. The procedure is required at least when power is first applied to the system. The procedure is also very helpful when things go astray within the processor and it is necessary to bring the system to a known state. (The latter condition occurs very frequently during program debugging.)

The procedure begins with the reset signal on the MC6800 MPU chip. When this signal is held at a logic 0 state for 8 clock times, the start-up procedure is initiated. The MC6800 puts the value *FFFE out on the address bus, and fetches a byte from that memory location. The value *FFFF is then put on the address bus, and a second byte is fetched from memory. These two bytes are then transferred to the program counter, and instruction execution begins in the normal fashion. The address of the very first instruction to be executed, then, is stored in memory locations *FFFE and *FFFF. The process is shown graphically in Figure 6.29. The more significant byte is stored in *FFFE, consistent with the MC6800 method of storing addresses. The addresses *FFFE and *FFFF must be in ROM or some other nonvolatile memory since these locations are often accessed after power has been off. If the address is in ROM, then execution will begin at the same location every time the MC6800 is restarted.

No matter what the system is doing, whenever a logic 0 is applied to the $\overline{\text{reset}}$ signal of the MC6800, the start-up procedure will be initiated. There are two other signals on the MC6800 which will cause a similar reaction. These are the two interrupt signals, the *interrupt request*, $\overline{\text{IRQ}}$, and

*FIGURE 6.29: Activity Following Reset* (Courtesy of Motorola Semiconductor Products, Inc.)

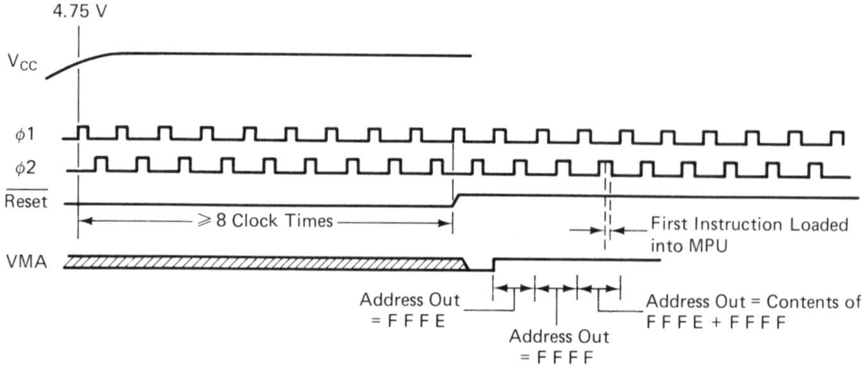


the *nonmaskable interrupt*, $\overline{\text{NMI}}$. These signals are generally used by peripheral I/O devices within the system when they require the immediate attention of the processor. This occurs, for example, during very high-speed data transfers between the processor and an I/O device such as a floppy disc or a communication device. There is a difference, though, between the circumstances under which a start-up occurs and the circumstances under which an interrupt occurs. When a start-up occurs, all activity of the processor is abandoned and execution begins at the predetermined address. When an interrupt occurs, the MC6800 may be engaged in meaningful activity, activity which should resume after the peripheral device has been serviced. In order for the meaningful activity to continue after the interrupt has been serviced, execution of the program must continue at the location in memory where the interrupt occurred, and all the registers and condition code register bits must be the same. The phrase "servicing an interrupt" refers to the execution of a short program which deals specifically with the cause of the interrupt. When an interrupt occurs, then, the program currently being executed must be temporarily abandoned, the interrupt service routine must begin, the interrupt service routine must end, and the original program must continue. This is shown graphically in Figure 6.30. Unlike a subroutine, which the programmer can execute under his control, an interrupt can occur at any time. Execution of the original program following an interrupt must continue as if the interrupt had never occurred.

The mechanism with which interrupts are handled will now be discussed. The MC6800 is interrupted when a logic 0 is applied to either the $\overline{\text{IRQ}}$ or the $\overline{\text{NMI}}$ signals of the MPU chip. The difference between the two signals is as follows: In order for the MC6800 to be interrupted by the $\overline{\text{IRQ}}$, the interrupt mask bit of the condition code register must be zero. If the programmer sets I to one, he/she is effectively nullifying the effect of any interrupt via $\overline{\text{IRQ}}$. The nonmaskable interrupt, as the name implies, cannot

*FIGURE 6.30: Interrupt Process*

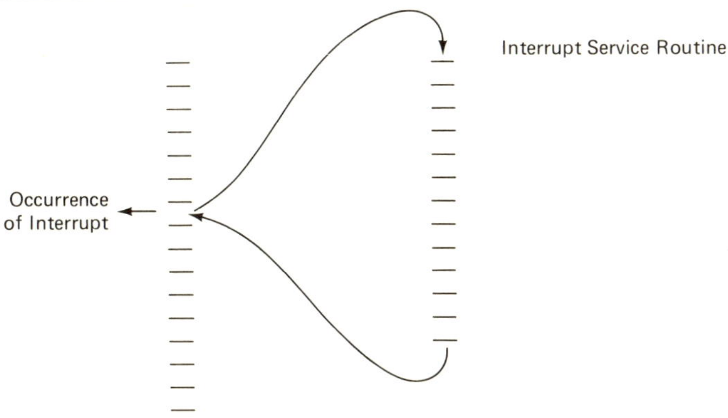


be masked out, or inhibited, by the programmer. When an interrupt occurs, the instruction currently being executed finishes. After this, the program counter is pushed onto the stack, followed by the index register, accumulator A, accumulator B, and the condition code register. In addition, the interrupt mask bit is set to one. When all registers have been saved, the program counter is replaced by the contents of *FFF8 and *FFF9 for $\overline{\text{IRQ}}$, or *FFFC and *FFFD for a $\overline{\text{NMI}}$. After all this has occurred, execution of the interrupt service routine begins. Figure 6.31 shows in logic equation form the actions at the occurrence of an interrupt.

*FIGURE 6.31: Register Save at Interrupt*

$M_{sp} \leftarrow PC_L$
$SP \leftarrow SP - 1$
$M_{sp} \leftarrow PC_H$
$SP \leftarrow SP - 1$
$M_{sp} \leftarrow IX_L$
$SP \leftarrow SP - 1$
$M_{sp} \leftarrow IX_H$
$SP \leftarrow SP - 1$
$M_{sp} \leftarrow A$
$SP \leftarrow SP - 1$
$M_{sp} \leftarrow B$
$SP \leftarrow SP - 1$
$M_{sp} \leftarrow CCR$
$SP \leftarrow SP - 1$
$I \leftarrow 1$
$PC \leftarrow$ *FFFX, *FFFX + 1

All registers are pushed onto the stack; the interrupt mask is set; the program counter is loaded from high address memory.

In addition to the two interrupts that can occur as a result of a hardware signal, there is an interrupt which can occur under the programmer's control. The *software interrupt* instruction, SWI, causes all the registers to be saved on the stack. Following execution of SWI, represented by the opcode *3F, the program counter is replaced by the contents of memory locations *FFFA and *FFFB. Although it is not an interrupt in the strict sense of the word, SWI does cause the interrupt sequence to occur. This can be very useful when debugging programs.

The interrupt service routine is just another program which begins at a predetermined location. This routine can load registers, push data on the stack, call subroutines, do anything that a normal program does. The only restriction on the interrupt service routine is that the original value in the stack pointer must be available at the termination of the routine. The *return from interrupt* instruction, RTI, is the means of terminating an interrupt. Represented by the opcode *3B, RTI simply pulls all the registers from the stack that were pushed on by the interrupt sequence. All the registers are returned to the values they had at the time the interrupt occurred. The last register to be pulled is the program counter. When the program counter contains the address of the instruction after the one which was interrupted, program execution resumes as if the interrupt had never occurred. Figure 6.32 shows the action of the RTI instruction.

There is one other instruction involving interrupts. This is the *wait for interrupt* instruction, WAI. Following execution of WAI, all CPU activity stops until an interrupt occurs or until a $\overline{\text{reset}}$ occurs. The WAI is the closest thing to a halt instruction in the MC6800. If the interrupt mask bit is set, only a nonmaskable interrupt or a $\overline{\text{reset}}$ can restart the CPU. If an interrupt

*FIGURE 6.32: RTI Instruction*

| | |
|---|---|
| $SP \leftarrow SP + 1$ | |
| $CCR \leftarrow M_{sp}$ | |
| $SP \leftarrow SP + 1$ | |
| $B \leftarrow M_{sp}$ | |
| $SP \leftarrow SP + 1$ | |
| $A \leftarrow M_{sp}$ | |
| $SP \leftarrow SP + 1$ | Registers previously pushed are now retrieved from the stack. |
| $IX_H \leftarrow M_{sp}$ | |
| $SP \leftarrow SP + 1$ | |
| $IX_L \leftarrow M_{sp}$ | |
| $SP \leftarrow SP + 1$ | |
| $PC_H \leftarrow M_{sp}$ | |
| $SP \leftarrow SP + 1$ | |
| $PC_L \leftarrow M_{sp}$ | |

does occur following a WAI, program execution continues with the next instruction after the interrupt has been serviced. WAI is a 1-byte instruction represented by the opcode *3E.

## *Concluding Remarks about Instructions*

At this point, all the MC6800 instructions have been covered. There are 72 different instructions, many of which operate on either accumulator, and many of which operate via several addressing modes. Taken collectively, these instructions make up what is known as the instruction set of the MC6800. The instruction set is a characteristic of microprocessors just as the data word length is a characteristic of microprocessors. The opcodes, logic equations, and effects on condition code register bits are all part of the instruction set.

The instruction set of the MC6800 is summarized in Figure 6.33. The instruction set summary, sometimes called the programmers' reference card, serves as a convenient reference for all aspects of MC6800 instructions. This summary is also available as a small pocket-sized card, hence the expression programmers' reference card.

All microprocessors, and indeed all computers, have their own unique instruction sets. Each of these instruction sets have their own strengths and weaknesses manifested in the types and varieties of available instructions. It is hoped that the preceding description of MC6800 instructions will serve as a basis for learning any other instruction set with which the reader wishes to become familiar. It is the opinion of the author that the MC6800 possesses a very good instruction set. The instructions are simple yet powerful. There are very few special-purpose instructions. All binary arithmetic and logical instructions may be performed directly. There are an adequate number of internal registers to efficiently implement many processes. Of course, the instruction set could be better, but the same remark can be made regarding any microprocessor.

It is interesting to note that from all the instructions in the MC6800, there are 197 valid opcodes. These opcodes encompass all the accumulator and addressing modes of the 72 basic instructions. The instruction register in the MC6800 is an 8-bit register, which implies that there are 256 different combinations of bits. Of these 256, 197 represent valid operations implemented by the microprocessor. An attempt to execute any of the other 59 values (that is, cause one of the values to be loaded into the instruction register from memory) will yield an unpredictable result. There is no reason to suspect that anyone would intentionally try to do so, but the possibility of trying to execute an unimplemented opcode remains. It is the programmer's responsibility to ensure that this does not occur.

The reader has now proceeded through descriptions of all the

*FIGURE 6.33: Instruction Set Summary* (Courtesy of Motorola Semiconductor Products Inc.)

## ACCUMULATOR AND MEMORY INSTRUCTIONS

| | | ADDRESSING MODES | | | | | | | | | | | | | | | BOOLEAN/ARITHMETIC OPERATION | COND. CODE REG. | | | | | |
|---|---|---|---|---|---|---|---|---|---|---|---|---|---|---|---|---|---|---|---|---|---|---|---|
| | | IMMED | | | DIRECT | | | INDEX | | | EXTND | | | IMPLIED | | | (All register labels refer to contents) | 5 | 4 | 3 | 2 | 1 | 0 |
| OPERATIONS | MNEMONIC | OP | ~ | = | OP | ~ | = | OP | ~ | = | OP | ~ | = | OP | ~ | = | | H | I | N | Z | V | C |
| Add | ADDA | 8B | 2 | 2 | 9B | 3 | 2 | AB | 5 | 2 | BB | 4 | 3 | | | | A + M → A | ↕ | • | ↕ | ↕ | ↕ | ↕ |
| | ADDB | CB | 2 | 2 | DB | 3 | 2 | EB | 5 | 2 | FB | 4 | 3 | | | | B + M → B | ↕ | • | ↕ | ↕ | ↕ | ↕ |
| Add Acmltrs | ABA | | | | | | | | | | | | | 1B | 2 | 1 | A + B → A | ↕ | • | ↕ | ↕ | ↕ | ↕ |
| Add with Carry | ADCA | 89 | 2 | 2 | 99 | 3 | 2 | A9 | 5 | 2 | B9 | 4 | 3 | | | | A + M + C → A | ↕ | • | ↕ | ↕ | ↕ | ↕ |
| | ADCB | C9 | 2 | 2 | D9 | 3 | 2 | E9 | 5 | 2 | F9 | 4 | 3 | | | | B + M + C → B | ↕ | • | ↕ | ↕ | ↕ | ↕ |
| And | ANDA | 84 | 2 | 2 | 94 | 3 | 2 | A4 | 5 | 2 | B4 | 4 | 3 | | | | A · M → A | • | • | ↕ | ↕ | R | • |
| | ANDB | C4 | 2 | 2 | D4 | 3 | 2 | E4 | 5 | 2 | F4 | 4 | 3 | | | | B · M → B | • | • | ↕ | ↕ | R | • |
| Bit Test | BITA | 85 | 2 | 2 | 95 | 3 | 2 | A5 | 5 | 2 | B5 | 4 | 3 | | | | A · M | • | • | ↕ | ↕ | R | • |
| | BITB | C5 | 2 | 2 | D5 | 3 | 2 | E5 | 5 | 2 | F5 | 4 | 3 | | | | B · M | • | • | ↕ | ↕ | R | • |
| Clear | CLR | | | | | | | 6F | 7 | 2 | 7F | 6 | 3 | | | | 00 → M | • | • | R | S | R | R |
| | CLRA | | | | | | | | | | | | | 4F | 2 | 1 | 00 → A | • | • | R | S | R | R |
| | CLRB | | | | | | | | | | | | | 5F | 2 | 1 | 00 → B | • | • | R | S | R | R |
| Compare | CMPA | 81 | 2 | 2 | 91 | 3 | 2 | A1 | 5 | 2 | B1 | 4 | 3 | | | | A − M | • | • | ↕ | ↕ | ↕ | ↕ |
| | CMPB | C1 | 2 | 2 | D1 | 3 | 2 | E1 | 5 | 2 | F1 | 4 | 3 | | | | B − M | • | • | ↕ | ↕ | ↕ | ↕ |
| Compare Acmltrs | CBA | | | | | | | | | | | | | 11 | 2 | 1 | A − B | • | • | ↕ | ↕ | ↕ | ↕ |
| Complement, 1's | COM | | | | | | | 63 | 7 | 2 | 73 | 6 | 3 | | | | $\overline{M}$ → M | • | • | ↕ | ↕ | R | S |
| | COMA | | | | | | | | | | | | | 43 | 2 | 1 | $\overline{A}$ → A | • | • | ↕ | ↕ | R | S |
| | COMB | | | | | | | | | | | | | 53 | 2 | 1 | $\overline{B}$ → B | • | • | ↕ | ↕ | R | S |
| Complement, 2's | NEG | | | | | | | 60 | 7 | 2 | 70 | 6 | 3 | | | | 00 − M → M | • | • | ↕ | ↕ | ① | ② |
| (Negate) | NEGA | | | | | | | | | | | | | 40 | 2 | 1 | 00 − A → A | • | • | ↕ | ↕ | ① | ② |
| | NEGB | | | | | | | | | | | | | 50 | 2 | 1 | 00 − B → B | • | • | ↕ | ↕ | ① | ② |
| Decimal Adjust, A | DAA | | | | | | | | | | | | | 19 | 2 | 1 | Converts Binary Add. of BCD Characters into BCD Format | • | • | ↕ | ↕ | ↕ | ③ |
| Decrement | DEC | | | | | | | 6A | 7 | 2 | 7A | 6 | 3 | | | | M − 1 → M | • | • | ↕ | ↕ | 4 | • |
| | DECA | | | | | | | | | | | | | 4A | 2 | 1 | A − 1 → A | • | • | ↕ | ↕ | 4 | • |
| | DECB | | | | | | | | | | | | | 5A | 2 | 1 | B − 1 → B | • | • | ↕ | ↕ | 4 | • |
| Exclusive OR | EORA | 88 | 2 | 2 | 98 | 3 | 2 | A8 | 5 | 2 | B8 | 4 | 3 | | | | A⊕M → A | • | • | ↕ | ↕ | R | • |
| | EORB | C8 | 2 | 2 | D8 | 3 | 2 | E8 | 5 | 2 | F8 | 4 | 3 | | | | B⊕M → B | • | • | ↕ | ↕ | R | • |
| Increment | INC | | | | | | | 6C | 7 | 2 | 7C | 6 | 3 | | | | M + 1 → M | • | • | ↕ | ↕ | ⑤ | • |
| | INCA | | | | | | | | | | | | | 4C | 2 | 1 | A + 1 → A | • | • | ↕ | ↕ | ⑤ | • |
| | INCB | | | | | | | | | | | | | 5C | 2 | 1 | B + 1 → B | • | • | ↕ | ↕ | ⑤ | • |
| Load Acmltr | LDAA | 86 | 2 | 2 | 96 | 3 | 2 | A6 | 5 | 2 | B6 | 4 | 3 | | | | M → A | • | • | ↕ | ↕ | R | • |
| | LDAB | C6 | 2 | 2 | D6 | 3 | 2 | E6 | 5 | 2 | F6 | 4 | 3 | | | | M → B | • | • | ↕ | ↕ | R | • |
| Or, Inclusive | ORAA | 8A | 2 | 2 | 9A | 3 | 2 | AA | 5 | 2 | BA | 4 | 3 | | | | A + M → A | • | • | ↕ | ↕ | R | • |
| | ORAB | CA | 2 | 2 | DA | 3 | 2 | EA | 5 | 2 | FA | 4 | 3 | | | | B + M → B | • | • | ↕ | ↕ | R | • |

| | | | | | | | | | | | | | | | | | | | | | | | |
|---|---|---|---|---|---|---|---|---|---|---|---|---|---|---|---|---|---|---|---|---|---|---|---|
| Push Data | PSHA | | | | | | | | | | | | | 36 | 4 | 1 | A → $M_{SP}$, SP − 1 → SP | • | • | • | • | • | • |
| | PSHB | | | | | | | | | | | | | 37 | 4 | 1 | B → $M_{SP}$, SP − 1 → SP | • | • | • | • | • | • |
| Pull Data | PULA | | | | | | | | | | | | | 32 | 4 | 1 | SP + 1 → SP, $M_{SP}$ → A | • | • | • | • | • | • |
| | PULB | | | | | | | | | | | | | 33 | 4 | 1 | SP + 1 → SP, $M_{SP}$ → B | • | • | • | • | • | • |
| Rotate Left | ROL | | | | | | | 69 | 7 | 2 | 79 | 6 | 3 | | | | M | • | • | ↕ | ↕ | (6) | ↕ |
| | ROLA | | | | | | | | | | | | | 49 | 2 | 1 | A } C ← b7 ← b0 (rotate through C) | • | • | ↕ | ↕ | (6) | ↕ |
| | ROLB | | | | | | | | | | | | | 59 | 2 | 1 | B | • | • | ↕ | ↕ | (6) | ↕ |
| Rotate Right | ROR | | | | | | | 66 | 7 | 2 | 76 | 6 | 3 | | | | M | • | • | ↕ | ↕ | (6) | ↕ |
| | RORA | | | | | | | | | | | | | 46 | 2 | 1 | A } C → b7 → b0 (rotate through C) | • | • | ↕ | ↕ | (6) | ↕ |
| | RORB | | | | | | | | | | | | | 56 | 2 | 1 | B | • | • | ↕ | ↕ | (6) | ↕ |
| Shift Left, Arithmetic | ASL | | | | | | | 68 | 7 | 2 | 78 | 6 | 3 | | | | M | • | • | ↕ | ↕ | (6) | ↕ |
| | ASLA | | | | | | | | | | | | | 48 | 2 | 1 | A } C ← b7 ← b0 ← 0 | • | • | ↕ | ↕ | (6) | ↕ |
| | ASLB | | | | | | | | | | | | | 58 | 2 | 1 | B | • | • | ↕ | ↕ | (6) | ↕ |
| Shift Right, Arithmetic | ASR | | | | | | | 67 | 7 | 2 | 77 | 6 | 3 | | | | M | • | • | ↕ | ↕ | (6) | ↕ |
| | ASRA | | | | | | | | | | | | | 47 | 2 | 1 | A } b7 → b0 → C (b7 retained) | • | • | ↕ | ↕ | (6) | ↕ |
| | ASRB | | | | | | | | | | | | | 57 | 2 | 1 | B | • | • | ↕ | ↕ | (6) | ↕ |
| Shift Right, Logic | LSR | | | | | | | 64 | 7 | 2 | 74 | 6 | 3 | | | | M | • | • | R | ↕ | (6) | ↕ |
| | LSRA | | | | | | | | | | | | | 44 | 2 | 1 | A } 0 → b7 → b0 → C | • | • | R | ↕ | (6) | ↕ |
| | LSRB | | | | | | | | | | | | | 54 | 2 | 1 | B | • | • | R | ↕ | (6) | ↕ |
| Store Acmltr. | STAA | | | | 97 | 4 | 2 | A7 | 6 | 2 | B7 | 5 | 3 | | | | A → M | • | • | ↕ | ↕ | R | • |
| | STAB | | | | D7 | 4 | 2 | E7 | 6 | 2 | F7 | 5 | 3 | | | | B → M | • | • | ↕ | ↕ | R | • |
| Subtract | SUBA | 80 | 2 | 2 | 90 | 3 | 2 | A0 | 5 | 2 | B0 | 4 | 3 | | | | A − M → A | • | • | ↕ | ↕ | ↕ | ↕ |
| | SUBB | C0 | 2 | 2 | D0 | 3 | 2 | E0 | 5 | 2 | F0 | 4 | 3 | | | | B − M → B | • | • | ↕ | ↕ | ↕ | ↕ |
| Subtract Acmltrs. | SBA | | | | | | | | | | | | | 10 | 2 | 1 | A − B → A | • | • | ↕ | ↕ | ↕ | ↕ |
| Subtr. with Carry | SBCA | 82 | 2 | 2 | 92 | 3 | 2 | A2 | 5 | 2 | B2 | 4 | 3 | | | | A − M − C → A | • | • | ↕ | ↕ | ↕ | ↕ |
| | SBCB | C2 | 2 | 2 | D2 | 3 | 2 | E2 | 5 | 2 | F2 | 4 | 3 | | | | B − M − C → B | • | • | ↕ | ↕ | ↕ | ↕ |
| Transfer Acmltrs | TAB | | | | | | | | | | | | | 16 | 2 | 1 | A → B | • | • | ↕ | ↕ | R | • |
| | TBA | | | | | | | | | | | | | 17 | 2 | 1 | B → A | • | • | ↕ | ↕ | R | • |
| Test, Zero or Minus | TST | | | | | | | 6D | 7 | 2 | 7D | 6 | 3 | | | | M − 00 | • | • | ↕ | ↕ | R | R |
| | TSTA | | | | | | | | | | | | | 4D | 2 | 1 | A − 00 | • | • | ↕ | ↕ | R | R |
| | TSTB | | | | | | | | | | | | | 5D | 2 | 1 | B − 00 | • | • | ↕ | ↕ | R | R |
| | | | | | | | | | | | | | | | | | | H | I | N | Z | V | C |

**LEGEND:**

OP Operation Code (Hexadecimal);
~ Number of MPU Cycles;
= Number of Program Bytes;
+ Arithmetic Plus;
− Arithmetic Minus;
· Boolean AND;
$M_{SP}$ Contents of memory location pointed to be Stack Pointer;

+ Boolean Inclusive OR;
⊕ Boolean Exclusive OR;
$\overline{M}$ Complement of M;
→ Transfer Into;
0 Bit = Zero;
00 Byte = Zero;

Note – Accumulator addressing mode instructions are included in the column for IMPLIED addressing

**CONDITION CODE SYMBOLS:**

H Half-carry from bit 3;
I Interrupt mask
N Negative (sign bit)
Z Zero (byte)
V Overflow, 2's complement
C Carry from bit 7
R Reset Always
S Set Always
↕ Test and set if true, cleared otherwise
● Not Affected

*FIGURE 6.33: Continued*

## INDEX REGISTER AND STACK MANIPULATION INSTRUCTIONS

| | | IMMED | | | DIRECT | | | INDEX | | | EXTND | | | IMPLIED | | | | COND. CODE REG. 5 | 4 | 3 | 2 | 1 | 0 |
|---|---|---|---|---|---|---|---|---|---|---|---|---|---|---|---|---|---|---|---|---|---|---|---|
| POINTER OPERATIONS | MNEMONIC | OP | ~ | # | OP | ~ | # | OP | ~ | # | OP | ~ | # | OP | ~ | # | BOOLEAN/ARITHMETIC OPERATION | H | I | N | Z | V | C |
| Compare Index Reg | CPX | 8C | 3 | 3 | 9C | 4 | 2 | AC | 6 | 2 | BC | 5 | 3 | | | | $X_H - M, X_L - (M+1)$ | • | • | ⑦ | ↕ | ⑧ | • |
| Decrement Index Reg | DEX | | | | | | | | | | | | | 09 | 4 | 1 | $X - 1 \rightarrow X$ | • | • | • | ↕ | • | • |
| Decrement Stack Pntr | DES | | | | | | | | | | | | | 34 | 4 | 1 | $SP - 1 \rightarrow SP$ | • | • | • | • | • | • |
| Increment Index Reg | INX | | | | | | | | | | | | | 08 | 4 | 1 | $X + 1 \rightarrow X$ | • | • | • | ↕ | • | • |
| Increment Stack Pntr | INS | | | | | | | | | | | | | 31 | 4 | 1 | $SP + 1 \rightarrow SP$ | • | • | • | • | • | • |
| Load Index Reg | LDX | CE | 3 | 3 | DE | 4 | 2 | EE | 6 | 2 | FE | 5 | 3 | | | | $M \rightarrow X_H, (M+1) \rightarrow X_L$ | • | • | ⑨ | ↕ | R | • |
| Load Stack Pntr | LDS | 8E | 3 | 3 | 9E | 4 | 2 | AE | 6 | 2 | BE | 5 | 3 | | | | $M \rightarrow SP_H, (M+1) \rightarrow SP_L$ | • | • | ⑨ | ↕ | R | • |
| Store Index Reg | STX | | | | DF | 5 | 2 | EF | 7 | 2 | FF | 6 | 3 | | | | $X_H \rightarrow M, X_L \rightarrow (M+1)$ | • | • | ⑨ | ↕ | R | • |
| Store Stack Pntr | STS | | | | 9F | 5 | 2 | AF | 7 | 2 | BF | 6 | 3 | | | | $SP_H \rightarrow M, SP_L \rightarrow (M+1)$ | • | • | ⑨ | ↕ | R | • |
| Indx Reg → Stack Pntr | TXS | | | | | | | | | | | | | 35 | 4 | 1 | $X - 1 \rightarrow SP$ | • | • | • | • | • | • |
| Stack Pntr → Indx Reg | TSX | | | | | | | | | | | | | 30 | 4 | 1 | $SP + 1 \rightarrow X$ | • | • | • | • | • | • |

*FIGURE 6.33: Continued*

## JUMP AND BRANCH INSTRUCTIONS

| OPERATIONS | MNEMONIC | RELATIVE | | | INDEX | | | EXTND | | | IMPLIED | | | BRANCH TEST | COND. CODE REG. | | | | | |
|---|---|---|---|---|---|---|---|---|---|---|---|---|---|---|---|---|---|---|---|---|
| | | | | | | | | | | | | | | | 5 | 4 | 3 | 2 | 1 | 0 |
| | | OP | ~ | # | OP | ~ | # | OP | ~ | # | OP | ~ | # | | H | I | N | Z | V | C |
| Branch Always | BRA | 20 | 4 | 2 | | | | | | | | | | None | • | • | • | • | • | • |
| Branch If Carry Clear | BCC | 24 | 4 | 2 | | | | | | | | | | C = 0 | • | • | • | • | • | • |
| Branch If Carry Set | BCS | 25 | 4 | 2 | | | | | | | | | | C = 1 | • | • | • | • | • | • |
| Branch If = Zero | BEQ | 27 | 4 | 2 | | | | | | | | | | Z = 1 | • | • | • | • | • | • |
| Branch If ⩾ Zero | BGE | 2C | 4 | 2 | | | | | | | | | | $N \oplus V = 0$ | • | • | • | • | • | • |
| Branch If > Zero | BGT | 2E | 4 | 2 | | | | | | | | | | $Z + (N \oplus V) = 0$ | • | • | • | • | • | • |
| Branch If Higher | BHI | 22 | 4 | 2 | | | | | | | | | | C + Z = 0 | • | • | • | • | • | • |
| Branch If ⩽ Zero | BLE | 2F | 4 | 2 | | | | | | | | | | $Z + (N \oplus V) = 1$ | • | • | • | • | • | • |
| Branch If Lower Or Same | BLS | 23 | 4 | 2 | | | | | | | | | | C + Z = 1 | • | • | • | • | • | • |
| Branch If < Zero | BLT | 2D | 4 | 2 | | | | | | | | | | $N \oplus V = 1$ | • | • | • | • | • | • |
| Branch If Minus | BMI | 2B | 4 | 2 | | | | | | | | | | N = 1 | • | • | • | • | • | • |
| Branch If Not Equal Zero | BNE | 26 | 4 | 2 | | | | | | | | | | Z = 0 | • | • | • | • | • | • |
| Branch If Overflow Clear | BVC | 28 | 4 | 2 | | | | | | | | | | V = 0 | • | • | • | • | • | • |
| Branch If Overflow Set | BVS | 29 | 4 | 2 | | | | | | | | | | V = 1 | • | • | • | • | • | • |
| Branch If Plus | BPL | 2A | 4 | 2 | | | | | | | | | | N = 0 | • | • | • | • | • | • |
| Branch To Subroutine | BSR | 8D | 8 | 2 | | | | | | | | | | } See Special Operations | • | • | • | • | • | • |
| Jump | JMP | | | | 6E | 4 | 2 | 7E | 3 | 3 | | | | | • | • | • | • | • | • |
| Jump To Subroutine | JSR | | | | AD | 8 | 2 | BD | 9 | 3 | | | | | • | • | • | • | • | • |
| No Operation | NOP | | | | | | | | | | 01 | 2 | 1 | Advances Prog. Cntr. Only | • | • | • | • | • | • |
| Return From Interrupt | RTI | | | | | | | | | | 3B | 10 | 1 | | (10) | | | | | |
| Return From Subroutine | RTS | | | | | | | | | | 39 | 5 | 1 | } See Special Operations | • | • | • | • | • | • |
| Software Interrupt | SWI | | | | | | | | | | 3F | 12 | 1 | | • | • | • | • | • | • |
| Wait for Interrupt* | WAI | | | | | | | | | | 3E | 9 | 1 | | • | (11) | • | • | • | • |

*WAI puts Address Bus, R/W, and Data Bus in the three-state mode while VMA is held low.

*FIGURE 6.33: Continued*

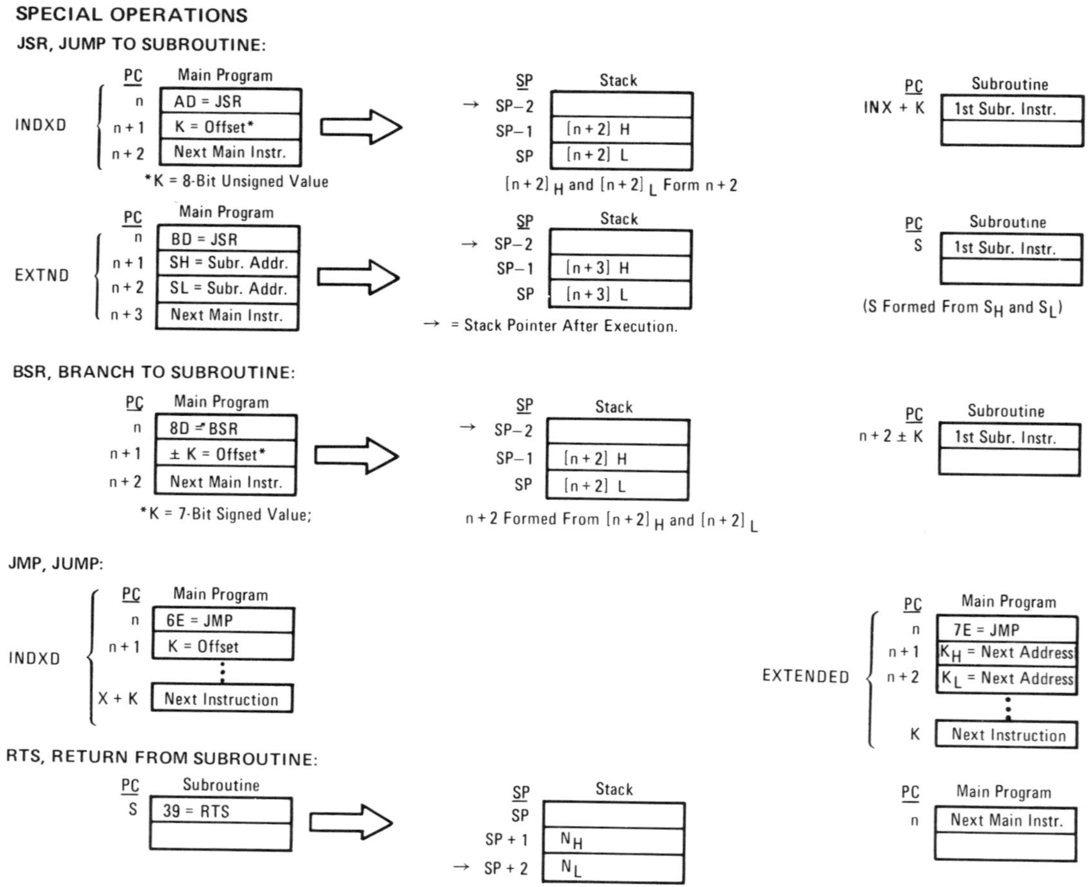

RTI, RETURN FROM INTERRUPT:

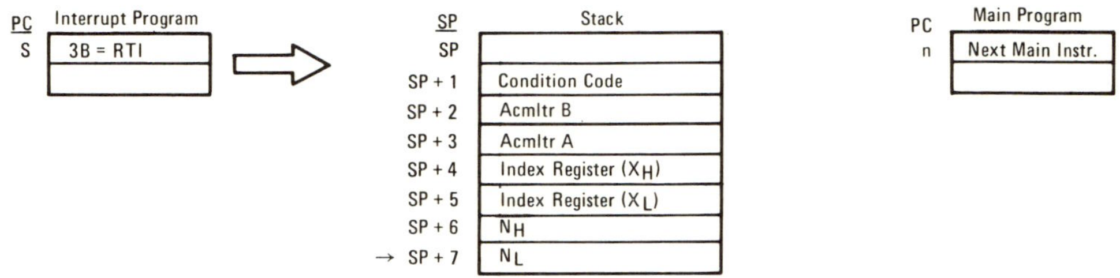


## CONDITION CODE REGISTER MANIPULATION INSTRUCTIONS

| | | IMPLIED | | | | COND. CODE REG. 5 | 4 | 3 | 2 | 1 | 0 |
|---|---|---|---|---|---|---|---|---|---|---|---|
| OPERATIONS | MNEMONIC | OP | ~ | # | BOOLEAN OPERATION | H | I | N | Z | V | C |
| Clear Carry | CLC | 0C | 2 | 1 | 0 → C | ● | ● | ● | ● | ● | R |
| Clear Interrupt Mask | CLI | 0E | 2 | 1 | 0 → I | ● | R | ● | ● | ● | ● |
| Clear Overflow | CLV | 0A | 2 | 1 | 0 → V | ● | ● | ● | ● | R | ● |
| Set Carry | SEC | 0D | 2 | 1 | 1 → C | ● | ● | ● | ● | ● | S |
| Set Interrupt Mask | SEI | 0F | 2 | 1 | 1 → I | ● | S | ● | ● | ● | ● |
| Set Overflow | SEV | 0B | 2 | 1 | 1 → V | ● | ● | ● | ● | S | ● |
| Acmltr A → CCR | TAP | 06 | 2 | 1 | A → CCR | (12) | | | | | |
| CCR → Acmltr A | TPA | 07 | 2 | 1 | CCR → A | ● | ● | ● | ● | ● | ● |

**CONDITION CODE REGISTER NOTES:** (Bit set if test is true and cleared otherwise)

1 (Bit V) Test: Result = 10000000?
2 (Bit C) Test: Result = 00000000?
3 (Bit C) Test: Decimal value of most significant BCD Character greater than nine? (Not cleared if previously set.)
4 (Bit V) Test: Operand = 10000000 prior to execution?
5 (Bit V) Test: Operand = 01111111 prior to execution?
6 (Bit V) Test: Set equal to result of N⊕C after shift has occurred.
7 (Bit N) Test: Sign bit of most significant (MS) byte = 1?
8 (Bit V) Test: 2's complement overflow from subtraction of MS bytes?
9 (Bit N) Test: Result less than zero? (Bit 15 = 1)
10 (All) Load Condition Code Register from Stack. (See Special Operations)
11 (Bit I) Set when interrupt occurs. If previously set, a Non-Maskable Interrupt is required to exit the wait state.
12 (All) Set according to the contents of Accumulator A.

instructions available in the MC6800. A thorough familiarity with all the instructions, however, does not guarantee that the reader can order the MC6800 to perform meaningful tasks. This can be accomplished only by putting the instructions together in a logical sequence. The computer is only a machine and, as such, does only what it is told to do, regardless of whether or not that's what the programmer wants it to do. This may seem like a humorous or inoccuous remark, but many is the time that the "impossible" things that the computer does is only the result of the programmer putting the wrong instructions together. This leads to the final section of this chapter.

## *Programming Examples*

Although this final section has little to do with the description of MC6800 instructions, it would be an injustice to simply describe the instructions without some indication of how they can be used. The real power of computers lies in putting instructions together to perform meaningful tasks in the shortest amount of time, and using as little memory as possible. The instructions are merely tools in this process. The tools themselves can't perform the tasks; they must be used skillfully by the programmer. This section is not intended to be a short course in programming (more will be said about it later), but presents a few common examples of programs or segments of programs so that some perspective can be added.

Suppose that a program is to be written which adds two 16-bit binary numbers. This is a very common example, one which is found in practically every microprocessor text (especially texts covering 8-bit microprocessors). Let us assume that the program begins in memory location *0084, and that the two numbers are stored in locations *0080 through *0083. Let us assume further that the more significant byte of the result is to be in accumulator B and the less significant byte of the result is to be in accumulator A. Locations *0080 and *0082 contain the more significant bytes of the addend and augend, and the less significant bytes are in locations *0081 and *0083. This is a very trivial example, since the entire task can be accomplished in four instructions, LDA and ADD followed by an LDA and ADC. Since the data for this example lies in the first 256 locations, the direct addressing mode can be used. Figure 6.34 shows memory locations *0080 through *008B, which contain both the data and the program. Note that when looking at all 12 bytes, it is virtually impossible to distinguish program from data without prior knowledge of where the program resides and what it is intended to do. This is almost always the case: when observing only memory contents, it is very difficult to distinguish programs from data, much less figure out what the program is supposed to do. Incidentally, following execution of the instruction in location *008A, the MC6800 will attempt to execute the contents of location *008C. Given only the contents of Figure 6.34, we have no idea what will happen next.

The second example performs addition of ten numbers. Assume that each of the numbers may be from zero to ten, and that they are stored in BCD format. The task is to obtain the sum of the numbers in BCD. Assume that the numbers are stored in memory locations *0110 through *0119, and that the program is to begin in location *0120. In order to perform this task, several additions are required. A program loop is the best way to handle a repetitive process because it involves execution of the same instructions repeatedly. The loop must begin in an orderly fashion and terminate at a specific time. Figure 6.35 shows a short program which performs the additions. In this program the sum will be maintained in accumulator A. The first instruction of the program loads the index register so that it points to the first data item. Next, the sum is initially set to zero, and the count of items is loaded into accumulator B. Now the addition begins: the contents of the location pointed to by the index register is added to accumulator A, and the sum is decimally adjusted. The index register is incremented so that it points to the next data item. The count in accumulator B is decremented, and control is passed back to the ADD instruction. The process is repeated until the count in accumulator B reaches zero. The loop method saves many memory instructions since ten ADDs and DAAs are not required. Note that the BCD sum is in accumulator A. If all the data items are 10, then the

*FIGURE 6.34: Memory Contents (short example)*

| Address | Contents |
|---|---|
| *007F | |
| *0080 | *06 |
| *0081 | *22 |
| *0082 | *17 |
| *0083 | *4A |
| *0084 | *96 |
| *0085 | *81 |
| *0086 | *9B |
| *0087 | *83 |
| *0088 | *D6 |
| *0089 | *80 |
| *008A | *D9 |
| *008B | *82 |
| *008C | ?? |

*FIGURE 6.35: Short Loop for Addition of 10 Numbers*

| Location | Mnemonic | Contents |
|---|---|---|
| *0120 | LDX (IMM) | *CE |
| *0121 | | *01 |
| *0122 | | *10 |
| *0123 | CLR A | *4F |
| *0124 | LDA B (IMM) | *C6 |
| *0125 | | *0A |
| *0126 | ADD A (IND) | *8B |
| *0127 | | *00 |
| *0128 | DAA | *19 |
| *0129 | INX | *08 |
| *012A | DEC B | *5A |
| *012B | BNE | *26 |
| *012C | | *F9 |

final sum will be 100, which will be indicated by zero in accumulator A and the carry bit set. This is acceptable since C is initially reset by the CLR A instruction, and is not affected by the DEC B at the end.

The third and final example involves a short routine which multiplies the contents of accumulator A by 10. Let us assume that this routine is to be a subroutine, called potentially by several other routines. If this is so, then the last instruction must be an RTS. Accumulator B will be used in this routine, but it may contain important data from the calling routines. In order to preserve the contents of B, the routine will begin with a PSH B and will have a PUL B immediately before the RTS. The routine is shown in Figure 6.36. The multiplicand is first transferred to accumulator B.

*FIGURE 6.36: Multiplication by 10*

| Location | Mnemonic | Contents |
|---|---|---|
| *0304 | | |
| *0305 | PSH B | *37 |
| *0306 | TAB | *16 |
| *0307 | ASL A | *48 |
| *0308 | ASL A | *48 |
| *0309 | ABA | *1B |
| *030A | ASL A | *48 |
| *030B | PUL B | *33 |
| *030C | RTS | *39 |

Accumulator A is multiplied by four by the two ASL instructions. Adding the original contents makes a multiply-by-five procedure, and the final ASL completes the multiply by 10. This routine will work for any values in the accumulator A, positive or negative, which do not create an overflow condition (i.e., absolute value less than 12).

### *EXERCISES*

*1.* Name the two 8-bit registers and the three 16-bit registers within the MC6800.

*2.* Explain briefly the immediate, direct, indexed, and extended addressing modes.

*3.* Why can indexed mode instructions address potentially anywhere in system memory?

*4.* What is the difference between the stack and the stack pointer? How big can the stack be?

*5.* In each of the following cases, write the contents of accumulator A after execution of each of the instructions. Assume that execution begins with the instruction in location *0080. Assume the index register contains *0076 and the carry bit is initially zero.

| | *Location* | *Mnemonic* | *Contents* |
|---|---|---|---|
| a) | *007E | | *44 |
| | *007F | | *3C |
| | *0080 | LDA A (IMM) | *86 |
| | *0081 | | *63 |
| | *0082 | ROLA | *49 |
| | *0083 | ROLA | *49 |
| | *0084 | AND A (DIR) | *94 |
| | *0085 | | *7F |
| b) | *007E | | *22 |
| | *007F | | *2F |
| | *0080 | LDA A (IND) | *A6 |
| | *0081 | | *02 |
| | *0082 | SUB A (IND) | *A0 |
| | *0083 | | *03 |
| | *0084 | ASL A | *48 |

*6.* Explain briefly the difference between a mnemonic and an opcode.

*7.* Name the three phases involved in instruction execution.

**8.** In each of the following cases, write the contents of accumulator B after execution of each of the instructions. Assume that the carry bit is initially zero, and that execution begins with the instruction in location *0080.

| | *Location* | *Mnemonic* | *Content* |
|---|---|---|---|
| a) | *007E | | *F0 |
| | *007F | | *4C |
| | *0080 | LDA B (IMM) | *C6 |
| | *0081 | | *5A |
| | *0082 | AND B (DIR) | *D4 |
| | *0083 | | *7F |
| | *0084 | ORA B (IMM) | *CA |
| | *0085 | | *76 |
| | *0086 | EOR B (DIR) | *D8 |
| | *0087 | | *7E |
| b) | *007E | | |
| | *007F | | *E8 |
| | *0080 | LDA B (DIR) | *D6 |
| | *0081 | | *7F |
| | *0082 | NEG B | *50 |
| | *0083 | INC B | *5C |
| | *0084 | COM B | *53 |
| | *0085 | DEC B | *5A |

**9.** Following execution of the instructions beginning in location *0140, what will be the contents of locations *013E and *013F?

| *Location* | *Mnemonic* | *Contents* |
|---|---|---|
| *013A | | *14 |
| *013B | | *86 |
| *013C | | *47 |
| *013D | | *CA |
| *013E | | * ? |
| *013F | | * ? |
| *0140 | LDX (IMM) | *CE |
| *0141 | | *01 |
| *0142 | | *30 |
| *0143 | LDA A (IND) | *A6 |
| *0144 | | *0B |
| *0145 | ADD A (IND) | *AB |
| *0146 | | *0D |
| *0147 | STA A (IND) | *A7 |
| *0148 | | *0F |
| *0149 | LDA A (IND) | *A6 |

| *Location* | *Mnemonic* | *Contents* |
|---|---|---|
| *014A | | *0A |
| *014B | ADC A (IND) | *A9 |
| *014C | | *0C |
| *014E | STA A (IND) | *A7 |
| | | *0E |

***10.*** In each of the following sequences, from what location will the next instruction be executed? Assume the index register contains *006C.

| | *Location* | *Mnemonic* | *Contents* |
|---|---|---|---|
| a) | *0142 | JMP | *7E |
| | *0143 | (EXT) | *02 |
| | *0144 | | *37 |
| b) | *0223 | BRA | *20 |
| | *0223 | | *1A |
| c) | *0228 | BRA | *20 |
| | *0229 | | *E7 |
| d) | *0200 | JMP | *6E |
| | *0201 | (IND) | *6C |

***11.*** Assuming accumulator A contains *3A, from what location will the next instruction be executed in the following examples?

| | *Location* | *Mnemonic* | *Contents* |
|---|---|---|---|
| a) | *00A4 | CMP A (IMM) | *81 |
| | *00A5 | | *26 |
| | *00A6 | BLE | *2F |
| | *00A7 | | *10 |
| b) | *0128 | EOR A (IMM) | *88 |
| | *0129 | | *C5 |
| | *012A | BNE | *26 |
| | *012B | | *F4 |
| c) | *0064 | ADD A (IMM) | *8B |
| | *0665 | | *4C |
| | *0666 | BVC | *28 |
| | *0667 | | *16 |
| d) | *0059 | TST A | *4D |
| | *005A | BMI | *2B |
| | *005B | | *FD |

***12.*** Under what conditions will the overflow bit be set during an ASL instruction? What does this mean in terms of signed binary numbers?

*13.* What happens when the MC6800 executes the following instruction?

BRA *20
*FE

*14.* What will be the value in the stack pointer after each of the following instructions?

| *Location* | *Mnemonic* | *Contents* |
|---|---|---|
| *0302 | LDS (IMM) | *8E |
| *0303 | | *04 |
| *0304 | | *20 |
| *0305 | PSH B | *37 |
| *0306 | PSH A | *36 |
| *0307 | PUL B | *33 |
| *0308 | JSR (EXT) | *BD |
| *0309 | | *12 |
| *030A | | *00 |

*15.* How many different memory locations can be accessed using direct addressing? Using indexed addressing?

*16.* What property of the stack pointer allows the stack to be anywhere in memory?

*17.* Assume the following register contents:

A = *6C IX = *2020 CCR = *D3

B = *02 SP = *A049

What will be the contents of memory locations *A040 through *A04F if a software interrupt (SWI) instruction is executed in memory location *011C? Use "XX" for unchanged.

*18.* Following a return from interrupt (RTI) instruction, will the interrupt mask bit be set or reset?

*19.* Specify the relative values for the following branch instructions:

a) Opcode at *057A, to branch to *0596
b) Opcode at *6440, to branch to *642C
c) Opcode at *0143, to branch to *0168

*20.* From what memory locations will program counter values be taken immediately following:

a) Software interrupt
b) $\overline{\text{Reset}}$
c) Interrupt request

***21.*** If the value of the stack pointer is *A03E, from what memory location will the following register be loaded if a return from interrupt instruction is executed?

Index register
Accumulator B
Program counter
Condition code register

***22.*** Given the following memory contents, write the mnemonics for a short program which will subtract the second 16-bit number from the first 16-bit number and store the result as indicated. Use as few bytes as possible.

*0260 More significant byte, first number
*0261 Less significant byte, first number
*0262 MSB, second number
*0263 LSB, second number

*026C MSB, result
*026D LSB, result

***23.*** If accumulator A contains *0C, what will it contain after execution of the following instructions? What happens if the same sequence is executed with *07 in accumulator A?

| | |
|---|---|
| AND A (IMM) | *84 |
| | *0F |
| ADD A (IMM) | *8B |
| | *30 |
| CMP A (IMM) | *81 |
| | *39 |
| BLS | *23 |
| | *02 |
| ADD A (IMM) | *8B |
| | *07 |

***24.*** Construct three examples of the branch if less than or equal to (BLE) instruction, as is shown for BGE in Figure 6.21.

***25.*** Modify the routine of Figure 6.36 so that a 16-bit value in A and B can be multiplied by 10.

# 7 Input/Output

The third and final component of a computer is input and output, or simply I/O. I/O is the communication link between the computer and the outside world. The outside world may actually be a human operator, an external device of some kind, or another computer. The word communication implies a transfer of information to or from the computer. The information may be data intended for manipulation, commands to be interpreted, or programs for subsequent execution. Information transferred from the computer may be results of manipulations, messages to an operator, or memory contents (including programs) intended for external storage and subsequent reloading. This chapter deals with a convention for handling data, a method for communicating that data, a few I/O devices, and a means of access to the rest of the computer.

## *ASCII Code and ASCII Transmission*

The emphasis in this chapter will be on the most basic type of I/O —communication between the computer and a human operator. In many cases, this communication is implemented by a terminal which has the capabilities of printing or displaying messages and of message or character entry. In message display, numbers, letters, punctuation marks, and special characters are printed or displayed so the operator can read them. Similarly, character entry is the process of sending the same kinds of numbers, letters, punctuation marks, and special characters to the computer. The computer, especially the CPU, understands only binary; it executes binary instructions and processes binary data. There must be a means, then, of converting English characters to and from binary. Without getting into the mechanics of how the terminal works, there must be a common set of rules such that when a key is struck on the terminal, the computer knows just what key it is. Similarly, these rules must dictate that when the computer sends some binary data to the terminal, a certain character will be printed.

There are several conventions for implementing this conversion. The most popular convention among microprocessors and microcomputer systems is ASCII, the American Standard Code for Information Interchange. In ASCII, all printable characters, all terminal controls, and a few special-purpose characters are assigned a binary value. The code is implemented with seven bits, allowing up to 128 unique characters. The entire ASCII character set is shown in tabular fashion in Figure 7.1. The more significant three bits are listed across the top of the table, while the less significant four bits are shown down the left side. The numbers in ASCII all begin with the hex character three. The uppercase letters begin with *41 and continue through *5A. Although only a few terminals are equipped to handle lowercase letters, the ASCII code provides for lowercase beginning with *61 and continuing through *7A. Punctuation marks occupy the column of characters beginning with *2, and terminal control and communications occupy the columns beginning with *0 and *1.

Now that a code for character communication has been established, there must be a physical means of transmitting information to and from the terminals. Virtually all keyboardlike terminals transmit and receive data serially, that is, one bit at a time. What this means, among other things, is that the terminal can communicate with other devices via only two wires:

*FIGURE 7.1: Complete ASCII Character Set*

| *Bits Shown in Transmission* | *Bits Shown in Transmission Sequence: 8, 7, 6, 5* | | | | | | | |
|---|---|---|---|---|---|---|---|---|
| *Sequence:4, 3, 2, 1* | *0000* | *0001* | *0010* | *0011* | *0100* | *0101* | *0110* | *0111* |
| 0000 | NUL | DLE | SP | 0 | @ | P | | p |
| 0001 | SOH | DC1 | ! | 1 | A | Q | a | q |
| 0010 | STX | DC2 | " | 2 | B | R | b | r |
| 0011 | ETX | DC3 | # | 3 | C | S | c | s |
| 0100 | EOT | DC4 | S | 4 | D | T | d | t |
| 0101 | ENQ | NAK | % | 5 | E | U | e | u |
| 0110 | ACK | SYN | & | 6 | F | V | f | v |
| 0111 | BEL | ETB | ' | 7 | G | W | g | w |
| 1000 | BS | CAN | ( | 8 | H | X | h | x |
| 1001 | HT | EM | ) | 9 | I | Y | i | y |
| 1010 | LF | SUB | * | : | J | Z | j | z |
| 1011 | VT | ESC | + | ; | K | [ | k | { |
| 1100 | FF | FS | , | < | L | \ | l | : |
| 1101 | CR | GS | – | = | M | ] | m | } |
| 1110 | SO | RS | . | > | N | ⌉ | n | ~ |
| 1111 | Si | US | / | ? | O | — | o | DEL |

the data line and a common line. In addition, most of these terminals are asynchronous—the characters are transmitted at irregular intervals.

There is another convention for the format in which data is transmitted across the two wires. There are actually two conventions—the teletype and the RS-232—but they are almost identical, and each is often referred to as ASCII communication. ASCII communication involves logic-level voltages, +5 and ground, as a function of time. When the terminal is physically connected to its host device, and when power is on in both devices, the normal state of the data line is a logic 1. This condition is known as the *idle state*, and it remains as long as both the terminal and host device have power. Transmission of a character is indicated by transition of the data line from a 1 to a 0. This is known as the *start bit*. Following the start bit are 8 information bits. If an ASCII character is being transmitted, the least significant bit will be transmitted first, followed by the other 6 bits in order. In many cases, the eighth information bit is ignored. Following the last information bit is a logic 1. This is called the *stop bit*, and its purpose is to return the data line to the idle state. The data line remains at logic 1 until the occurrence of the next start bit. One of the major differences between teletype transmission and RS-232 transmission is that teletype includes two stop bits, while RS-232 includes only one. Teletype and RS-232 transmissions are shown graphically in Figure 7.2; part (a) shows teletype transmission of the character "9", and part (b) shows RS-232 transmission of the character "?".

Both parts of the figure show 8 information bits, 7 of which are used

*FIGURE 7.2: Two Methods of ASCII Data Transmission: (a) Teletype Transmission, (b) RS-232 Transmission*

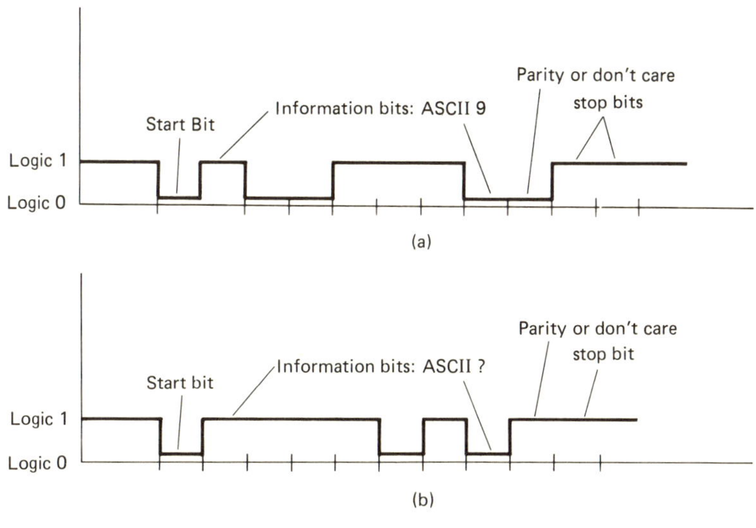

for conveying the ASCII character. In many cases, the eighth bit is used as a *parity* bit. Parity is a means of error checking. Characters are often transmitted over long distances and through unreliable equipment. In these cases, bits may be "dropped," that is, ones may be changed to zeros and vice versa, and the data originally sent is not what is actually received. Although little can be done to remedy this, the situation can be detected and an attempt at retransmission can be made. Parity is the addition of a bit for error-detection purposes. There are two types of parity, odd and even, and this refers to the total number of logical ones (including parity) in the character. Each ASCII character contains a fixed number of ones, and the parity bit is set to 1 or 0 according to odd or even parity. If odd parity was used in the characters of Figure 7.2, the parity bits would be 1 and 0, respectively. Even parity in the same two examples would yield 0 and 1 parity bits.

In data communications lingo, the terms *mark* and *space* are often heard. Mark refers to a logic 1 bit, and space refers to a logic 0. The transmission of a character in an asynchronous serial medium, then, is indicated by the first mark-to-space transition.

Although characters are transmitted asynchronously, the bits within each character are transmitted at regular intervals. Most teletypelike terminals operate at a maximum speed of 10 characters per second, or 10 cps. That means that there are 110 bits transmitted per second, or 110 bps. Bits per second is often referred to as *baud*, so the teletypelike device operates at 110 baud. (Actually, baud means voltage level changes per second. In rare cases, the voltage may take more than two possible values, allowing more than one bit to be transmitted at a given time. Very technically speaking, baud is not the same as bits per second, but the two terms have been used interchangeably lately.) Most teletypelike devices operate at only 110 baud and cannot go any faster.

RS-232 devices, on the other hand, are not limited to one speed. They may operate at 10 characters per second, which, for these devices, is the same as 100 baud. But RS-232 devices also commonly operate at 150, 300, 600, 1200, 2400, and even 9600 baud. The reason for the difference is that the teletypelike devices are mechanical printing devices, while the RS-232 devices are usually cathode ray tube (CRT) screens which operate electronically. The CRT devices physically resemble television screens. While these operate very fast, they cannot provide a hard copy like the teletypelike devices can. There are a few RS-232 devices which operate mechanically, but most are currently limited to a speed of 300 baud.

Now that a code for character representation has been discussed, along with a means of serially transmitting that data to and from a terminal, we can turn to how that serial data interfaces to a microcomputer system in which all data is handled in parallel, 8 bits at a time. There is just such a device which implements the parallel to serial conversion and it is called a universal asynchronous receiver/transmitter, or UART for short. A UART can take parallel information from a computer system and transmit it serially to a terminal, and it can receive serial data from a terminal and convert it to parallel for the computer. A typical UART is shown in Figure 7.3.

Most UARTs have two separate, often independent functions, a transmit function and a receive function, as shown in the figure. In the transmit portion, there are 8 inputs reserved for parallel data output from the computer, and there is one output for the serial data to the terminal. Four function-select inputs are shown, but there may actually be more. The functions that they select are what make the UART universal.

One of the selectable functions is the number of data bits, exclusive of parity. Two function-select bits are usually reserved to select the transmission of 5, 6, 7, or 8 data bits. Another function-select bit is used to select either one or two stop bits, so that the same UART can be used with either teletype or RS-232 devices. Two more function-select bits are reserved for the use of the parity bit. One of these bits indicates whether or not parity is involved, and the second bit indicates whether odd or even parity is used. Logic circuitry within the UART can both generate parity prior to transmission and check parity upon reception. Many UARTs have separate function-select inputs for the transmit and receive sections, but some only have one set of function selects which govern the operation of both sections.

Two clock inputs are shown, one for the transmit section and one for the receive section. These clocks specify the frequency at which bits within the characters are transmitted or must be received. In many cases, the frequency at which characters are transmitted is only a fraction of the input clock frequency. If this is the case, then function-select bits are reserved so that the fraction can be specified. The most common case is two

*FIGURE 7.3: Universal Asynchronous Receiver/Transmitter (UART)*

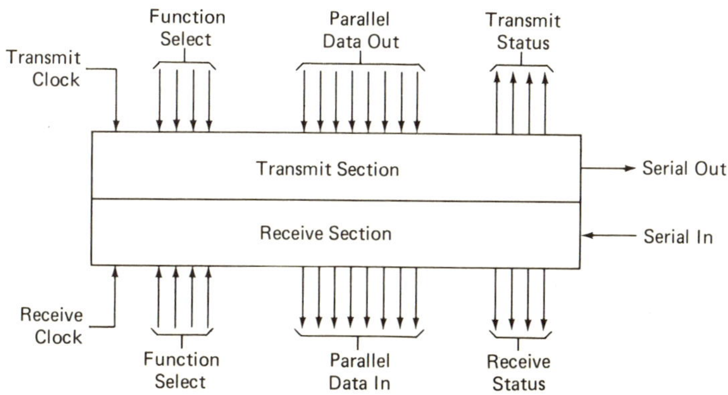

function-select bits can determine whether the input frequency is divided by 1 (i.e., the transmission frequency is the input frequency), by 16, or by 64. A very common case is an input clock frequency of 1760 cycles per second with a divide-by-16 function, yielding a data transmission rate of 110 baud.

There are actually two registers involved in the transmitting or receiving of characters in a UART. In the transmit section, one 8-bit register accepts data in parallel from the host. This data is immediately transferred to a second register which shifts the bits (plus start bit and appropriate parity and stop bits) out through the serial lead. The shift register is ready to accept data as long as it has no data to shift. This means that two data words can be stored one right after the other into the first register. The second word will remain in the first register until the first word is shifted out. There are also two registers in the receive portion. As soon as a word is shifted in (all data and stop bits) through the serial input lead, it is transferred to another 8-bit register which is available to the host. A word which has been received may remain in the second register while a second word is being serially received.

This leads to a discussion of the status bits. There is usually only one status bit associated with the transmit portion of a UART. This bit is called *transmit data register empty*, or TDRE. This bit is set when a character has been shifted completely out through the serial-out lead, and it indicates that another character may be stored in the parallel input register. There are four status bits associated with data reception. The first of these is called *receiver data register full*, or RDRF. It indicates that a character has been totally received and that it is available through the parallel output register. The other three status bits involve error conditions. One is called a *data overrun condition*. It indicates that one character has been received and transferred to the parallel output register, a second character has been totally accepted into the input shift register, and a third character is being accepted into the shift register, all before the first character has been accepted by the host. This results in the loss of at least the second character received. The second error indicator is called *framing error*. This is set when the receiving shift register expects to see a stop bit (i.e., logic 1), but in fact sees a 0. The third error indicator is *parity error* and indicates that the received character plus its parity bit does not yield the number of ones that is specified by the function-select bits. Another possible status bit is that which indicates a "break" condition on the transmission line. A break condition exists when all zeros are received for the start bit, the information bits, and one or both stop bits. A break condition is functionally equivalent to power being removed from the transmitting device.

The UART is a very flexible and powerful device for implementing input and output for a computer. It can accommodate a variety of terminal devices and data transmission arrangements. UARTs are available as

40-pin integrated circuit packages from several vendors. In addition, many microprocessor manufacturers provide UART-like devices as part of their families of devices.

## *I/O in the M6800 System*

Throughout the discussion of the MC6800 instruction set, no input/output instructions were covered. This is because the M6800 system uses a concept called "memory-mapped I/O." In many microprocessors, specific I/O instructions exist which transfer data through the 8 data bits and use all or a portion of the address bus to select specific I/O devices. In the M6800 system, however, I/O devices are connected to the microprocessor (via the address bus) as though they are memory addresses. In this scheme, data is transferred into the microprocessor via load accumulator instructions, and is transferred out of the microprocessor via store accumulator instructions. The advantage of this scheme is an overall simplicity and uniformity of data transfer to and from the microprocessor. The disadvantage of the scheme lies in the fact that those addresses which are used for I/O devices are not available for memory locations; this could result in a smaller total system memory.

Two I/O components in Motorola's M6800 family of devices are of a type generally referred to as interface chips: they implement the transition from the microprocessor to an actual I/O device. The first of the two interface devices to be considered is the Motorola MC6850, Asynchronous Communications Interface Adapter, or ACIA. The ACIA is Motorola's equivalent of the UART, and it is used primarily for the transmission and reception of serial data. A portion of the product specification sheet for the MC6850 is shown in Figure 7.4. Physically, the MC6850 is a 24-pin integrated circuit which is compatible, circuitwise, with the other devices in the M6800 family.

An expanded block diagram of the ACIA is shown in Figure 7.5. There are several leads which connect the ACIA to the rest of the computer system. Among these leads are the 8-bit data bus. This data bus, like the data busses of all the MC6800 compatible devices, is both bidirectional and three-state. Through this data bus passes not only the data which ultimately comes from and goes to the peripheral devices, but also all the necessary control and status information. The ACIA has three chip-select lines, two of which are high active and one which is low active. These chip selects perform the same function as they do in the Motorola memory chips. There is a register select lead, RS, which selects among the registers internal to the ACIA. There is a read/write lead, R/W, which governs the direction of data transfer between the microprocessor and the ACIA. There is also an enable lead which dictates when data will be transferred; this lead is usually

*FIGURE 7.4: MC6850 Product Specification Sheet* (Courtesy of Motorola Semiconductor Products Inc.)

## ASYNCHRONOUS COMMUNICATIONS INTERFACE ADAPTER (ACIA)

The MC6850 Asynchronous Communications Interface Adapter provides the data formatting and control to interface serial asynchronous data communications information to bus organized systems such as the MC6800 Microprocessing Unit.

The bus interface of the MC6850 includes select, enable, read/write, interrupt and bus interface logic to allow data transfer over an 8-bit bi-directional data bus. The parallel data of the bus system is serially transmitted and received by the asynchronous data interface, with proper formatting and error checking. The functional configuration of the ACIA is programmed via the data bus during system initialization. A programmable Control Register provides variable word lengths, clock division ratios, transmit control, receive control, and interrupt control. For peripheral or modem operation three control lines are provided. These lines allow the ACIA to interface directly with the MC6860L 0-600 bps digital modem.

- Eight and Nine-Bit Transmission
- Optional Even and Odd Parity
- Parity, Overrun and Framing Error Checking
- Programmable Control Register
- Optional ÷1, ÷16, and ÷64 Clock Modes
- Up to 500 kbps Transmission
- False Start Bit Deletion
- Peripheral/Modem Control Functions
- Double Buffered
- One or Two Stop Bit Operation

**MOS**

(N-CHANNEL, SILICON-GATE)

ASYNCHRONOUS COMMUNICATIONS INTERFACE ADAPTER

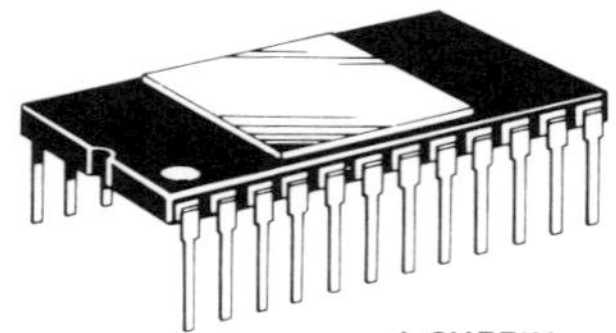

L SUFFIX
CERAMIC PACKAGE
CASE 716

NOT SHOWN: P SUFFIX
PLASTIC PACKAGE
CASE 709

*FIGURE 7.5: ACIA Expanded Block Diagram* (Courtesy of Motorola Semiconductor Products Inc.)

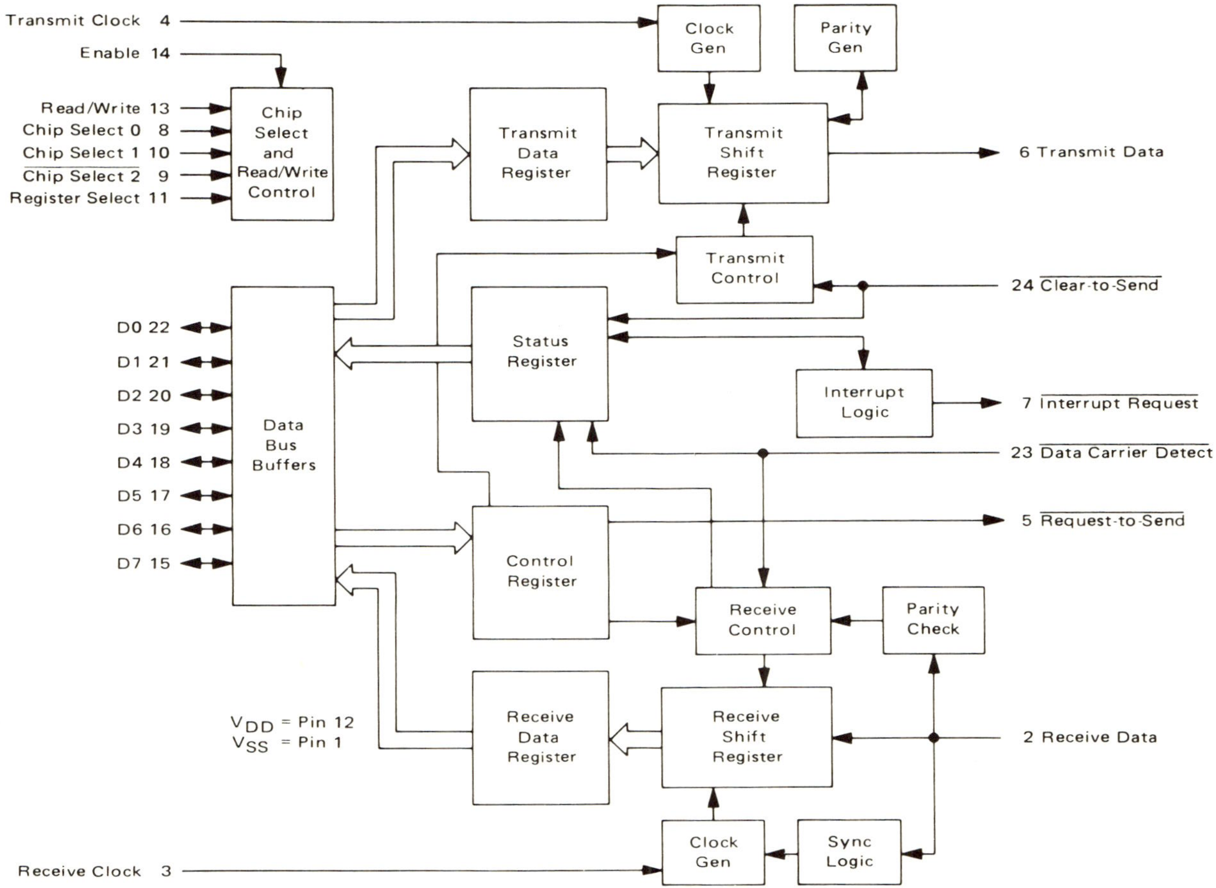

connected to the system $\phi 2$ clock. Finally, there is the $\overline{\text{IRQ}}$ lead which, when connected to the MC6800's $\overline{\text{IRQ}}$ lead, can optionally initiate an interrupt sequence in the microprocessor.

The ACIA has two clock inputs, one for transmission and one for reception. This is standard in most UART-like devices.

On the peripheral device side of the ACIA are five signals. Two of these are the familiar transmit data and receive data signals. The data which passes through these signals is the serial data in transmission. The other three signals are used for interfacing an ACIA to a modem (modulator-demodulator). These signals are the data carrier detect ($\overline{\text{DCD}}$), request-to-send ($\overline{\text{RTS}}$), and clear-to-send ($\overline{\text{CTS}}$). Each of these signals is active low. Modems and their operation are beyond the scope of this text.

There are four registers internal to the ACIA which are accessible to the programmer. These are the transmit data register, the receive data register, the control register, and the status register. The transmit data and control registers are write-only (i.e., their contents cannot be read), and the receive data and the status registers are read-only. The registers are selected by the register select input and the read/write input. The read/write input is connected to the microprocessor's read/write signal, so that any read operation (via load accumulator) will access either the receive data register or the status register. The RS input is normally connected to the system address bus bit 0, so that the registers may be accessed as one of two addresses. The register contents and their meanings are shown in Figure 7.6.

The transmit and the receive data registers are accessed when RS = 1. Bit 0 of each of these registers is the least significant bit, the bit which will be transmitted first in either direction. If seven bits plus parity is selected, then bit 7 will be transmitted as a "don't care," and will be read as a zero in the receive data register.

The control and status registers are accessed when RS = 0. The control register determines the characteristics of data transmission. The total control register is broken down into four fields, each governing a separate phase of operation. Bits 0 and 1 govern the bit data rate as a function of the transmit and receive clocks. Divide by 1, divide by 16, and divide by 64 are possible. Both transmission ratios are governed by these two bits. When both bits are 1, a master reset occurs which terminates all data transmission activity and resets all the status register bits except bits 2 and 3. None of the other control register bits are affected by master reset. Control register bits 2, 3, and 4 govern the number of data bits, stop bits, and parity as shown in the smaller table. Control register bits 5 and 6 govern the state of the $\overline{\text{RTS}}$ line (which is an output from the ACIA), and also govern whether or not an $\overline{\text{IRQ}}$ will be sent to the microprocessor when a character has been completely transmitted (i.e., when transmit data register empty goes high). Setting $\overline{\text{RTS}}$ low effectively marks the commu-

*FIGURE 7.6: ACIA Register Definition*

| | Buffer Address | | | |
|---|---|---|---|---|
| *Data Bus Line Number* | $RS \cdot \overline{R/W}$ *Transmit Data Register (Write Only)* | $RS \cdot R/W$ *Receive Data Register (Read Only)* | $\overline{RS} \cdot \overline{R/W}$ *Control Register (Write Only)* | $\overline{RS} \cdot R/W$ *Status Register (Read Only)* |
| *0* | Data Bit 0* | Data Bit 0 | Counter Divide Select 1 (CR0) | Receive Data Register Full (RDRF) |
| *1* | Data Bit 1 | Data Bit 1 | Counter Divide Select 2 (CR1) | Transmit Data Register Empty (TDRE) |
| *2* | Data Bit 2 | Data Bit 2 | Word Select 1 (CR2) | $\overline{\text{Data Carrier Detect}}$ ($\overline{\text{DCD}}$) |
| *3* | Data Bit 3 | Data Bit 3 | Word Select 2 (CR3) | $\overline{\text{Clear-to-Send}}$ ($\overline{\text{CTS}}$) |
| *4* | Data Bit 4 | Data Bit 4 | Word Select 3 (CR4) | Framing Error (FE) |
| *5* | Data Bit 5 | Data Bit 5 | Transmit Control 1 (CR5) | Receiver Overrun (OVRN) |
| *6* | Data Bit 6 | Data Bit 6 | Transmit Control 2 (CR6) | Parity Error (PE) |
| *7* | Data Bit 7*** | Data Bit 7** | Receive Interrupt Enable (CR7) | Interrupt Request (IRQ) |

*Leading bit = LSB = Bit 0
** Data bit will be zero in 7-bit plus parity modes.
*** Data bit is "don't care" in 7-bit plus parity modes.

| *CR1* | *CR0* | *Function* |
|---|---|---|
| 0 | 0 | ÷ 1 |
| 0 | 1 | ÷ 16 |
| 1 | 0 | ÷ 64 |
| 1 | 1 | Master Reset |

(b)

*FIGURE 7.6: Continued*

| CR4 | CR3 | CR2 | Function |
|---|---|---|---|
| 0 | 0 | 0 | 7 Bits + Even Parity + 2 Stop Bits |
| 0 | 0 | 1 | 7 Bits + Odd Parity + 2 Stop Bits |
| 0 | 1 | 0 | 7 Bits + Even Parity + 1 Stop Bit |
| 0 | 1 | 1 | 7 Bits + Odd Parity + 1 Stop Bit |
| 1 | 0 | 0 | 8 Bits + 2 Stop Bits |
| 1 | 0 | 1 | 8 Bits + 1 Stop Bit |
| 1 | 1 | 0 | 8 Bits + Even Parity + 1 Stop Bit |
| 1 | 1 | 1 | 8 Bits + Odd Parity + 1 Stop Bit |

(c)

| CR6 | CR5 | Function |
|---|---|---|
| 0 | 0 | $\overline{RTS}$ = low, Transmitting Interrupt Disabled. |
| 0 | 1 | $\overline{RTS}$ = low, Transmitting Interrupt Enabled. |
| 1 | 0 | $\overline{RTS}$ = high, Transmitting Interrupt Disabled. |
| 1 | 1 | $\overline{RTS}$ = low, Transmits a Break level on the Transmit Data Output. Transmitting Interrupt Disabled. |

(d)

nication line active, while setting it high marks it inactive. Transmitting a break condition is also possible via control register bits 5 and 6. Control bit 7 governs whether or not an $\overline{IRQ}$ will be generated when a character has been received. If bit 7 is high, the $\overline{IRQ}$ will be generated. Any of the following conditions will generate the $\overline{IRQ}$: receiver data register full, data overrun, or a low to high transition of data carrier detect.

The status register indicates all possible conditions related to character transmission and reception. Both normal and error conditions are recorded, and the conditions are recorded whether or not interrupts are generated. Bit 0 is receiver data register full, RDRF, and it is set when a character has been fully received and is ready to be taken by the MC6800. RDRF will be reset when the MC6800 reads the receiver data register. Bit 1 is the transmit data register empty, TDRE. It indicates that a new character may be stored in the write data register. Bit 2 of the status register is the data carrier detect bit, or $\overline{DCD}$. When low, it indicates that a carrier is present from a modem and that characters may be transmitted in either direction. (This and certain other bits are intended for, but not restricted to, use with modems; the ACIA may, of course, be used without a modem.) If the actual $\overline{DCD}$ input goes high and then returns to low, the $\overline{DCD}$ status bit will remain high until the status register is used by the microprocessor. The clear-to-send bit, bit 3 of the status register, indicates the state of the $\overline{\text{CTS}}$ input from the modem. A low $\overline{\text{CTS}}$ input indicates the normal state of the modem, while a high $\overline{\text{CTS}}$ indicates no transmission is permitted. A high $\overline{\text{CTS}}$ prevents TDRE from going high. Framing error, bit 4, is set when an expected stop bit is not received. Framing error is reset upon reception of every valid character, or by a master reset. Bit 5 of the status register is receiver overrun, or OVRN. OVRN indicates that more than two valid characters have been received without a character being read by the microprocessor. OVRN will be reset by reading a character from the receive data register or by a master reset. Parity error, bit 6 of the status register, indicates a parity error in the received character. Parity error can only be set if a parity option is selected in the control register. Bit 6 will remain set until the invalid character is read from the read data register. The final bit of the status register is the $\overline{\text{IRQ}}$ bit. This bit will be set when any interrupt condition along with its applicable enable occur. Bit 7 will be high anytime the $\overline{\text{IRQ}}$ output is low, and it will be reset by any read to the receive data register or write to the transmit data register.

There is a specific reason for having a separate interrupt bit in the status register. If two or more ACIAs are used in the same system, their $\overline{\text{IRQ}}$ lines will be physically tied together and will also be tied to the MC6800 $\overline{\text{IRQ}}$ input. If an interrupt occurs on any of these ACIAs, the microprocessor has no way of knowing which one requested the interrupt. It must then load the status register to determine which ACIA or ACIAs require service. The process of loading all the registers is known as *polling*.

Consider the following example in which a system contains an ACIA. Assume that the control/status registers occupy memory address *2000, and that the data registers occupy address *2001. The following two instructions will initialize the ACIA for divide-by-16 clock ratio, 7 data bits + odd parity + 2 stop bits, $\overline{\text{RTS}}$ low, and no interrupts:

```
LDA A (IMM)    *86    Load proper code.
               *05
STA A (EXT)    *B7    Store in control register.
               *20
               *00
```

The following instructions will continuously check for the RDRF signal. When RDRF finally goes high, the three error bits are checked, and if no error occurs, the data word is loaded into accumulator B.

```
LDA A (EXT)    *B6    Load status register.
               *20
               *00
BIT A (IMM)    *85    Check RDRF.
               *01
```

| | | |
|---|---|---|
| BEQ | *27 | If not set, branch back to load. |
| | *F9 | |
| BIT A (IMM) | *85 | Check 3 errors. |
| | *70 | |
| BNE | *26 | If any set, branch to error routine. |
| | *XX | |
| LDA B (EXT) | *F6 | Load data word. |
| | *20 | |
| | *01 | |

The preceding is a somewhat unrealistic example of ACIA handling because most of the MC6800's instructions are spent repeatedly checking the RDRF. In a real system, either the interrupts would be enabled, or the RDRF would be checked only periodically. The instructions following the RDRF are realistic, however. The errors should be checked before the data word is loaded.

While the ACIA implements parallel-to-serial data conversion and transfer, the Peripheral Interface Adapter, PIA, is used for parallel-to-parallel data transfers. The PIA, Motorola's MC6820, is useful for interfacing the M6800 system to digital-to-analog converters and bit monitoring and control devices.

The product specification sheet for the Peripheral Interface Adapter is shown in Figure 7.7.

The interface between the PIA and the rest of the computer system is much the same as the interface between the ACIA and the computer system. An 8-bit three-state bidirectional data bus conveys all data and control information between the MC6800 and the PIA. There are three chip-select leads, two active high and one active low. There is an enable signal and a read/write signal going to the PIA, and there is an $\overline{\text{IRQ}}$ coming from the PIA. There are two register select inputs for selecting the various internal registers. Finally, there is a master reset input, $\overline{\text{reset}}$, which is used for total initialization and which is intended to be connected to the MC6800's $\overline{\text{reset}}$ input.

On the peripheral side of the PIA, the signals are divided into two halves, the A-side and the B-side. Each side contains an 8-bit bidirectional data register called the peripheral data register, or PDR, and two control bits. The two sides are logically identical, but the B-side data register and one of the B-side control bits are three-state and are also TTL compatible. This makes for a minor difference between the operation of the two sides.

The two control bits on each side of the PIA are used for general control and hardware handshaking related to the transfer of data through the PDR. The first control bits, CA1 and CB1, are always inputs and respond to a level transition from a peripheral device. The second control bits, CA2 and CB2, can be either inputs or outputs. As inputs, their

*FIGURE 7.7: Peripheral Interface Adapter Product Specification Sheet (PIA)* (Courtesy of Motorola Semiconductor Products Inc.)

## PERIPHERAL INTERFACE ADAPTER (PIA)

The MC6820 Peripheral Interface Adapter provides the universal means of interfacing peripheral equipment to the MC6800 Microprocessing Unit (MPU). This device is capable of interfacing the MPU to peripherals through two 8-bit bidirectional peripheral data buses and four control lines. No external logic is required for interfacing to most peripheral devices.

The functional configuration of the PIA is programmed by the MPU during system initialization. Each of the peripheral data lines can be programmed to act as an input or output, and each of the four control/interrupt lines may be programmed for one of several control modes. This allows a high degree of flexibility in the over-all operation of the interface.

- 8-Bit Bidirectional Data Bus for Communication with the MPU
- Two Bidirectional 8-Bit Buses for Interface to Peripherals
- Two Programmable Control Registers
- Two Programmable Data Direction Registers
- Four Individually-Controlled Interrupt Input Lines; Two Usable as Peripheral Control Outputs
- Handshake Control Logic for Input and Output Peripheral Operation
- High-Impedance 3-State and Direct Transistor Drive Peripheral Lines
- Program Controlled Interrupt and Interrupt Disable Capability
- CMOS Drive Capability on Side A Peripheral Lines

## MOS

(N-CHANNEL, SILICON-GATE)

## PERIPHERAL INTERFACE ADAPTER

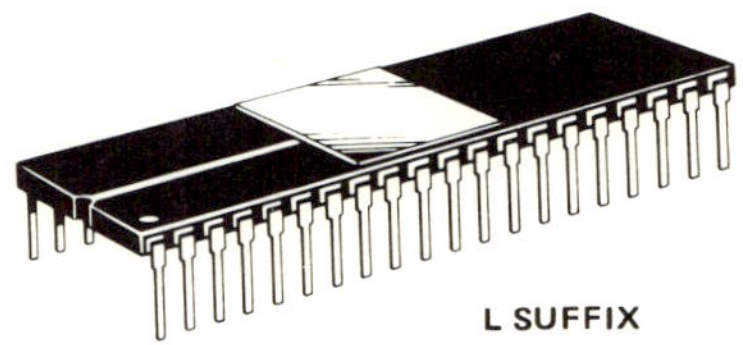

L SUFFIX
CERAMIC PACKAGE
CASE 715

NOT SHOWN: P SUFFIX
PLASTIC PACKAGE
CASE 711

behavior is roughly the same as CA1 and CB1. As outputs, their function can be either under direct program control or under control of the interfaced peripheral device.

Because the output side of the PIA is essentially divided in half, the internal structure of the PIA is also divided in half. There are three major registers in both the A-side and the B-side of the PIA. These are the peripheral data register (PDR) through which all data coming from or going to the outside world passes; the data direction register (DDR), which specifies whether each bit of the PDR is an input or an output; and the control register (CR) which controls the operation of the particular half. All six of these registers are 8-bit registers, and all of them are accessible through the 8-bit data bus. An expanded block diagram of the PIA is shown in Figure 7.8.

Before describing the internal registers in detail, it is interesting to note that there are 6 internal registers (all of which are read/write registers) and only two register select bits for selecting. Register select bit 1 (RS1) selects either the A-side (RS1 = 0) or the B-side (RS1 = 1). Register select bit 0 (RS0) selects either the control register (RS0 = 1) or either the data direction register or the peripheral data register, depending on whether control register bit 2 is a 0 or 1, respectively. The control register is, therefore, used in the selection of the other registers. This is all shown in tabular form in Figure 7.9. In normal operation, the register select bits are connected to system address bits so that all the internal registers may be accessed as different memory locations are accessed.

The data direction registers govern whether or not the individual bits of the peripheral data registers will be inputs or outputs. A logic 1 in a bit in DDR will cause the corresponding bit of PDR to be an output, while a logic 0 in DDR will cause the corresponding bit to be an input. Thus, in each of the sides of the PIA, there are 256 possible combinations of inputs and outputs.

The control registers are primarily concerned with operation of the peripheral control bits and the generation of interrupts to the MPU. Figure 7.10 illustrates the general format of the control register. Bit 2 of each control register specifies whether the peripheral data register or data direct register will be accessed as the even address. Bits 7 and 6 record the occurrence of interrupts from peripheral control bits 1 and 2, respectively. These bits are set by active transitions on the inputs and are reset by the issuance of a read to the control register. Bits 6 and 7 are set by active transitions whether or not interrupts to the MPU are enabled.

Bits 0 and 1 govern the operation of control bit 1, as shown in Figure 7.11. Note that the active transition can be either positive or negative, and interrupts to the MPU can be enabled or disabled for either case.

Bits 3, 4, and 5 govern the operation of control bit 2. Bit 5 specifically governs whether control bit 2 will be an input (bit 5 = 0) or an output (bit

5 = 1). If bit 5 is in fact low, control bit 2 will behave exactly like control bit 1, with control register bits 4 and 3 performing the same functions as control register bits 1 and 0. The only difference between control bit 2 as an input and control bit 1 is that control bit 2 affects control register bit 6. With bit 5 high, control bit 2 is an output. Control bit 2 on the A-side performs a different function than the B-side control bit 2. The basic difference in the two sides is that the A-side control bit 2 reacts to peripheral data read operations, while the B-side control bit 2 reacts to peripheral data write operations. Note also that with both control bits 2, an option is available wherein the control bit follows the contents of control

*FIGURE 7.8: PIA Expanded Block Diagram* (Courtesy of Motorola Semiconductor Products Inc.)

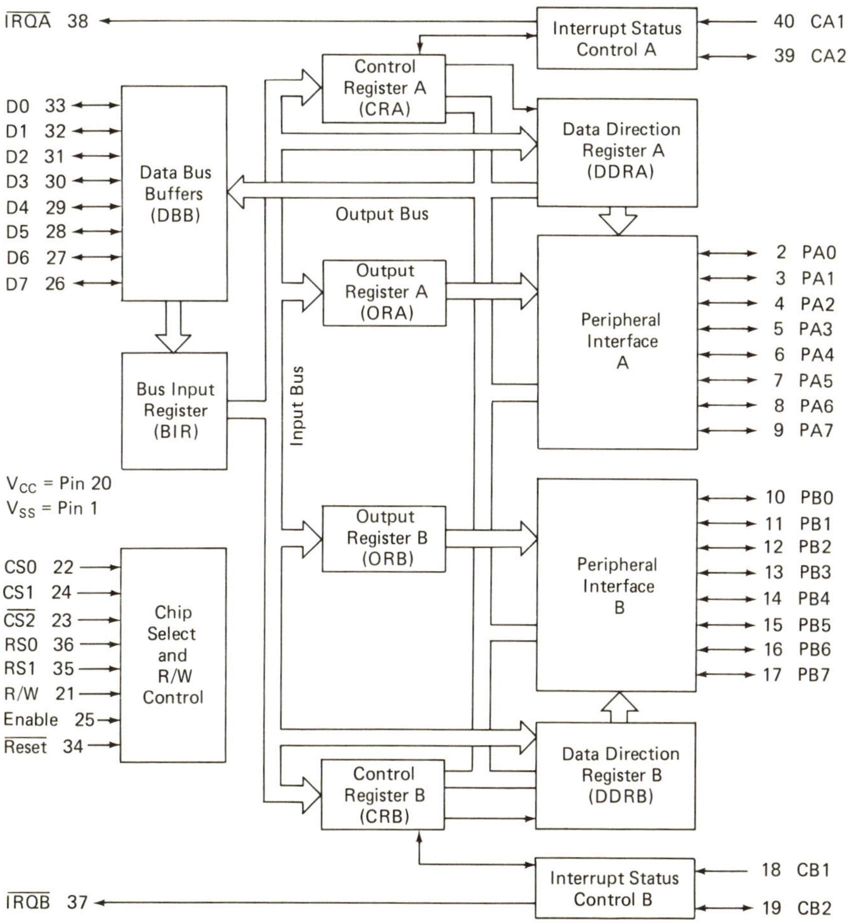

register bit 3. (A more thorough discussion of the operation of the PIA is beyond the scope of this book. The reader is referred to the full product specification sheet for further details.)

The $\overline{\text{reset}}$ input of the MC6820 resets all internal registers to zeros. With the internal registers at zero, all bidirectional peripheral leads become inputs, and all interrupts are disabled. This has the effect of making the MC6820 a totally passive device until it is programmed for useful service.

The following is a brief example of PIA initialization. For the purpose of this example, assume that the A-side peripheral data/data direction register can be accessed at location *B020, the A-side control register at *B021, the B-side PDR/DDR at *B022, and the B-side control register at

*FIGURE 7.9: Internal Addressing within the PIA*

| | | *Control Register Bit* | | |
|---|---|---|---|---|
| *RS1* | *RS0* | *CRA-2* | *CRB-2* | *Location Selected* |
| 0 | 0 | 1 | X | Peripheral Register A |
| 0 | 0 | 0 | X | Data Direction Register A |
| 0 | 1 | X | X | Control Register A |
| 1 | 0 | X | 1 | Peripheral Register B |
| 1 | 0 | X | 0 | Data Direction Register B |
| 1 | 1 | X | X | Control Register B |

X = Don't care

*FIGURE 7.10: Control Word Format*

| | 7 | 6 | 5 | 4 | 3 | 2 | 1 | 0 |
|---|---|---|---|---|---|---|---|---|
| CRA | IRQA1 | IRQA2 | CA2 Control | | | DDRA Access | CA1 Control | |

| | 7 | 6 | 5 | 4 | 3 | 2 | 1 | 0 |
|---|---|---|---|---|---|---|---|---|
| CRB | IRQB1 | IRQB2 | CB2 Control | | | DDRB Access | CB1 Control | |

*FIGURE 7.11: Control of Control Bit 1*

| *CRA-1 (CRB-1)* | *CRA-0 (CRB-0)* | *Interrupt Input CA1 (CB1)* | *Interrupt Flag CRA-7 (CRB-7)* | *MPU Interrupt Request $\overline{IRQA}$ ($\overline{IRQB}$)* |
|---|---|---|---|---|
| 0 | 0 | ↓ Active | Set high on ↓ of CA1 (CB1) | Disabled — $\overline{IRQ}$ remains high |
| 0 | 1 | ↓ Active | Set high on ↓ of CA1 (CB1) | Goes low when the interrupt flag bit CRA-7 (CRB-7) goes high |
| 1 | 0 | ↑ Active | Set high on ↑ of CA1 (CB1) | Disabled — $\overline{IRQ}$ remains high |
| 1 | 1 | ↑ Active | Set high on ↑ of CA1 (CB1) | Goes low when the interrupt flag bit CRA-7 (CRB-7) goes high |

Notes:
1. ↑ indicates positive transition (low to high).
2. ↓ indicates negative transition (high to low).
3. The interrupt flag bit CRA-7 is cleared by an MPU read of the A data register, and CRB-7 is cleared by an MPU read of the B data register.
4. If CRA-0 (CRB-0) is low when an interrupt occurs (interrupt disabled) and is later brought high, $\overline{IRQA}$ ($\overline{IRQB}$) occurs after CRA-0 (CRB-0) is written to a "one."

*B023. In this example, the B-side peripheral data register will be initialized so that the less significant four bits are outputs and the more significant four bits are inputs. The B-side control bit 1 will be set on a positive-going transition, but no interrupts will be enabled. The following is the sequence of instructions necessary for initialization:

| | | |
|---|---|---|
| CLR A | *4F | Clear bit 2 of control register |
| STA A (EXT) | *B7 | to allow access to data direction |
| | *B0 | register. |
| | *23 | |
| LDA A (IMM) | *86 | Set bits in DDR for proper inputs |
| | *0F | and outputs. |

| | | |
|---|---|---|
| STA A (EXT) | *B7 | |
| | *B0 | |
| | *22 | |
| LDA A (IMM) | *86 | Store proper value in control |
| | *06 | register. |
| STA A (EXT) | *87 | |
| | *B0 | |
| | *23 | |

Following execution of the last instruction, normal operation of the PIA, as intended in its application, may begin. The first two instructions are often omitted; the initialization should occur only once in a working system, and this should be immediately following a system reset. If a hardware reset occurred, then the control register will already be zero.

## *Summary of Input/Output*

In chapter 7, the basics of input and output were covered. Input and output, involving communication between the computer and a human operator, was emphasized. The ASCII code and serial ASCII transmission, and a general communications device, the UART, were also covered. Memory-mapped I/O, and I/O in the M6800 system were discussed. The chapter ended with descriptions of the MC6850 Asynchronous Communications Interface Adapter and the MC6820 Peripheral Interface Adapter.

The chapter covered only the very basic concepts and devices. Applications of these concepts, as well as advanced ones, will be described in subsequent chapters.

### *EXERCISES*

*1.* What message does the following sequence of bytes contain?

*4D, *49, *43, *52, *4F, *2D, *54, *45, *58, *54

*2.* Convert the following message to the equivalent hexadecimal:

PERIPHERAL I/O

*3.* For the following ASCII characters, fill in the parity bit if first even then odd parity were used:

a) __0001101    b) __0110110    c) __1001000

*4.* Assuming RS-232 data transmission, draw the sequence of bits for transmission of the ASCII character X.

*5.* Assuming teletype transmission, draw the sequence of bits for transmission of the ASCII character " (double quotes).

*6.* What is the duration of 1 bit in RS-232 transmission at the rate of 1200 characters per second? At the rate of 330 characters per second?

*7.* In a system using an ACIA for teletype transmission, what transmit clock frequency is required for 10 characters per second with a divide-by-16 clock ratio?

*8.* What value must be stored in the ACIA control register in order to implement the following functions:

Divide-by-64 clock ratio
Receiver interrupt enabled
7 data bits + even parity + 1 stop bit
$\overline{\text{RTS}}$ low, transmit interrupt enabled

*9.* Assuming that a $\overline{\text{reset}}$ has just occurred, write a sequence of instructions that will initialize the PIA for the following functions:

A-side bits 0–3 outputs,
CA1 active on positive going transmission
(interrupt enabled)
All B-side bits outputs
CB2 output, follows bit 3

# 8 Two Computers

At this point, the three individual subsystems within a computer have been discussed. Memory, the CPU and instructions, and basic input/output have been covered in separate chapters. The purpose of this chapter is to present two examples of operational computers.

The Motorola Design Evaluation Kit 1, the D1 kit, and the Motorola Design Evaluation Kit 2, the D2 kit, will be considered. The kits provide both hardware and software and are therefore complete computers. The primary purpose of these two computers is to provide the purchaser with an inexpensive means of evaluating the Motorola family of products for industrial purposes. Both kits are excellent laboratory computers. They are significantly different from each other, and each possesses distinct advantages and disadvantages. The D1 kit will be discussed first because of its simplicity.

## *Design Evaluation Kit 1*

The D1 kit includes 1 MC6800 microprocessor, 2 MC6820 PIAs, 1 MC6850 ACIA, 2 MCM6810 RAMs, 1 MCM6830 ROM, and a printed circuit (PC) board on which to mount all the devices. The MCM6810 ROM contains the MIKBUG debugging program. A programming manual and an applications manual are also provided. In addition, space is provided on the PC board for up to four additional MCM6810 RAM chips. The basic layout of the D1 kit with its components is shown in Figure 8.1. Items not included with the D1 kit are the power supply, discrete components such as resistors, capacitors, and potentiometers, non-microprocessor related integrated circuits, optical couplers, cables, sockets, and connectors. These components represent only about one-fourth of the cost of the system. Also not provided is a teletype or other terminal which, of course, represents a substantial investment, but which can also be used in other applications or systems.

The full interconnection schematic of the D1 kit is shown in Figure

*FIGURE 8.1: Semiconductor Positioning Diagram of D1 Kit* (Courtesy of Motorola Semiconductor Products Inc.)

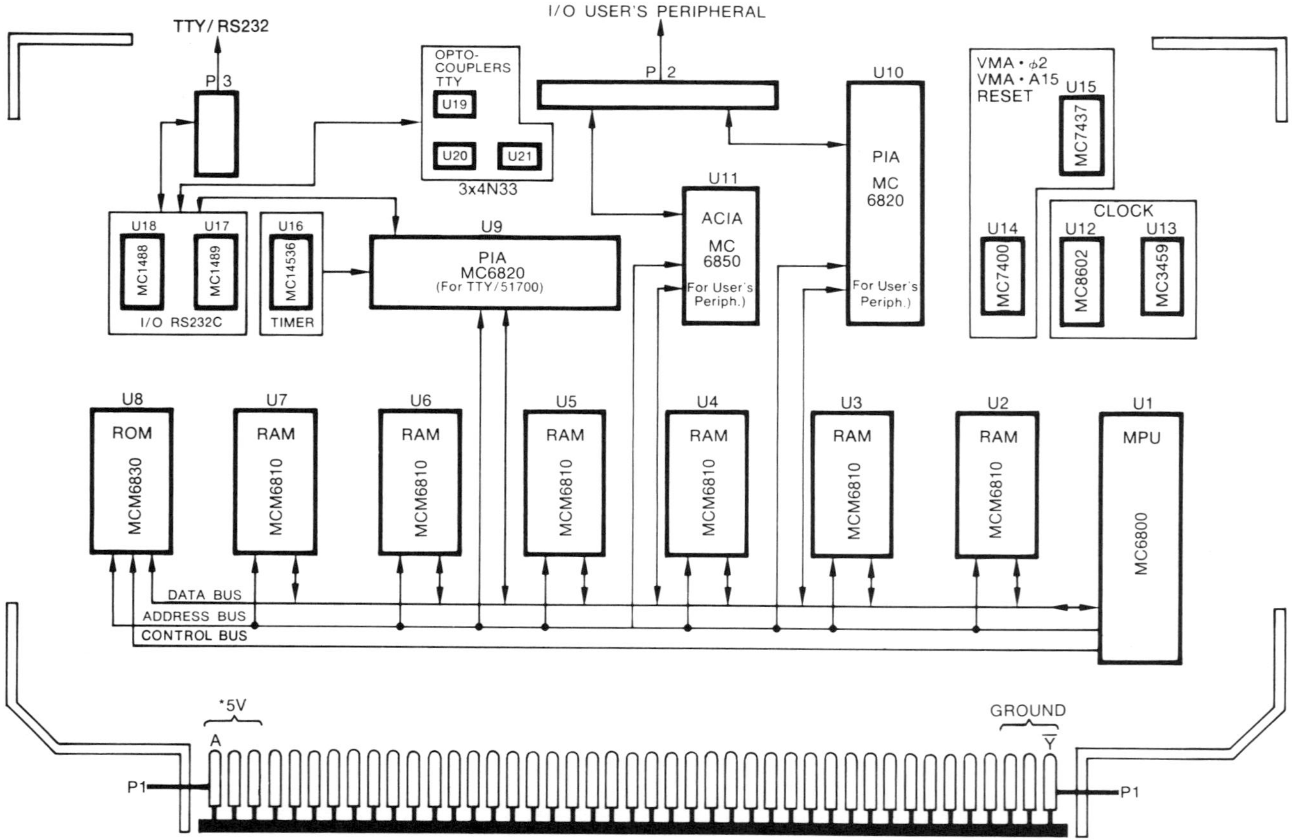

8.2. The major component of the kit is, of course, the MC6800 MPU, shown in part (a); the MPU is labeled as integrated circuit U1. The 16 lines of the address bus and the 8 lines of the data bus come from the left side of the microprocessor. The busses proceed to a connector identified as the P1 connector (to extend the system from the PC board) and to memory devices in part (c). The control signals leave the MPU from the right. From the MPU, they go both to the P1 connector and to other parts of the system. Some of the control signals are gated to clock outputs and to certain address lines.

The system clocks are implemented by the two monostable vibrators (one-shots) in U12, shown in part (b). The negative outputs of the one-shots, $\overline{Q}$, are subsequently gated through the NAND gates of U13. These gates function as inverters and act as buffers, because the one-shot outputs cannot drive all the clock inputs within the system. The $\phi 1$ and $\phi 2$ clocks go both to the MPU and to the P1 connector. The frequencies of the clocks are governed by the potentiometers at the top of the clock circuit. The $\phi 2$ clock is gated with both VMA and with A15.

The system reset function is implemented by a momentary contact pushbutton with an RS latch which serves as a debouncer. The $\overline{\text{reset}}$ signal goes to both PIAs, the MPU, and the P1 connector. The $\overline{\text{reset}}$ can also be generated by a remote switch through the P3 connector.

All system memory is shown in part (c). Memory is divided into three parts: the ROM which contains the debugging program, one MCM6810 RAM which is used directly by the debugging program as scratchpad memory, and between one and five MCM6810 RAMs that are available to the user for writing and testing programs.

The ROM, supplied by Motorola, is the MCM6830L7 ROM. It contains 1K bytes, and all the chip selects are active high. The ROM contains two programs: MIKBUG, which occupies the lower-numbered 512 bytes, and MINIBUG, which occupies the higher-numbered 512 bytes. In this exercise, the MIKBUG program is used. Consequently, address input 9 of the ROM chip is connected to ground, preventing access to the MINIBUG program. Three of the chip selects (shown as "E" on the schematic) are connected directly to the address bus. Address bits 15, 14, and 13 must all be high in order for the ROM to be accessed. The fourth chip select is connected to the system read/write signal, so the ROM is accessed only by a "read". Address bits 8 through 0 are connected to ROM address inputs 8 through 0, and address bits 12 through 9 are not connected and are therefore "don't cares."

The first RAM chip beginning at the left, sometimes called the "MIKBUG" RAM, is used extensively by the MIKBUG program. Addressing of this RAM is also accomplished by the chip selects. There are four active low chip selects and two active high chip selects on each MCM6810. The two active high chip selects are connected to address bits

*FIGURE 8.2: Full Interconnection Schematic of D1 Kit* (Courtesy of Motorola Semiconductor Products Inc.)

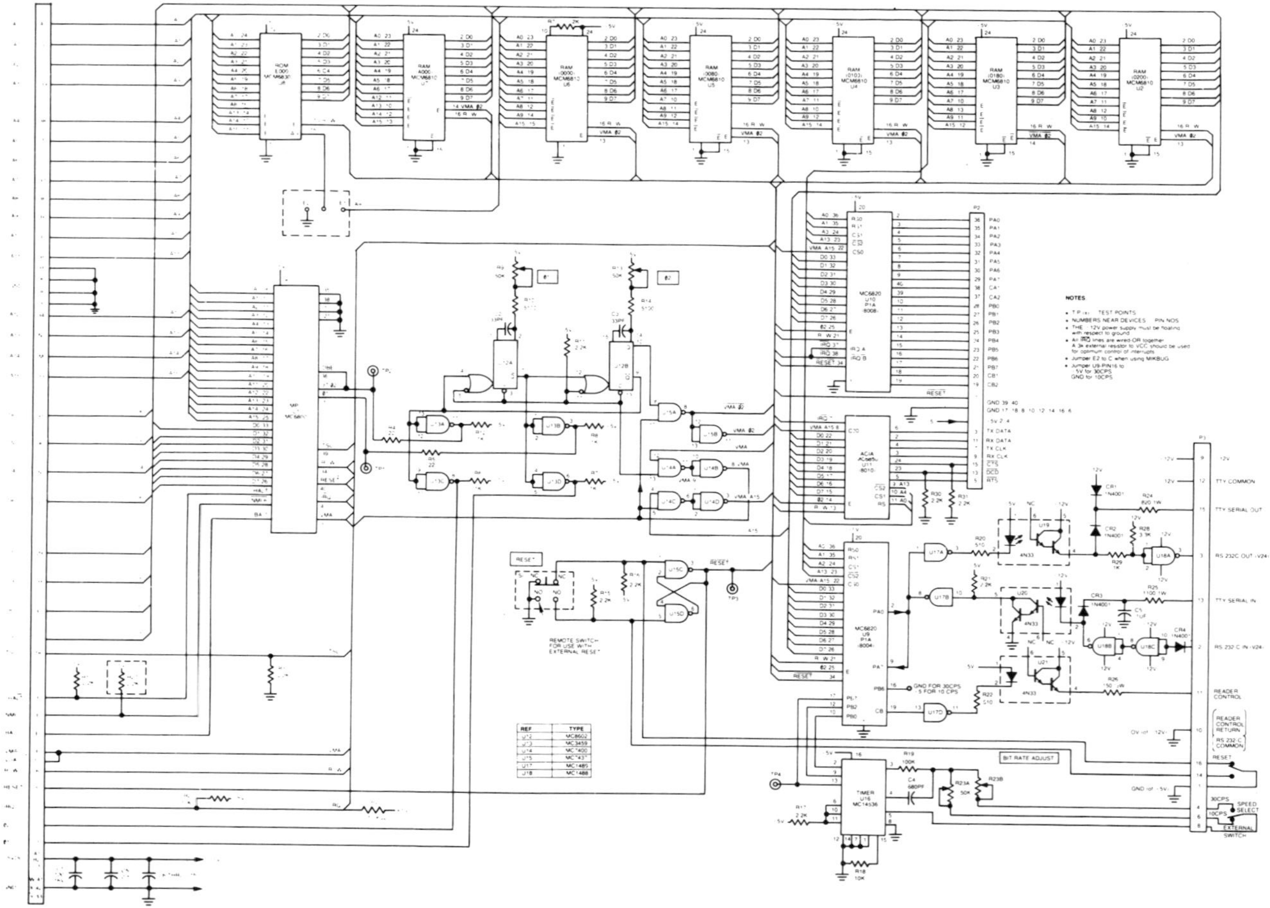

*FIGURE 8.2: (a) Major Component MC6800 MPU*

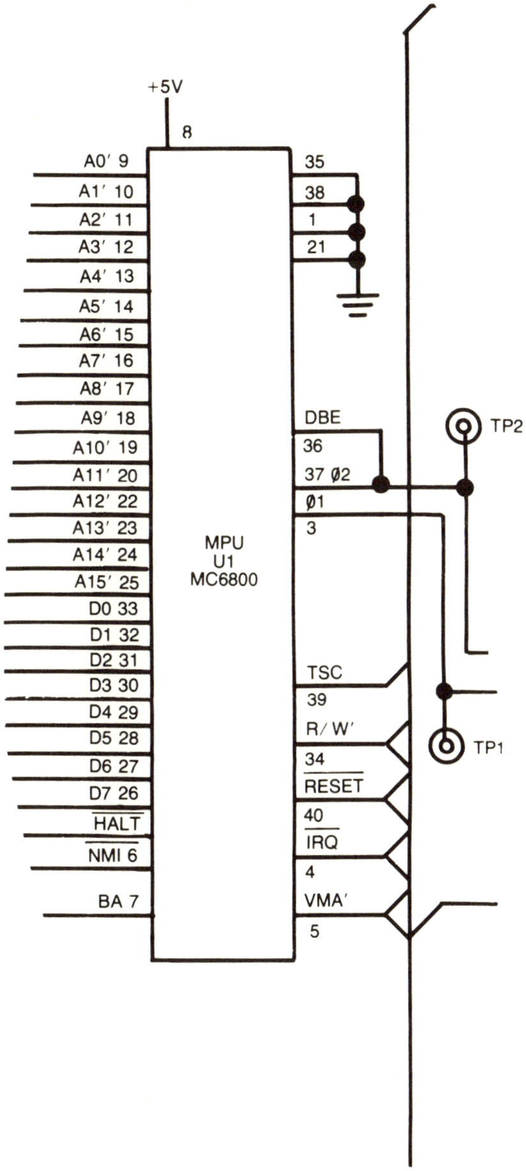

*FIGURE 8.2: (b) Clock and Reset Circuitry*

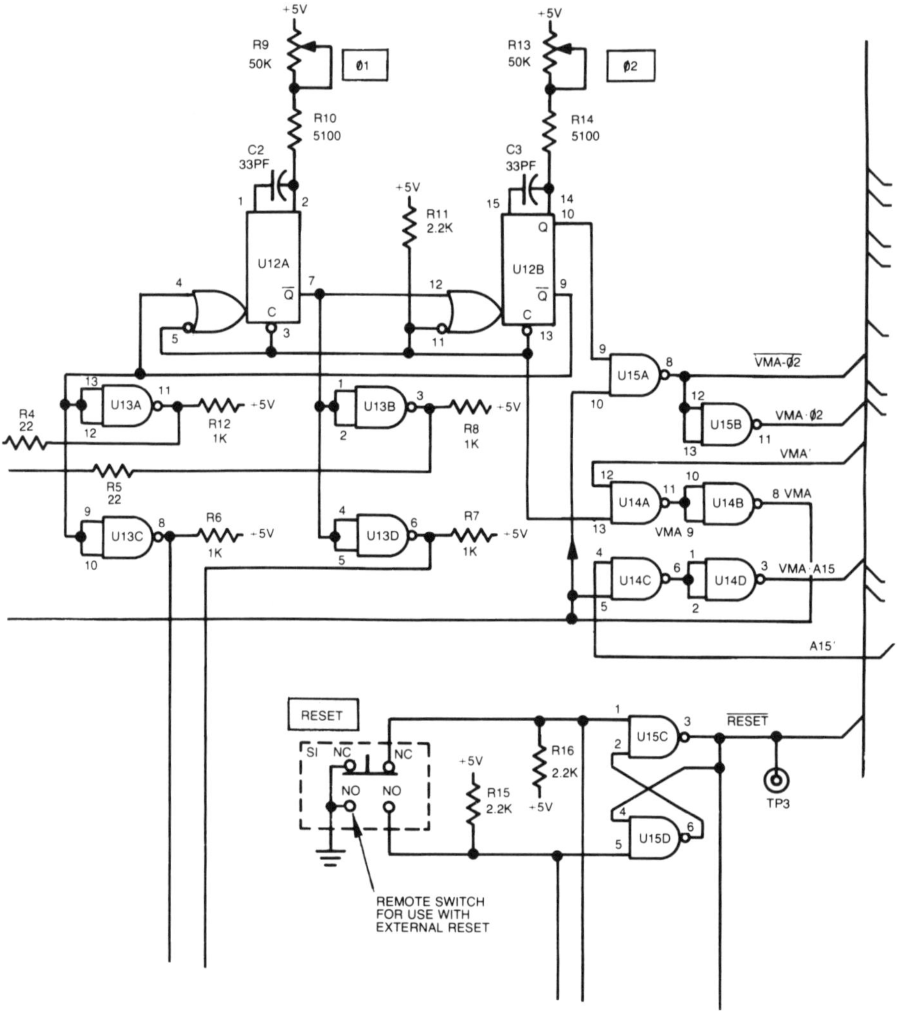

*FIGURE 8.2: (c) System Memory*

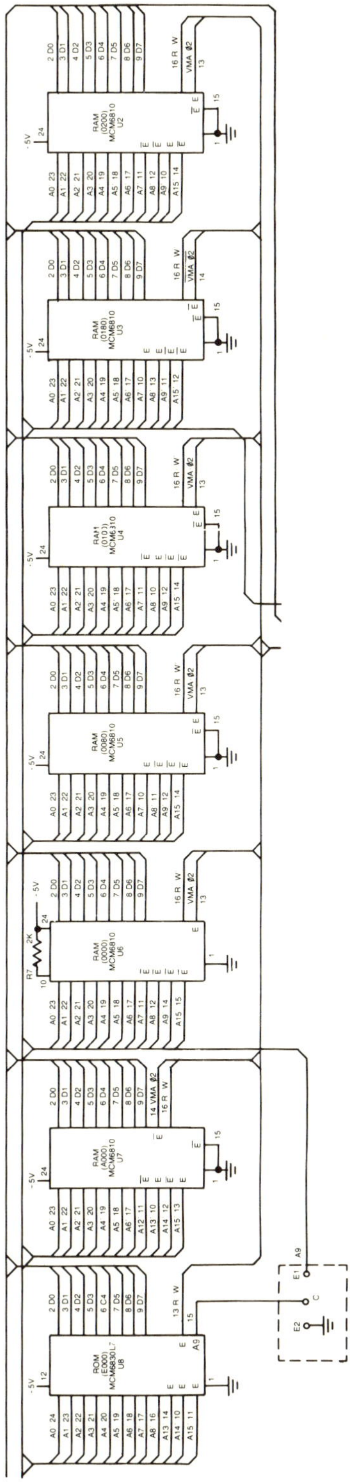

*FIGURE 8.2: (d) User I/O Interfaces*

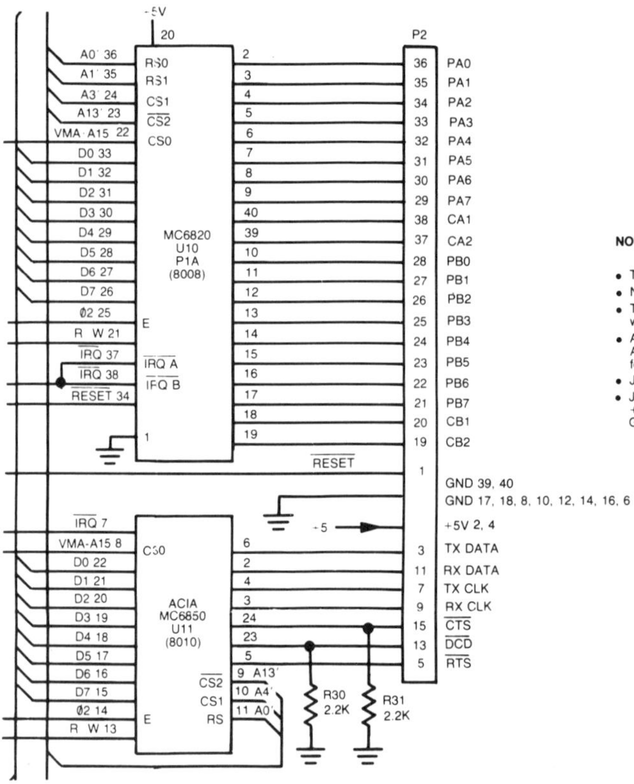


**NOTES:**

- T P (x) = TEST POINTS
- NUMBERS NEAR DEVICES = PIN NOS.
- THE ±12V power supply must be floating with respect to ground.
- All $\overline{\text{IRQ}}$ lines are wired-OR together. A 3k external resistor to VCC should be used for optimum control of interrupts.
- Jumper E2 to C when using MIKBUG.
- Jumper U9-PIN16 to +5V for 30CPS GND for 10CPS

FIGURE 8.2: *(e) Teletype Interface Circuitry*

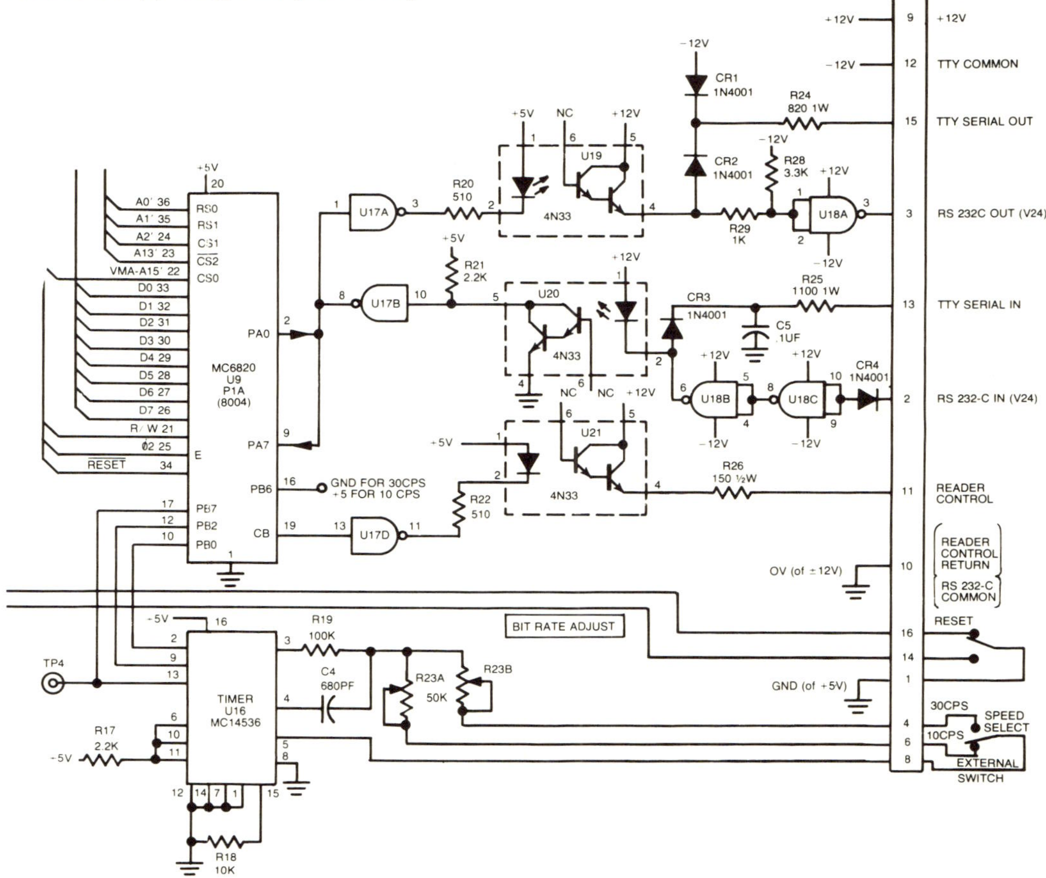

15 and 13. Two of the active low chip selects are connected to address bits 14 and 12. The third chip select is connected to the $\overline{VMA \cdot \phi 2}$ signal, and the fourth is simply connected to ground where it is always enabled. The VMA • $\phi$2 input to the RAM ensures that data will only be read from or written to the RAM when the memory address is valid and not changing. This prevents the wrong memory location from being accessed during a write operation. VMA and $\phi$2 are not inputs to the ROM chip because no data can be lost due to an invalid address. Address bits 6 through 0 are connected to the RAM address inputs 6 through 0, and address bits 11 through 7 are "don't cares."

The next 5 RAM chips are available to the user for writing programs. The intention here is that the address of this block of memory start at 0 and continue in increments of 128. This is accomplished by careful manipulation of address bits 9, 8, and 7. First, address bit 15 is connected to an active low chip select on each of the chips. Then address bits 9, 8, and 7 are connected to the chip selects to yield the following: the first chip is addressed at *0000 (bits 9, 8, 7 = 0, 0, 0), the second chip is addressed at *0080 (bits 9, 8, 7 = 0, 0, 1), the third chip is addressed at *0100 (bits 9, 8, 7 = 0, 1, 0), and so on. This allows 768 bytes of available user memory on the PC board. VMA and $\phi$2 are also connected to an available chip select on each RAM chip. The total allocation of memory in the D1 kit will be shown following a discussion of the system I/O chips.

Input/output capability in the D1 kit is provided by two MC6820 PIAs and an MC6850 ACIA, shown in parts (d) and (e). The PIA in part (e) is reserved for interfacing a terminal device, while the PIA and ACIA in part (d) are available for the user for evaluation purposes. In each of these three devices, VMA • A15 is connected to one active high chip select, and address bit 13 is connected to the active low chip select. Also, the $\phi$2 clock is used as the enable input, and the interrupt outputs are all tied to the MC6800 $\overline{IRQ}$ input. In the two PIAs, address bits 0 and 1 are connected to RS0 and RS1, respectively, and in the ACIA, address bit 0 is connected to the RS input. The effect of this last condition is that all internal registers in a particular device occupy consecutive memory locations for addressing purposes. The system data bus is connected to the data leads of the three I/O interface chips (as it is to the memory chips, as well). The peripheral signals from the user PIA (chip U10) and the ACIA are connected to the outside world via the P2 connector.

The terminal interface via the system PIA (chip U9) is rather tricky. Note first of all that the teletype (TTY) inputs and outputs and the RS-232C inputs and outputs are isolated from the PIA by the 4N33 optical isolators. What these devices do is ensure that there are no physical connections between the outside world and the microprocessor system. This means that, for example, if a 120 volt AC wire were to accidentally short to the TTY-in line, the semiconductor devices would not be affected. The

4N33s provide isolation up to about 1500 volts. Since the PIA is basically a parallel-to-parallel interface and TTY transmission is serial, the I/O data is transmitted to and from the D1 kit in parallel, one bit at a time. Peripheral data is transmitted via the PIA A-side peripheral data register. Bit 0 is used for transmitting, and bit 7 is used for receiving. Since the PIA cannot generate its own timing as the ACIA does, an external timing chip, U16, is used to generate the bit transmission rate. Two potentiometers are provided, one to generate a 10-cps bit rate, and the other to generate a 30-cps rate. The timer is interfaced via the B-side peripheral data register. The B-side control bit 2 is used for the control of a paper tape reader which is often available with a teletype.

The purchaser of a D1 kit must provide a power supply. Only +5 volts at 1 amp is required for the MC6800 and the memory and I/O chips, but the terminal interface requires +12 and −12 volts at about 100 milliamps and 50 milliamps, respectively.

Before discussing software, it is appropriate to discuss the connections of the system address bus as connected to all the devices. Figure 8.3 shows the system address map. This map correlates physical connections to memory addresses that the programmer would use. There is an address range for each addressable device. The address bit values which are fixed at either 1 or 0 are fixed because the address bit is connected to a chip select. The advantage of this method is that no other hardware is required to generate correct addresses. The disadvantage is that the system is not easily expandable because higher-numbered addresses may have the same 1s and 0s in certain address bits, and would, therefore, access more than one memory device.

## *Software Considerations—MIKBUG*

The software associated with the D1 kit is available in the MCM6830L7 ROM provided with the kit. Although the ROM contains both the MIKBUG and the MINIBUG programs, the MIKBUG program will be emphasized because it is simpler and more user oriented. MIKBUG occupies the lower 512 bytes of the ROM. In the D1 configuration, this maps to memory locations *E000 through *E1FF. MIKBUG requires a few bytes of read/write memory, and these bytes are available on the RAM which occupies the addresses *A000 through *A07F. This RAM is used for the stack, for temporary storage required by MIKBUG, and for a few locations with which the user can communicate with MIKBUG.

All of the software provided in the D1 kit is provided so that the purchaser (user) can write and test relatively short programs, and thus evaluate Motorola's family of products. The MIKBUG program is designed primarily to implement five commands which are accessible to the user at the teletype. These commands allow the user to examine and/or change memory one byte at a time, display the registers used by the user's program, print (and optionally punch on paper tape) relatively large sections of memory, go to a program written by the user, and load into memory a program previously punched on paper tape. These commands

*FIGURE 8.3: System Address Map*

| Device, location | Address line values | | | | | | | | | | | | | | | | Effective address range |
|---|---|---|---|---|---|---|---|---|---|---|---|---|---|---|---|---|---|
| | 15 | 14 | 13 | 12 | 11 | 10 | 9 | 8 | 7 | 6 | 5 | 4 | 3 | 2 | 1 | 0 | |
| | | | | | | | | | | | | | | | | | |
| RAM U6 | 0 | | | | | | 0 | 0 | 0 | x | x | x | x | x | x | x | *0000 –*007F |
| RAM U5 | 0 | | | | | | 0 | 0 | 1 | x | x | x | x | x | x | x | *0080 –*00FF |
| RAM U4 | 0 | | | | | | 0 | 1 | 0 | x | x | x | x | x | x | x | *0100 –*017F |
| RAM U3 | 0 | | | | | | 0 | 1 | 1 | x | x | x | x | x | x | x | *0180 –*01FF |
| RAM U2 | 0 | | | | | | 1 | 0 | 0 | x | x | x | x | x | x | x | *0200 –*027F |
| PIA U9 | 1 | | 0 | | | | | | | | | | | 1 | x | x | *8004 –*8007 |
| PIA U10 | 1 | | 0 | | | | | | | | | | 1 | | x | x | *8008 –*800B |
| ACIA U11 | 1 | | 0 | | | | | | | | | 1 | | | | x | *8010 –*8011 |
| RAM U7 | 1 | 0 | 1 | 0 | | | | | | x | x | x | x | x | x | x | *A000 –*A07F |
| ROM U8 | 1 | 1 | 1 | | | | 0 | x | x | x | x | x | x | x | x | x | *E000 –*E1FF |
| | | | | | | | | | | | | | | | | | |

are executed by entering on the teletype the keys M, R, P, G, and L, respectively.

When the reset button is pressed, a carriage return, line feed, and an asterisk (*) are printed on the teletype. This indicates that MIKBUG is ready to accept commands from the user. At normal completion of any of the commands, the carriage return, line feed, and asterisk are again printed. The asterisk in the left-hand column is the signal that commands may be entered.

### *M Command*

The M command is executed by entering "M" on the teletype. MIKBUG responds by printing a space. The user then types a four-character hex address. After this, MIKBUG prints a space and the two-hex character contents of the location. The user then has three options: (1) keep the current contents and examine the next higher-numbered memory location; (2) change the contents and examine the next memory location; or (3) exit the M command. The first option is selected by entering any teletype key except the space bar. Following entry of the key, MIKBUG will issue a carriage return, line feed, and two spaces. MIKBUG will then print the next sequential address followed by the contents, and the user will then have the three options. The second option is selected by entering a space followed by the desired two-character hex contents of the addressed location. MIKBUG will store the contents into the location, and will then issue a carriage return, line feed, and two spaces. The next sequential address will be printed, followed by the contents of that address, and at this time the user may again choose any of the three options. The third option is selected by entering a space followed by any nonhexadecimal character. At this time, MIKBUG issues a carriage return, line feed, and an asterisk. Although slow and somewhat prone to error, entire programs may be keyed into memory by this method. Figure 8.4 shows an example of examining and changing memory contents using the M command. Incidentally, when power is first applied to the system, contents of the memory locations will be random and unpredictable. Because the RAMs are volatile storage devices, turning the power supply off means that any programs in RAM will be lost.

### *R Command*

The R command, executed by entering an R on the teletype, displays the contents of the MC6800 registers. This may seem a little misleading since the registers themselves are used in the process of using the teletype. The registers being displayed are a copy of the registers either immediately before or immediately after execution of the user's program. A copy of the

```
*M 0000
*0000 6D M         M—retain contents
*0001 7E  20       space 20—change contents to *20
*0002 28 M         M—retain contents
*0003 3C  .        space period—exit M command
```

*FIGURE 8.4:*
*Use of MIKBUG's M Command*

MC6800 registers is stored in memory, and it is this copy which is printed. The condition code register (CCR), accumulator B, accumulator A, index register (IX), program counter (PC), and stack pointer (SP) are printed by the R command. CCR, A, and B are printed as two-character hex each, and IX, PC, and SP are printed as four-character hex. All register contents are followed by a space as shown in Figure 8.5. Upon entry of the R command, the copy of the register contents is printed, and then carriage return, line feed, and asterisk are printed. If the R command is entered immediately after power is turned on, the register contents that are displayed are just random contents of memory.

The M command may be used to alter the contents of the registers as they are stored in memory. The copy of CCR is stored in location *A043. Similarly, the copy of accumulator B is stored in *A044, accumulator A in *A045, index register in *A046 and *A047, and program counter in *A048 and *A049. Although the copy of the stack pointer is printed, it is not stored along with the other registers. After the reset button is pushed, the stack pointer will have been initialized, by MIKBUG, to *A042.

### *P Command*

The P command is used to print relatively large numbers of memory locations on the teletype. If the teletype is equipped with a paper tape reader/punch, then the contents may optionally be punched onto paper tape. Whereas the M command may be used to examine one memory location at a time, the P command can print up to 16 locations per line for a virtually unlimited number of times. Prior to entry of the character P, the start address and end address of the data to be printed must be stored in memory. The start address is taken from memory locations *A002 and *A003, and the end address is taken from *A004 and *A005. These locations may be specified with the M command. When data is printed on the teletype, the following information is printed: carriage return, line feed, the characters "S1", byte count, address of data, up to 16 bytes of data, and checksum. When more than 16 bytes of memory are to be printed, they are

```
*R 00 ED 1F C0 E4 80 16 A0 42
*
```

*FIGURE 8.5:*
*The R Command*

printed on successive lines, 16 bytes at a time. An example of the P command is shown in Fig. 8.6.

An analysis of a single line of the P command is shown in Figure 8.7. The two characters "S1" appear first. Next comes the byte count, which, expressed in hexadecimal, includes the two bytes of the address, the bytes of data, and the checksum. The 2-byte address follows. This is the address where the first of the data bytes is stored. Each of the data bytes follows. The last two characters on the line form the checksum. A checksum is included for error-checking purposes, and it ensures that the data which was punched is in fact that which is read. In the P command, the checksum is computed by taking the 1's complement of the sum of the byte count, address bytes, and data bytes. As the bytes are being printed, they are added to a cumulative sum, all carries and overflows ignored. After the last data byte is added to the cumulative sum and printed, the checksum is complemented (1's complement) and printed. The checksum is maintained, not merely for printing purposes, but because the P command is closely related to the L command.

### *L Command*

The L command is used for loading data into memory from paper tapes. The tapes must have been punched previously in the proper format, and the proper format is that in which the P command prints and punches

*FIGURE 8.6:*
*Printed Output of the P Command*

```
*M A002
*A002 00 01
*A003 00 00
*A004 FC 01
*A005 D9 0F
*A006 ED .
*P
S1130100FFE589AEEDBBEFEFD9DFAB46F9EDF96F53
*
```

*FIGURE 8.7:*

```
*M A002
*A002 01  00
*A003 00 M
*A004 01  00
*A005 0F  3F
*A006 ED  .
*P
S11300006D20283CDC08ACE700DDA474FAB8F08C61
S1130010B8CA58BE851EF01C786CC86429A77CF445
S1130020F876F434DA07FCC47EFED1F2EEFF8CFBE2
S1130030166D42BEEE3E789954DE4C7C725DD2DC85
*
```

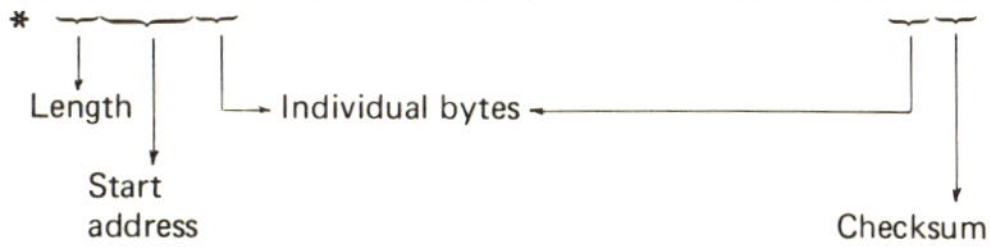

data. There are actually three formats in which information can be punched on paper tape. Each is called a *record type*, and a given paper tape contains one or more records. The most important record type is the *data record*, that which is created by the P command. The data record contains the "S1" characters, the byte count, address, data, and checksum. The other two record types are the *start record* and *end record*. The start record begins with the characters "S0", and usually contains the name of the program or data to be loaded. The end record begins with the characters "S9". Although other information may be contained in the end record, the characters "S9" are the most important because MIKBUG will print a carriage return, line feed, and asterisk when the "S9" is encountered.

Upon entry of the L command, MIKBUG will turn on the paper tape reader and begin examining characters coming through the reader. MIKBUG ignores all characters until an "S" is encountered. Unless the next character is a "1" or a "9", MIKBUG will continue ignoring characters until the next "S" is encountered. If an "S1" is encountered, the data is read from the tape and loaded into memory according to the start address and byte count. When all the data has been read and stored, and if the computed checksum agrees with the checksum punched on the tape, MIKBUG continues reading the tape in search of the next "S". If an "S9" is encountered, MIKBUG turns off the paper tape reader, then prints a carriage return, line feed, and an asterisk, and waits for entry of the next command.

So with the P and L commands, memory contents may be dumped to paper tape and subsequently reloaded at a later time. There is one minor problem associated with this procedure. The P command can only punch S1 records, so after the L command has read all such records, the user must manually type in "S9" or push the reset button in order to enter the next command. This, however, is very minor indeed. Also, paper tapes may be punched by programs other than MIKBUG, as long as the data is in the proper format. More will be said about such programs later.

### *G Command*

The final command is the G command. This is probably the most important command, since it allows the user to evaluate the programs which have been written and entered. Upon entry of the G command, control passes from MIKBUG to the user's program. The mechanism for doing this is the RTI instruction. Entering the G command causes the RTI instruction to be executed. Recalling the discussion of chapter 6, RTI causes the MC6800 registers to be loaded with the contents of memory in the seven memory locations pointed to by the stack pointer. So when the G command is entered, the condition code register, accumulators A and B, index register, and program counter are loaded with the contents in memory. When the program counter is loaded, execution continues at the location specified by the program counter. The user should end the program with a software interrupt, *3F. This provides a normal return to MIKBUG. In addition, MIKBUG prints a copy of the registers as they were when the SWI was executed. Recalling operation of SWI, the registers are stored in the seven memory locations, beginning with the location pointed to by SP and continuing downward. As long as the stack pointer is not altered by the user's program, the registers are saved in the same locations from which they were taken at entry of the G command. There is one departure from normal in MIKBUG. After the user's program executes SWI, MIKBUG decrements the copy of the program counter by 1 so it points to the location of SWI, rather than the next location. This will be shown in the register printout.

Consider Figure 8.8. The R command reflects random memory contents. A short program is entered at location *00A0. The copy of PC is set to *00A0, and G is executed. The register printout, which immediately follows G, shows the results of the instructions executed: CLR A, CLR B, and LDX (IMM). Note that the new copy of PC is the location of the *3F.

### *Debugging*

MIKBUG provides for debugging of programs. The program is entered via either the M command or the L command. When the program is loaded, the starting address of the program is deposited in the copy of PC. The G command is entered, and the program is executed. At successful completion of the program, the registers are printed. As is most often the case, the program will not be written correctly the first time. The evidence of this is entry of the G command and a seemingly endless wait for the register printout. This is often referred to as the program being "blown away," and the only recovery from this is pressing the reset button. After a quick verification that the program still resides in memory, the program can be checked in small segments. The opcode of any of the program's

*FIGURE 8.8:*
*Short Program in the Evaluation Kit*

```
*R 00 ED 1F C0 E4 80 16 A0 42
*M 00A0
*00A0 B9  4F
*00A1 A2  5F
*00A2 DB  CE
*00A3 DE  02
*00A4 D9  80
*00A5 EB  3F
*00A6 BB  .
*M A048
*A048 80  00
*A049 16  A0
*A04A 80  .
*G C0 00 00 0280 00A5 A042
*
```

instructions can be replaced with *3F. If the copy of PC is again given the start address of the program, that portion of the program between the beginning and the temporary *3F can be checked. Entry of G will quickly determine whether the segment is working. If it is, the *3F can be replaced with the original opcode, and the *3F can be moved further into the program. The offending portion(s) of the program can be uncovered in this manner.

### *MIKBUG Subroutines*

The primary purpose of MIKBUG is the implementation of the five commands which allow the user to enter and test programs. Other valuable facilities available in MIKBUG are subroutines which, while designed to enable MIKBUG to implement the commands, are also available to the user. These subroutines offer capabilities to the user's program while not taking up valuable RAM memory. Probably the two most common of these subroutines are OUTEEE and INEEE. Subroutine OUTEEE, located at *E1D1, outputs the byte in accumulator A to the teletype. If the contents of accumulator A are an ASCII character, the character will be printed on the teletype. Subroutine INEEE, located at *E1AC, waits for a character to be input from the teletype, then returns with the 7-bit equivalent of the character in accumulator A. Consider the sample program of Figure 8.9. If executed, it will first print a question mark, then a space, and will then wait for a teletype character to be struck. Upon return from the subroutine call

*FIGURE 8.9: Short Program Involving MIKBUG Subroutines*

```
*86   LDA A (IMM)   *3F
*3F
*BD   JSR   (EXT)   OUTEEE
*E1
*D1
*86   LDA A (IMM)   *20
*20
*BD   JSR   (EXT)   OUTEEE
*E1
*D1
*BD   JSR   (EXT)   INEEE
*E1
*AC
•         •
•         •
•         •
```

to INEEE, the character which was entered will be in accumulator A.

Table 8.1 shows a list of several of the subroutines available in MIKBUG, their locations, and a brief description of their functions.

## *Input/Output and Interrupt Considerations—D1 Kit*

At this point, use of a teletype or other ASCII terminal has been alluded to quite often, but the matter of transmission of information to and from the terminal has not been discussed. The following is a description of how a character is input via the teletype. Recall that the interface device is a PIA, rather than an ACIA. Since a parallel interface device is used, the bits must be accepted one at a time. Recall also that bit 0 of the PIA A-side is output and bit 7 is input. The PIA B-side interfaces a one-shot used as a timer. When bit 0 of the B-side changes to a one, then to a zero, the timer starts.

*TABLE 8.1: MIKBUG Subroutines Available to the User*

| *Name* | *Location* | *Function* |
|---|---|---|
| INEEE<br>INCH | *E1AC<br>*E078 | Input a character from the teletype, return the ASCII equivalent in accumulator A. |
| OUTEEE<br>OUTCH | *E1D1<br>*E075 | Output the contents of accumulator A to the teletype. |
| OUTHL | *E067 | Output the leftmost four bits of accumulator A to the teletype as one hexadecimal character. |
| OUTHR | *E06B | Output the rightmost four bits of accumulator A to the teletype as one hex character. |
| PDATA1 | *E07E | Output the contents of memory to the teletype; begin with the location pointed to by IX, and continue until a *04 is encountered. |
| INHEX | *E0AA | Input a hex character (0–9, A–F) from the teletype, return with 4 bits in accumulator A. |
| OUT2H | *E0BF | Output the contents of the memory byte pointed to by IX to the teletype as two hex characters. |
| OUT2HS | *E0CA | Same as OUT2H, but follow two hex characters with a space. |
| OUT4HS | *E0C8 | Output the contents of two memory locations pointed to by IX to the teletype as four hex characters followed by a space. |
| OUTS | *E0CC | Output a space to the teletype. |

When bit 7 of the B-side goes to one, the timer has expired. The timer is fixed by analog circuitry to delay 1-bit time within an ASCII character (9.09 milliseconds for 10-character-per-second teletype, for example). Bit 2 of the B-side selects whether the delay will be for a half-bit time (bit 2 = 0) or a full-bit time (bit 2 = 1). The INEEE subroutine begins by saving the user's accumulator B and index register. The index register is then loaded with *8004, the address of the PIA A-side data registers. MIKBUG then waits for the occurrence of a start bit by testing A-side bit 7 for a zero. (The author estimates that 95% of MIKBUG operation is spent in the two-instruction loop waiting for the user to input a character.) When the start bit occurs, the timer is started for a one-half bit delay. When time is up, the timer is adjusted for full-bit delays. The following procedure is then repeated 8 times: a full-bit delay is executed; the carry bit is set; the carry bit is rotated to bit 0 of the PIA A-side, while the input bit, bit 7, is rotated into the carry bit; the input bit is then rotated into bit 7 of accumulator A. If this is indeed repeated 8 times, the bit encountered first will be in accumulator A bit 0, the bit encountered second will be in bit 1, and so on. In this manner, a full 8-bit character is transferred to accumulator A. When the last data bit is in, either 1- or 2-bit times are delayed, corresponding to the number of stop bits required. The user's accumulator B and IX are restored, and control returns to the user's program. This procedure is shown in Figure 8.10.

This is an ingenious but quite cumbersome method of inputting a character. A similar routine is used for outputting a character, one bit at a time. It is the author's understanding that the D1 kit and MIKBUG were designed before Motorola had the ACIA in production, and it is for this reason that the PIA was used for a serial interface. The ACIA was then inserted as an evaluation device when it became available. The user may interface a second teletype via the ACIA if so desired. In this case, of course, none of the MIKBUG subroutines could be used for the second teletype.

In chapter 6, the initialization of the MC6800 was discussed. When a reset signal is applied to the MC6800, the MPU stops, and the contents of memory locations *FFFE and *FFFF are fetched from memory and deposited in the program counter. In the D1 kit, the MIKBUG ROM occupies memory locations *E000 through *E1FF. Careful inspection of the system address map shows that when all 1s are on the address bus, the highest numbered address in the ROM will respond, that is, the address of the first instruction to be executed is contained in memory locations *E1FE and *E1FF.

One of the purposes of the evaluation kit is that the user be able to evaluate the use of interrupts. The software interrupt is evaluated in conjunction with the G command. The hardware interrupts, $\overline{\text{IRQ}}$ and $\overline{\text{NMI}}$, may be evaluated in regard to both hardware and software. Hardwarewise, the interrupt signals are available on the connectors, and the $\overline{IRQ}$ may be used via the ACIA and user PIA. When either of these interrupts reaches the MC6800, the address of the interrupt routine is fetched from ROM, either from addresses *FFFC and *FFFD or from addresses *FFF8 and *FFF9. This poses a problem since these addresses are in ROM (and therefore can't be changed), and the user may wish to evaluate his/her own interrupt routine. The problem is easily resolved. The $\overline{IRQ}$ and $\overline{NMI}$ interrupt vectors each point to a routine which loads into the index register

*FIGURE 8.10: Entry of the Character "9": Progression of Bits in Subroutine INEEE*

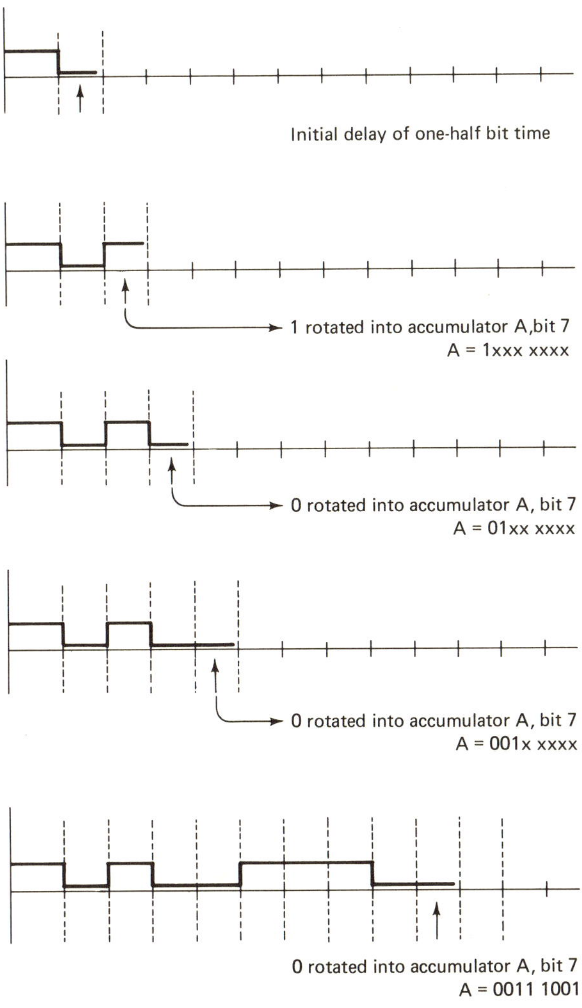

the contents of two locations in RAM, then executes a jump indexed instruction with an offset of zero. What this does is allow the user to specify the addresses of interrupt routines in RAM locations. The address of the $\overline{\text{IRQ}}$ interrupt routine is stored in locations *A000 and *A001, while the address of the $\overline{\text{NMI}}$ interrupt routine is stored in locations *A006 and *A007.

## The Motorola Design Evaluation Kit 2

The D2 kit is another Motorola product which allows a user to evaluate the Motorola product family. The D2 kit includes an MC6800 microprocessor, a ROM containing the JBUG program, 2 MCM6810 RAMs, 2 MC6820 PIAs, and an MC6850 ACIA. While the semiconductor products included are identical to those of the D1 kit, the form and specific functions of the two kits are quite different.

The D2 kit comes in a three-ring binder which contains all the components necessary for construction of the kit. The only items required for complete operation are a +5 volt power supply and a few sockets. Assembly time is generally only a few hours. Assembly instructions and operating manuals are also provided.

The JBUG monitor program is used to provide all the user functions in the D2 kit.

### *Hardware Considerations*

The D2 kit includes two printed circuit boards. One, called the microcomputer module, contains the microprocessor, memory and related logic. The second, called the keyboard/display module, contains all operator I/O hardware and the interface circuitry for nonoperator I/O. The two modules are connected by a 50-pin ribbon connector. The schematic for the microcomputer module is shown in Figure 8.11.

The processor and memory portions of the D2 kit are similar to the D1 kit. The MC6800 MPU, chip U6, is shown in Figure 8.11a. The 16 address signals leave the MPU on the left, and the 8 data lines and the control signals leave from the right. All of these signals are used on-board, and they all go to the P1 connector on the far left. The signals on the P1 connector of the D2 kit are identical to the signals on the P1 connector of the D1 kit. Many of the signals may optionally be buffered to have greater electrical drive capability. Between the microprocessor and the P1 connector are optional MC8T97 drivers, chips U1 through U3, for the address bus signals and MC8T26 bidirectional drivers, chips U4 and U5, for the data bus signals. These drivers are intended for use with off-board system expansion.

The addressing capability is provided by a 1-of-8 decoder, the MC74155, chip U11, shown in part (b). This chip is enabled by the system VMA signal, and decodes address bits 15, 14, and 13. This decoder will enable any of eight 2K(hex) regions of memory. The I/O devices, as well as all the memory units, use these signals for enables. In addition, the four user RAMs (U14, U18, U19, and U20) use address bits 7, 8, and 9 for further decoding. (The total system address map is shown in Figure 8.12.) The two devices labeled PROM, chip U12 in part (b) and chip U10 in part (c), are optional with on-board space provided. The devices labeled $\overline{2/3}$ and $\overline{4/5}$ are optional, but must be implemented off-board.

The system reset function is provided by a debounced momentary contact pushbutton. The two system clocks are implemented by a Motorola MC6871B Microprocessor Clock chip. This chip requires only a +5 volt and a ground input to generate the required two phase nonoverlapping clocks. In addition, the MC6871B has inputs, $\overline{\text{H1}}$ and $\overline{\text{H2}}$, which can stretch the $\phi 1$ or $\phi 2$ clock pulses. These inputs are used with slow memories which cannot be accessed within a single $\phi 2$ clock period. A Motorola MC14040 Binary Counter chip is used to provide a 4800 Hz clock pulse for use with the ACIA and the cassette tape storage system.

On-board system memory is shown in 8.11c. The first memory module is the MCM6830 ROM, chip U8, which occupies addresses *E000 through *E3FF. This ROM contains the JBUG program which performs the same functions as MIKBUG. The next chip on the right, chip U10, is an optional PROM which occupies addresses *C000 through *C3FF. The next chip, U13, is an MCM6810 RAM chip. This RAM occupies addresses *A000 through *A07F and is used by JBUG. The next four chips, U14, U16, U18 and U19, are all MCM6810 RAM chips which are provided for the user's programs. The first two of these are provided with the kit, and the second two are optional.

The I/O capability of the D2 kit is provided by two MC6820 PIAs and an MC6850 ACIA. The PIAs are shown in part (d). The top PIA, chip U20, is available for user evaluation. The lower PIA, chip U21, is reserved for use with the keyboard and LED display. The ACIA, shown in part (e), is reserved for use with the tape cassette storage unit. Also shown in part (e) is the MC8316 Binary Counter and two D flip-flops. This circuit is used to implement the trace function. The function and circuit will be described in the software section.

A sketch of the keyboard input and 7-segment indicator display is shown in Figure 8.13. Address and data are displayed in hexadecimal on the LEDs. All operator commands and data are input via the 24-key keyboard. A key is reserved for each of the 16 hexadecimal digits, and a key is reserved for each of the 8 operator commands. A portion of the schematic for the keyboard display module is shown in Figure 8.14.

The interface between the microprocessor and the keyboard and

*FIGURE 8.11: D2 Kit Microcomputer Module Schematic* (Courtesy of Motorola Semiconductor Products Inc.)

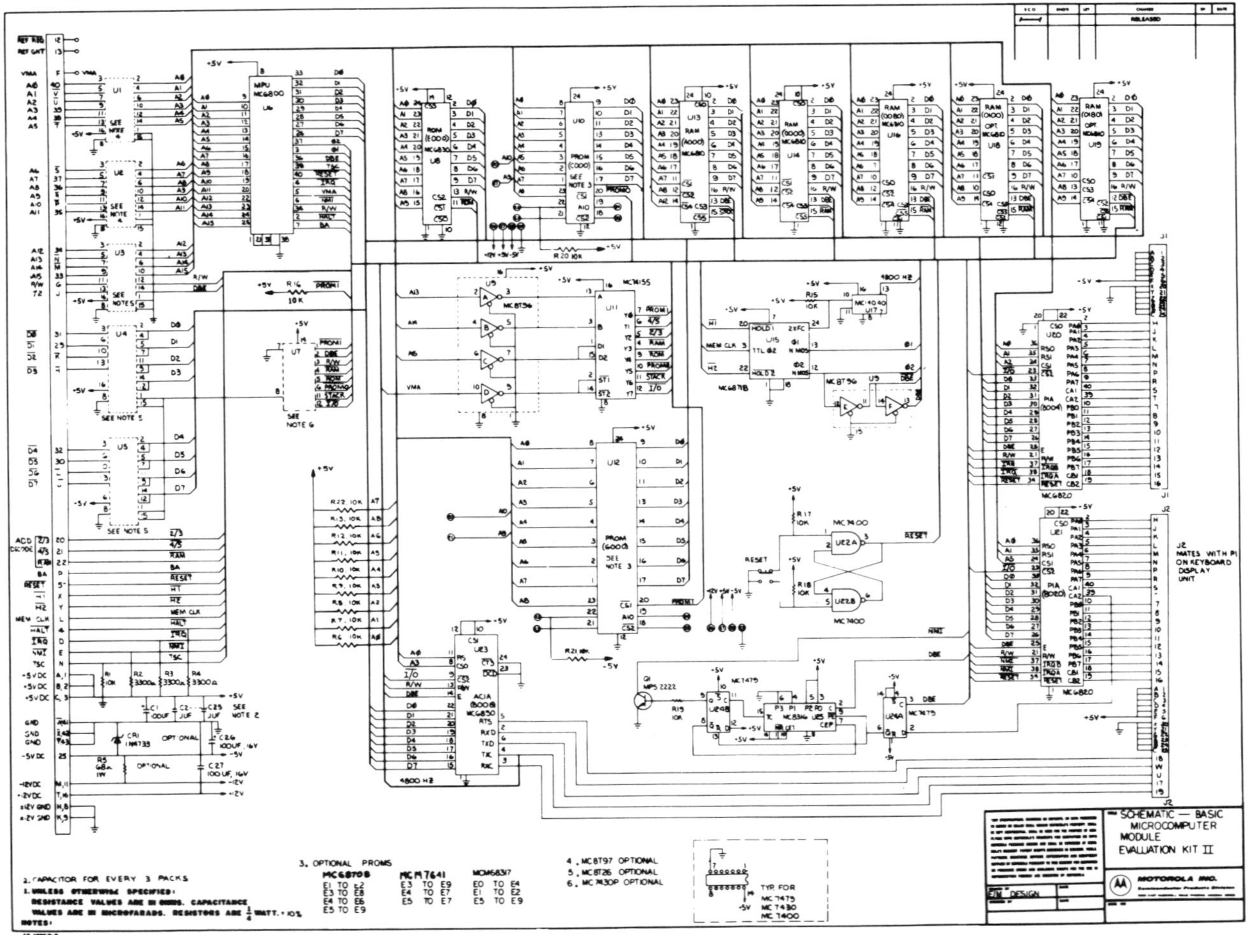

*FIGURE 8.11: (a) Major Component MC6800 and Buffer*

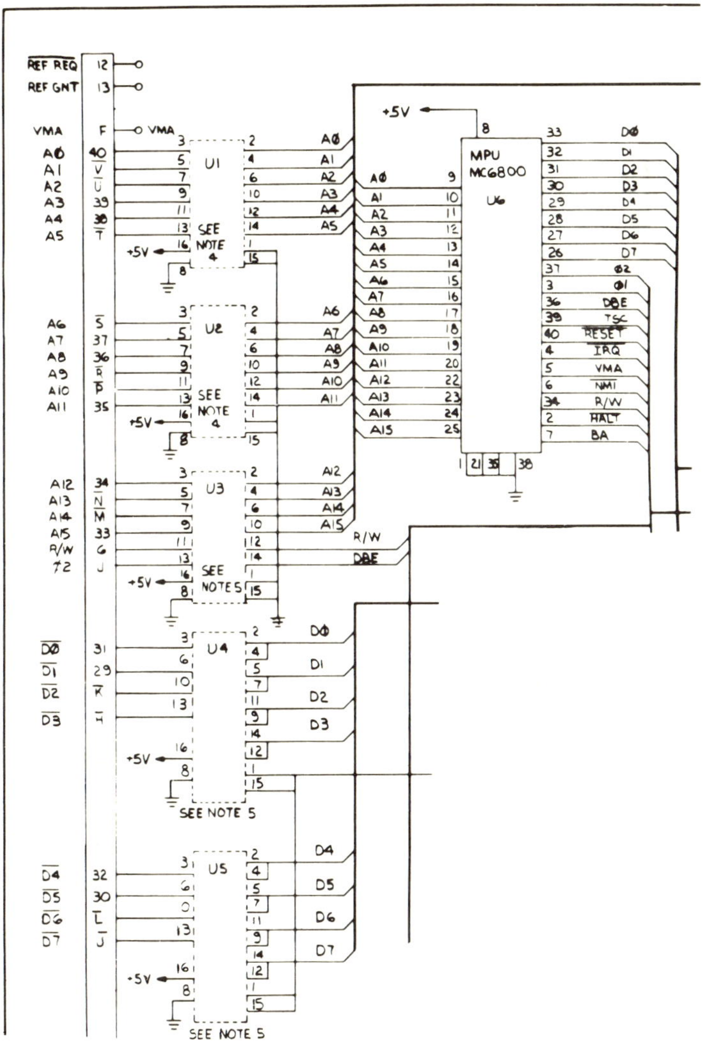

*FIGURE 8.11: (b) Addressing, Decoding Reset Circuitry and Optional Memory*

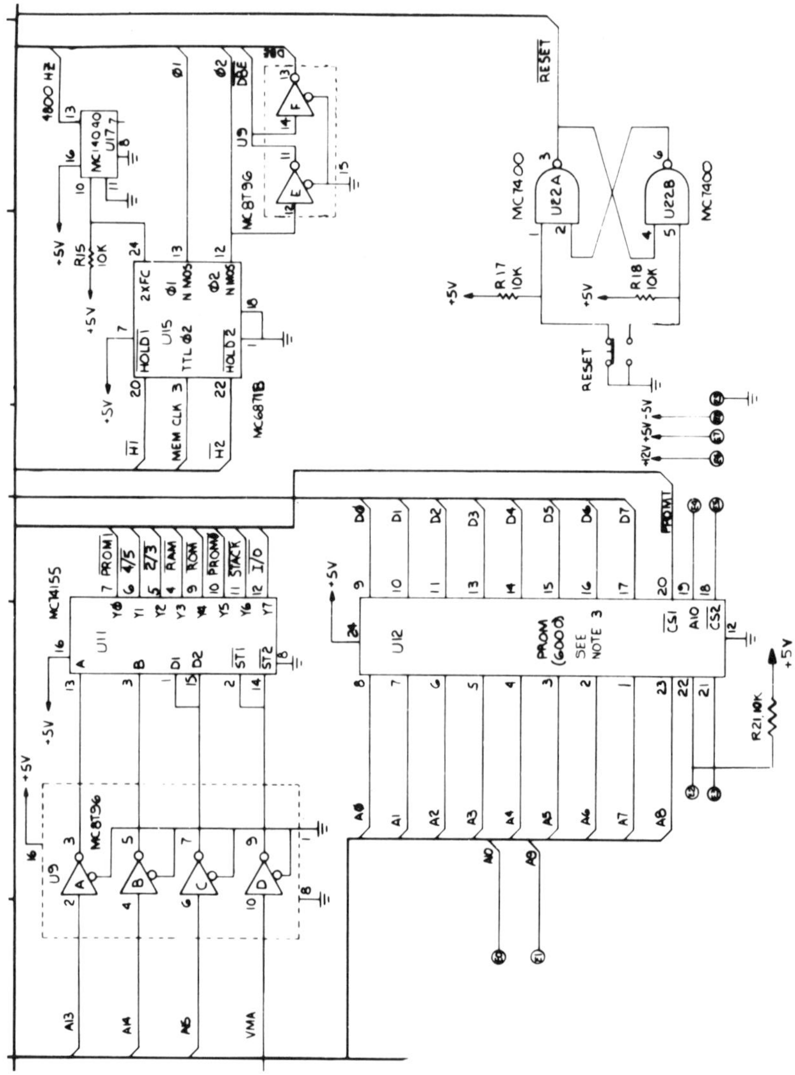

*FIGURE 8.11: (c) Basic System Memory*

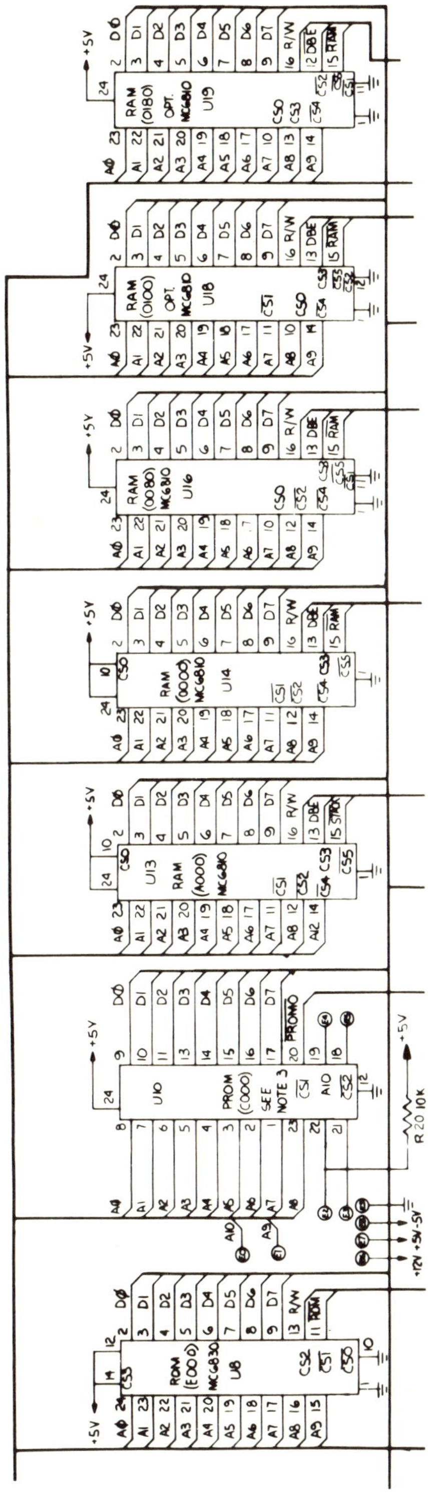

*FIGURE 8.11: (d) Cassette Interface and Trace Function Circuitry*

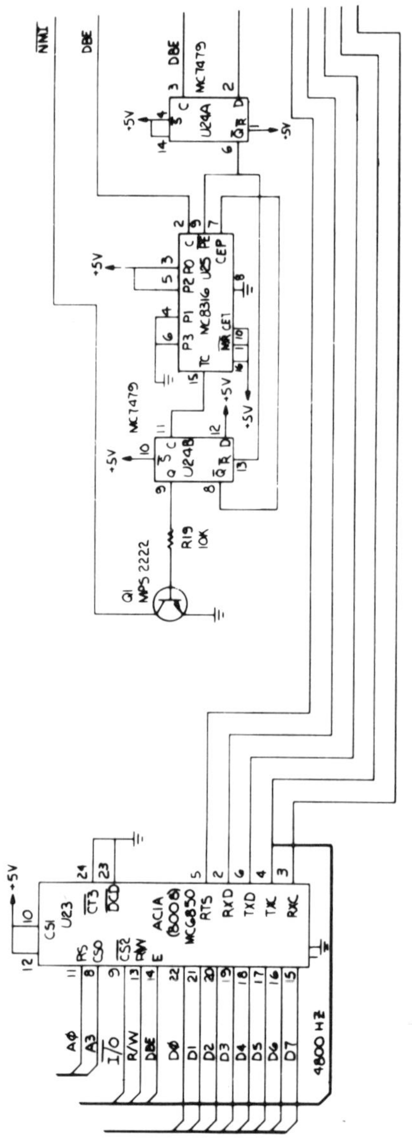

*FIGURE 8.11: (e) Keyboard and User I/O Interface*

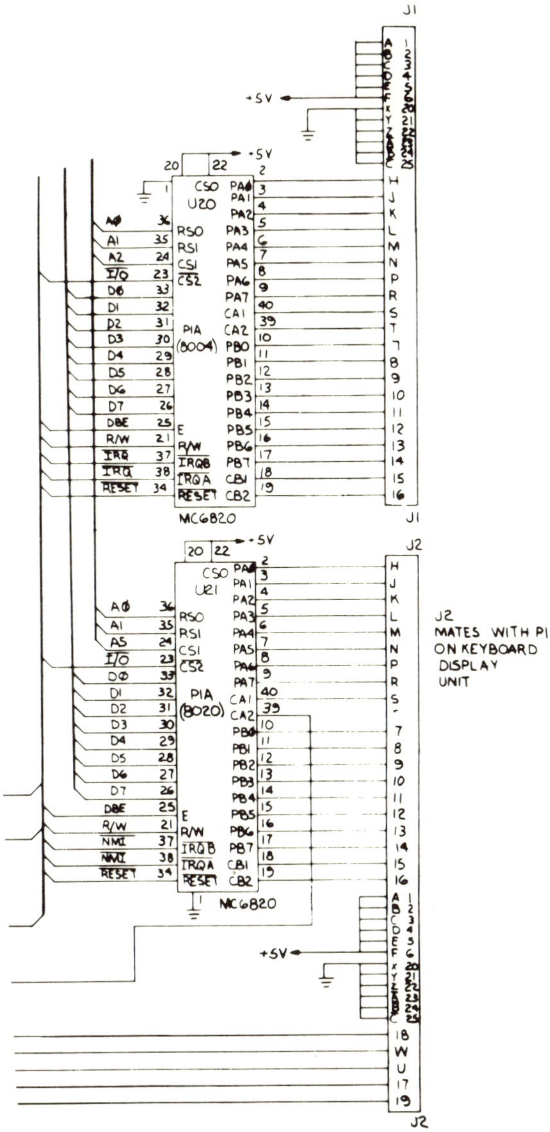

*FIGURE 8.12: D2 Evaluation Kit Address Map* (Courtesy of Motorola Semiconductor Products, Inc.)

| *SIGNALS DECODED* | | | | | | | | | | | | | | | | | | | | | | |
|---|---|---|---|---|---|---|---|---|---|---|---|---|---|---|---|---|---|---|---|---|---|---|
| *Device* | *Addresses* | $\phi 2$ | *R/W* | *Symbol* | | *VMA* | *A15* | *A14* | *A13* | *A12* | *A11* | *A10* | *A9* | *A8* | *A7* | *A6* | *A5* | *A4* | *A3* | *A2* | *A1* | *A0* |
| ROM | E000-E3FF | 1 | 1 | $\overline{\text{ROM}}$ | = | 1 | 1 | 1 | 1 | | | | x | x | x | x | x | x | x | x | x | x |
| PROM | C000-C3FF | | | $\overline{\text{PROM}}$ | = | 1 | 1 | 1 | 0 | | | + | x | x | x | x | x | x | x | x | x | x |
| RAM (Stack) | A000-A07F | 1 | x | $\overline{\text{STACK}}$ | = | 1 | 1 | 0 | 1 | 0 | | | | 0 | 0 | x | x | x | x | x | x | x |
| PIA | 8020-8023 | 1 | x | $\overline{\text{I/O}}$ | = | 1 | 1 | 0 | 0 | | | | | | | | 1 | | 0* | 0* | x | x |
| ACIA | 8008-8009 | 1 | x | $\overline{\text{I/O}}$ | = | 1 | 1 | 0 | 0 | | | | | | | | 0* | | 1 | 0* | | x |
| PIA | 8004-8007 | 1 | x | $\overline{\text{I/O}}$ | = | 1 | 1 | 0 | 0 | | | | | | | | 0* | | 0* | 1 | x | x |
| PROM | 6000-7FFF | | | $\overline{\text{6/7}}$ | = | 1 | 0 | 1 | 1 | | | + | x | x | x | x | x | x | x | x | x | x |
| USER | 4000-5FFF | | | $\overline{\text{4/5}}$ | = | 1 | 0 | 1 | 0 | | | | | | | | | | | | | |
| USER | 2000-3FFF | | | $\overline{\text{2/3}}$ | = | 1 | 0 | 0 | 1 | | | | | | | | | | | | | |
| RAM (User) | 0000-007F | 1 | x | $\overline{\text{RAM}}$ | = | 1 | 0 | 0 | 0 | | | | 0 | 0 | 0 | x | x | x | x | x | x | x |
| RAM (User) | 0080-00FF | 1 | x | $\overline{\text{RAM}}$ | = | 1 | 0 | 0 | 0 | | | | 0 | 0 | 1 | x | x | x | x | x | x | x |
| RAM (User) | 0100-017F | 1 | x | $\overline{\text{RAM}}$ | = | 1 | 0 | 0 | 0 | | | | 0 | 1 | 0 | x | x | x | x | x | x | x |
| RAM (User) | 0180-01FF | 1 | x | $\overline{\text{RAM}}$ | = | 1 | 0 | 0 | 0 | | | | 0 | 1 | 1 | x | x | x | x | x | x | x |

x = Decoded by the device addressed
* = Required but not decoded by the device addressed
\+ = Decoded by 2K x 8 bit optional RAM

*FIGURE 8.13:*
*(a) Keyboard Input and (b) LED Output*

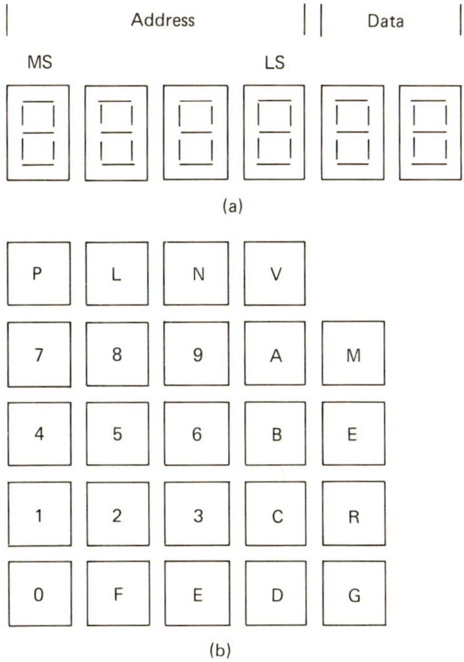


*FIGURE 8.14: Portion of Keyboard/Display Module Schematic* (Courtesy of Motorola Semiconductor Products Inc.)

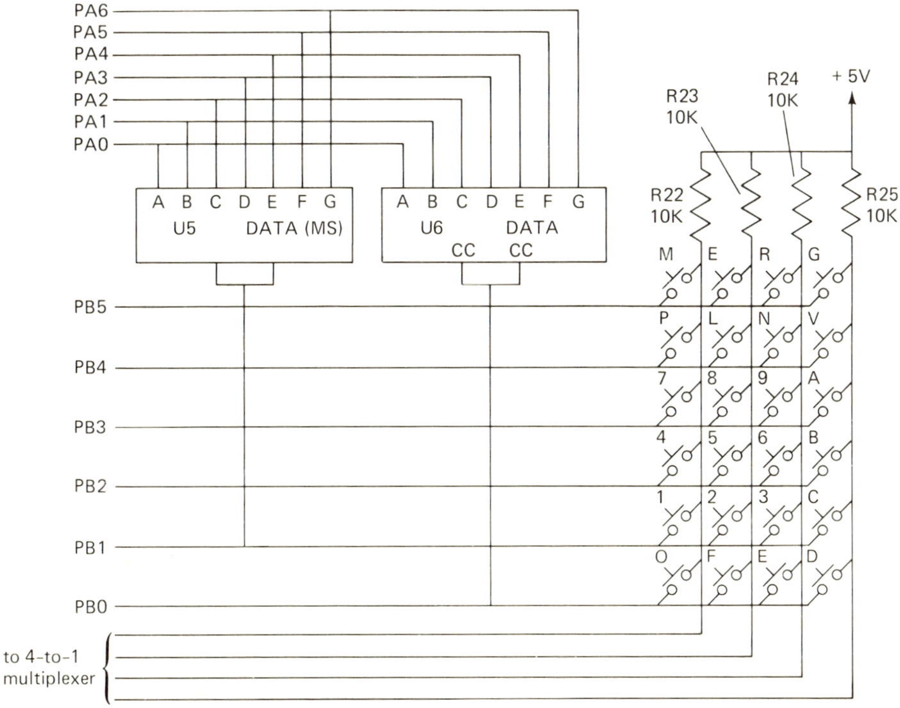

LEDs is the PIA, chip U21, shown in Figure 8.11d. The seven bits of data to each of the LEDs are transmitted via PA0 through PA6. One of the LEDs is selected by applying a logic 1 to only one of PB0 through PB5. Display of meaningful information is handled by routines internal to JBUG.

The keyboard is partitioned into 6 rows of 4 columns each. JBUG determines which key has been struck by applying a logic 1 to each of the 6 rows (via PB0 through PB5), and then by checking each column for a logic 1. The leads from the 4 columns are input to a 4-to-1 multiplexer (not shown in the portion of the schematic). Selection of one of the 4 columns is implemented by PB6 and PB7, and the selected column is returned to the microprocessor via PA7. A keyboard debounce feature is included in the routine.

Not shown in the keyboard/display module schematic is the circuitry which implements a cassette tape interface.

### *Software Considerations—JBUG*

All software provided with the D2 kit is available in the JBUG program which occupies all 1K bytes of the MCM6830 ROM. JBUG uses an MCM6810 RAM for scratchpad memory, and this RAM resides in memory locations *A000 through A07F. The purpose of JBUG is identical to that of MIKBUG: to allow the user to prepare and debug programs which ultimately allow the user to evaluate the Motorola product family. JBUG, like MIKBUG, accomplishes this via commands.

When the reset button is pushed, JBUG performs its initialization routines, and then indicates its readiness to accept commands by displaying a dash (–) on the leftmost LED. The eight commands in JBUG are P, L, M, R, G, N, V, and E. These commands are executed by depressing the appropriate key on the keyboard. The first five are similar in function to the MIKBUG commands.

The P command causes memory-resident data to be punched to cassette tape. The starting address of data must be stored in memory locations *A002 and *A003, and the ending address of the data must be stored in *A004 and *A005. Data is written to the tape via the ACIA in blocks of up to 256 bytes each. Upon completion of the punch function, the dash will be displayed on the leftmost LED, and memory locations *A002 and *A003 will contain a 16-bit value one greater than the value in *A004 and *A005. The L command causes data on cassette tape to be transferred into memory. On completion of the L command, the dash will be displayed on the leftmost LED, and memory locations *A002 and *A003 will contain the starting address of the last block of data.

The M command provides the memory examine/change function. To display the contents of any memory location, the keys xxxxM are entered, where xxxx is the hexadecimal address of the location to be examined. At this point, the leftmost four LEDs will display the address, and the rightmost two displays will display the two-character hex contents of the location. Following display of the contents, the contents may be altered by striking any two hexadecimal keys. The display will show the current address and the new contents. The contents may again be changed if desired. Entry of the G command will cause the next higher-numbered memory location to be examined. The new address and contents will be displayed. Each time the G key is struck, the next memory location will be accessed and its contents displayed. Striking the E key causes the memory examine/change mode to be terminated and causes the dash to be displayed on the leftmost LED.

The R command causes the contents of the MPU registers to be displayed. As in the D1 kit, the values displayed are only copies of the registers stored in memory, presumably following a software interrupt. Striking the R key causes the four character contents of the program counter to be displayed on the leftmost four LEDs. Typing the G key will cause the next register, the index register, to be displayed. Repeatedly striking the G key will cause the registers to be displayed in the following order: PC, IX, accumulator A, accumulator B, condition code register, and stack pointer. The display is circular: if the stack pointer is being displayed, striking G causes the program counter to be displayed again. The contents of the registers may be changed only by the M command. The registers are stored in memory as follows:

| | | |
|---|---|---|
| *A008 | = | high-order byte of stack pointer |
| *A009 | = | low-order byte of SP |
| SP + 1 | = | condition code register |
| SP + 2 | = | accumulator B |
| SP + 3 | = | accumulator A |
| SP + 4 | = | high-order byte of index register |
| SP + 5 | = | low-order byte of IX |
| SP + 6 | = | high-order byte of program counter |
| SP + 7 | = | low-order byte of PC |

Striking the E key at any point in the register display sequence causes the register display mode to be terminated and causes the dash to be displayed.

The escape, or E, key causes an orderly exit from any JBUG or user function. This applies not only to the M and R commands, but also to user programs which have "gone astray."

The G key has two functions within JBUG. The first of these is the continue function for the M and R commands. The second provides for execution of a user program. Entering xxxxG causes user program execution to begin execution at location xxxx. The user program will continue until a SWI instruction is executed, until the E key is depressed, or until the reset button is depressed. Another option of the second function provides for continued user program execution after a breakpoint has been encountered. This option is ordered by entering only G with no leading address.

The V key allows the user to insert breakpoints in his/her program. When debugging a program, if the user wishes to check temporary results at a certain point, he/she can replace an opcode with a SWI instruction. This will temporarily return control to JBUG so that memory or registers may be examined. In order to continue, the user must replace the SWI with the original opcode. Use of the V command simplifies this process. In order to insert a breakpoint, the user may enter xxxxV, where xxxx is the address at which the user wishes to stop the program. Up to five breakpoints may be inserted with V. Entry of V with no preceding address causes all the breakpoints to be cleared (i.e., removed). When a SWI is encountered, JBUG temporarily removes the breakpoints so the original opcodes are in place. The current value of the program counter is displayed in the leftmost four LEDs, and the opcode (the original opcode) is displayed in the rightmost two LEDs. At this point, the user is in the register examine mode. By depressing the G key, the registers can be displayed in sequence. To continue program execution, the E key must be entered (to terminate register examination), and the G key must be entered again. Upon entry of G (with or without a starting address), the breakpoints are again inserted, and user program execution continues.

The N key allows an instruction-by-instruction trace of a program. Upon entry of N, the instruction at the current value of the program counter is executed. Immediately following execution of this one instruction, the new value of the program counter and its contents are displayed, and JBUG is in the register examine mode. Following termination of the register examine mode, program debugging may continue. JBUG employs an interesting technique for implementing the single instruction trace function. Chip U25 of Figure 8.12e is a binary counter which is clocked by the $\phi 2$ clock. The counter is initiated by the CA2 output of the system PIA. Eleven clock pulses are counted before logic 0 is applied to the $\overline{\text{NMI}}$ input. When the N key is entered, JBUG starts the counter and executes the RTI. The RTI instruction, which takes 10 clock cycles, causes the instruction at the stored value of PC to be executed. The $\overline{\text{NMI}}$ will go low after the first machine cycle of the current instruction. Since the current instruction is always finished before an interrupt sequence begins, and since all instructions are at least two machine cycles, the N key allows one and only one instruction to be executed. Because the trace is a hardware function, instructions in either RAM or ROM may be traced.

In addition to the eight commands, JBUG provides one other useful feature. This feature is the calculation of relative values for branch instructions. Manual calculation can be tricky and error prone. The following is the procedure to determine relative values:

1. Obtain the dash by depressing the E key.
2. Determine the value of the stack pointer via the R command.
3. Enter the high-order byte of the destination address in accumulator B and the low-order byte in accumulator A.
4. Enter the address of the branch opcode into the index register.
5. Exit the M command and enter E000G.
6. Upon return, examine the registers with the G command:
   Accumulator A contains the relative value.
   Accumulator B contains: *FF if the branch is valid and negative; *00 if the branch is valid and positive; anything else if the branch is out of range.

Interrupts in the D2 kit are handled about the same as they are in the D1 kit. Two bytes are reserved in the JBUG RAM for the address of the user's $\overline{\text{IRQ}}$ routine, and two bytes are reserved for the address of the user's $\overline{\text{NMI}}$ routine. The user should bear in mind, however, that JBUG uses $\overline{\text{NMI}}$ for trace and breakpoint functions. Tampering with $\overline{\text{NMI}}$ may nullify some of JBUG's debugging capabilities.

## *Summary and Comparisons*

Both the D1 and D2 kits are excellent examples of operational computers. Each is self-contained and has all the elements of a computer. Either kit would be ideal in a laboratory environment. In addition, both systems possess several examples of how ingenuity in both hardware and software can be used to accomplish a task with available hardware.

The most striking characteristic of the D1 kit is its simplicity. Only the essential functional elements are included in the system. An example of this simplicity is the direct connections of the address bus to implement system addressing. A second advantage is the availability of hard copy input and output. When a teletype is used as the terminal, records of activities can be maintained (and lab reports can be submitted). A third advantage associated with hardware is the PC board. The D1 kit can be included in larger systems. It can even be used in industrial systems if the MIKBUG ROM is replaced by a special-purpose ROM. In the software area, a major advantage of the D1 kit is the availability of the I/O subroutines to user programs; they need not occupy user RAM. Finally, the paper tape input feature allows the D1 kit to share programs written on other systems. An excellent example of this will be shown in chapter 9.

Unfortunately, two of the advantages of the D1 kit can also impose disadvantages. First, a teletype or CRT is required for operation. The purchaser who does not already have such a terminal must buy or rent one. Second, and more important, the simplicity of the D1 kit makes it very difficult to expand. In order to expand user memory, for example, all on-board user RAM must be removed. The final disadvantage is the primitive set of commands, making extensive program debugging very inconvenient.

The primary advantage of the D2 kit is that it is totally self-contained. Only a power supply is required for full operation. This makes evaluation of the Motorola product line very convenient. Another advantage is that the JBUG commands are quite powerful. The multiple breakpoint and trace features are extremely useful in program debugging. A very significant advantage is its expandability. Space is provided on the board for buffers and additional memory. The decoding of the address bus allows convenient expansion of memory. The expansion feature permits testing of new Motorola devices as well as predesigned subsystems.

The D2 kit also has a few disadvantages. A very minor one is that there is room for only four user RAM chips on board. This means that only small user programs can be written without adding a relatively substantial amount of hardware. Another disadvantage is that very few subroutines in JBUG are useful to the programmer. Any user input and output involving the keyboard and LEDs must be written by the user and located in user RAM. Perhaps the major disadvantage of the D2 kit is its lack of a terminal or hard copy device. With the exception of the cassette tape interface, neither hardware nor software is provided for use with a printing device.

## *SUGGESTED LABORATORY EXERCISES*

*1.* Push the reset button and verify that the system is running. Display the contents of the registers with the R command. Identify each register, and identify each of the six condition code register bits. Modify all the registers (except the stack pointer) by changing the appropriate memory locations with the M command. Verify the changes with the R command. Write and enter a short program which will clear accumulators A and B and which will load the index register with *0180. Execute the program (don't forget to set the breakpoint or enter the *3F) and verify execution with the R command. Note the value of the program counter.

*2.* Write a program which will add two 24-bit signed binary numbers. Store the addend and augend in a set of specific memory locations, and store the sum in another specific set of memory locations.

*3.* Write a subroutine which takes exactly one second to execute. Use this subroutine in a program which takes $x$ seconds to execute. Let $x$ be in accumulator A.

4. Write a program beginning in location *0050 which will examine the contents of a random memory location. If the byte is *00, branch to location *0020 and stop. If the byte is positive, branch to location *0040 and stop. If the byte is negative, take the 2's complement of the byte, the branch to location *007A and stop.

5. Write a program which will add two 4-digit BCD numbers. Store the addend and augend in specific memory locations, and store the 5-digit sum in another set of memory locations.

# 9 Software Design and Development

This chapter addresses itself to the general problem of using the microprocessor to perform meaningful work. This task is accomplished primarily by designing programs. Putting the hardware together is the first step: selecting the microprocessor, specifying the ROM and RAM, selecting the appropriate I/O interface devices. The importance of this step should not be minimized, but the key element of the microcomputer is the software. It is the programs which provide the power and flexibility in microprocessor-based systems. This fact is demonstrated by the change in the relative cost of hardware and software development. In the 1950s, when computers evolved from a research machine to a problem-solving tool, hardware development costs represented about 80% of the total cost of the project. It is estimated that by 1980, hardware development will represent less than 20% of the total cost. Cost, the most important item in industrial considerations, dictates emphasis on software.

## Designing Software

In earlier chapters, there were instances when a few instructions were connected together to give an example of a certain operation or principle. Although connecting instructions together is an acceptable procedure for constructing short routines, it is not the procedure for designing large programs, complex programs, or groups of programs. There is actually a three-step procedure which should be followed whenever programs of any major consequence are required: specify the requirements of the program, design the program using flowcharts, and, finally, prepare the program in a form acceptable to the computer. This three-step procedure applies to large-scale computers as well as to microprocessors.

### *Requirements Specification*

The first step is probably the most important. Specifying the requirements of the program is another way of establishing exactly what the program is to do. If you don't know precisely what the program is to do, no matter how well the program is written, it probably won't work right. The requirements of the program include the inputs, the process, and the outputs. What exactly are the inputs? Are they numbers, letters, or binary values? In what form are the inputs: are they keys struck by an operator, values received from I/O interface devices, binary values in memory, elapsed time? Are any inputs error conditions? Are any "don't care" or "not applicable" inputs to be ignored? Do different types of inputs apply to different processes? Must the inputs be available in a specific sequence or at certain times? Are there initial conditions which must be established by the program before any inputs are considered? Many of these same questions can be asked about the outputs of the program: how many outputs, what form, what type, error conditions? And what of the processes to be applied to the inputs? Are there multiple processes? Does each process apply to all the inputs or only to some of them? Is there a process for all the inputs?

This description of the requirements, though not complete, demonstrates the significance of this step. There is a knack to recognizing and specifying requirements, and expertise usually comes with practice and experience. Specification is the most important part of software design and should always come first.

### *Flowcharting*

The second part of the design cycle is design of the processes involved. Traditionally, this part is accomplished by drawing flowcharts. A flowchart shows graphically the flow of the program from beginning to end or from inputs to outputs. A flowchart has often been associated with documenting a program, a step which occurs when the project is complete. Many a novice programmer has looked with disdain on flowcharts, only to become entangled in a mass of seemingly unrelated instructions. When proper attention is paid to charting the flow of the program, transition from initial to final phases of the program proceeds very smoothly.

Flowcharting involves the use of graphic symbols. The symbols usually represent conditions, processes, and decisions. Several of the common symbols are shown in Figure 9.1. The process symbol represents a single instruction or a small series of instructions which performs a single operation. The predefined process symbol represents a subroutine which is called. The decision symbol denotes the alternate actions which are taken after a test is made. A decision is usually implemented by a branch instruction. The terminal symbol represents the beginning or end of a program, but can also represent the occurrence of an interrupt. The I/O symbol obviously designates an I/O operation, and the connectors are shown because it is often easier to construct flowcharts with connectors rather than to have lines going from symbol to symbol.

*FIGURE 9.1: Flowchart Symbols*

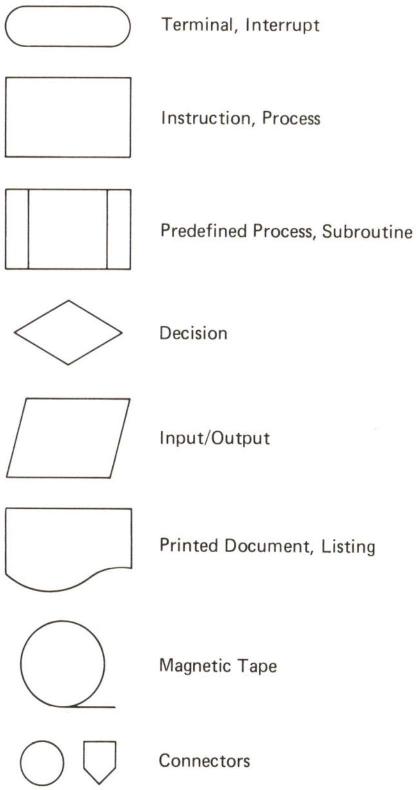


A sample flowchart is given in Figure 9.2. This short routine will accept a character from the teletype, determine if the character is a decimal digit, and return with the value (i.e., not the ASCII character). If the entered character was not a digit, then control passes to some other routine which handles an error condition. This is a simple example, but it demonstrates the use of the flowcharting symbols.

The second example, Figure 9.3, is a more lengthy and detailed flowchart. The flowchart is for a subroutine which will convert an 8-bit unsigned binary number and print it as 3 decimal digits. Note that the subroutine will print 3 digits, even leading zeros. Also, the subroutine will not print a carriage return and line feed, or any other formatting characters.

Flowcharting is currently the most common form of planning a program. It is an excellent means of preplanning, of thinking about the program before it is written. The flowchart doesn't have to be drawn with a straight edge or template; it doesn't have to be formal, but it should be thorough. If proper attention is paid to planning the program beforehand, the overall effort becomes much easier. In addition, the flowchart serves as

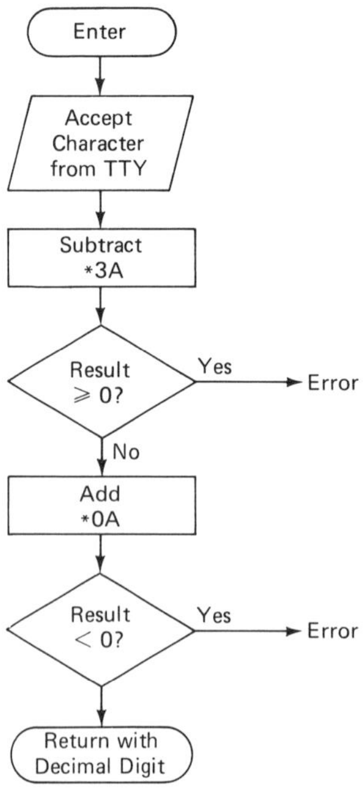


*FIGURE 9.2:*
*Flowchart for Inputting a Decimal Digit*

a record of program design. When the program modification is required several months later, the flowchart serves as an easy way to remember the logic of the program.

### *Execution Preparation*

The final stage in designing a program is preparation for execution by the computer. This should be the easiest stage if proper attention has been given to the first two stages. This stage involves converting the logic of the program into the binary code that is stored in memory and executed by the processor.

In the D1 and D2 kits under the control of MIKBUG and JBUG, new programs could only be entered by the operator, one byte at a time. In this case, the operator or designer prepares the program in binary. This is a very time-consuming process and is prone to error. It is up to the designer to convert the operations to the proper opcode with the proper addressing mode. The operator must remember all the hex addresses of the temporary storage and must figure out the relative values for the branch instructions. As if all this weren't bad enough, making an addition or change to the program requires that virtually the entire program be reentered. This often means that many addresses and branch relative values must be recalculated.

*FIGURE 9.3: Flowchart for Printing an 8-bit Binary Number*

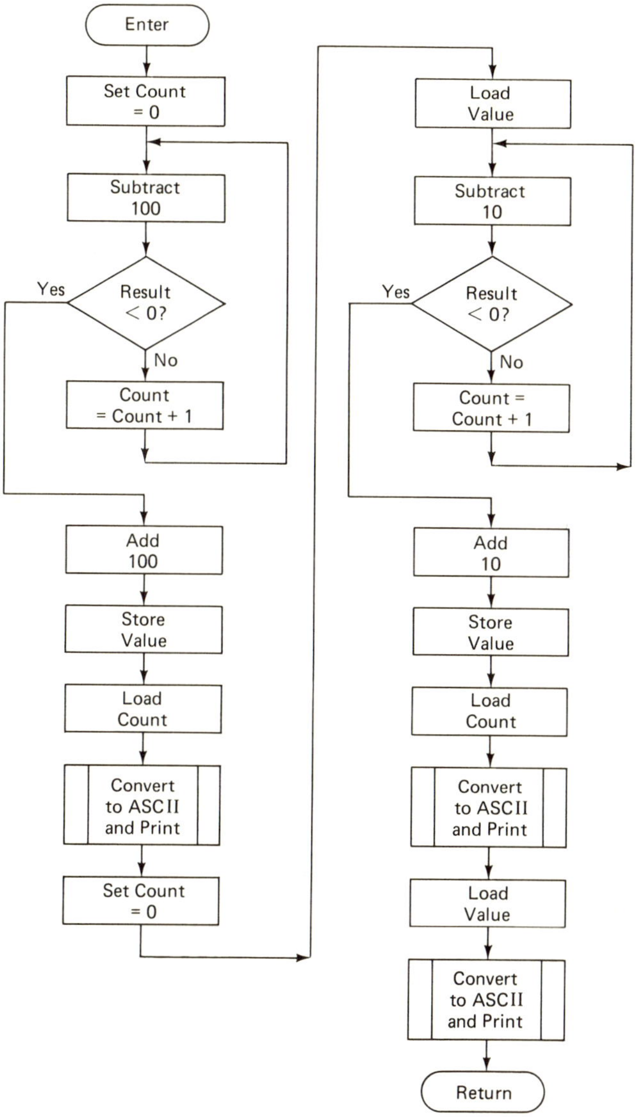

The binary data directly executable by the computer is called *machine code* or *machine language*, and preparing programs in this fashion is called *machine language programming*. The machine code for the flowchart of Figure 9.3 is shown in Figure 9.4. The subroutine begins at location *0200. The two storage locations for count and value are located at the end of the subroutine. When the code was written, the locations of the variables were

*FIGURE 9.4: Machine Code Program for Decimal Output*

| Location | Contents | Mnemonic | Location | Contents | Mnemonic |
|---|---|---|---|---|---|
| *0200 | 7F | CLR | *0220 | 05 | *0226 |
| 1 | 02 | Count | 1 | 7C | INC |
| 2 | 38 | | 2 | 02 | Count |
| 3 | 80 | SUB A | 3 | 38 | |
| *0204 | 64 | 100 | *0224 | 20 | BRA |
| 5 | 25 | BCS | 5 | F7 | *021D |
| 6 | 05 | *020C | 6 | 8B | ADD A |
| 7 | 7C | INC | 7 | 0A | 10 |
| *0208 | 02 | Count | *0228 | B7 | STA A |
| 9 | 38 | | 9 | 02 | Value |
| A | 20 | BRA | A | 39 | |
| B | F7 | *0203 | B | B6 | LDA A |
| *020C | 8B | ADD A | *022C | 02 | Count |
| D | 64 | 100 | D | 38 | |
| E | B7 | STA A | E | BD | JSR |
| F | 02 | Value | F | XX | Print |
| *0210 | 39 | | *0230 | XX | |
| 1 | B6 | LDA A | 1 | B6 | LDA A |
| 2 | 02 | Count | 2 | 02 | Value |
| 3 | 38 | | 3 | 39 | |
| *0214 | BD | JSR | *0234 | BD | JSR |
| 5 | XX | Print | 5 | XX | Print |
| 6 | XX | | 6 | XX | |
| 7 | 7F | CLR | 7 | 39 | RTS |
| *0218 | 02 | Count | *0238 | | Count |
| 9 | 38 | | 0239 | | Value |
| A | B6 | LDA A | | | |
| B | 02 | Value | | | |
| *021C | 39 | | | | |
| D | 80 | SUB A | | | |
| E | 0A | 10 | | | |
| *021F | 25 | BCS | | | |

unknown, so the addresses had to be filled in at the end. The relative values for the branch instructions were all calculated by hand. This method of program preparation may possibly be acceptable for small or nonimportant applications; however, it is clearly inadequate for designing software of any consequence.

## *Assembly Language Programming*

The next step up in program preparation is assembly language programming. Alphabetic symbols are used to represent addresses, opcodes, and operands. A program called an *assembler* is used to convert the symbols to binary code. An assembler is a special case of a type of program called a translator, which converts input statements (called source code) to the binary code executable by the computer (called object code).

An assembly language program consists of a series of statements. A statement comprises a label, an opcode, an operand, and comments. The label, if present, is a symbol which is equivalent to the address of the instruction. The instruction may be the beginning of a subroutine or the beginning of a loop. The label will always be associated with an address value. The opcode is the mnemonic representation of the instruction. The operand is that which is operated upon by the opcode. It may be an immediate value, or it may be a label which refers to an address. The comments, if present, serve to explain or clarify the process.

While each MC6800 instruction can be represented by one assembly language statement, each such statement does not necessarily implement one MC6800 instruction. A trivial example of this is the comment statement. Any statement which has an asterisk (*) in the first column is ignored by the assembler and is treated as a comment. The other examples of this are called *pseudo-operations*, or pseudo-op statements. These statements do not cause any machine code to be generated, but give information to the assembler. They are called pseudo-ops because they appear in the opcode field. The most common pseudo-ops, or assembler directives, are NAM, ORG, EQU, RMB, FCB, FDB, FCC, and END.

The NAM pseudo-op informs the assembler that an assembly language program is about to begin; the operand of the NAM statement is considered the name of the program. The ORG statement tells the assembler where to put the next byte of generated object code; the operand of an ORG statement is usually a hexadecimal value which represents an address. The EQU pseudo-op directs the assembler to equate the label with the address in the operand field. The RMB (reserve memory byte) directs the assembler to set aside some number of bytes without inserting any object code; the operand of RMB specifies how many bytes are to be reserved. The FCB (form constant byte) pseudo-op reserves memory locations with constant values inserted; the operand is the value to be inserted. FDB (form double byte) is similar to FCB, except that FDB inserts 16-bit values. FCC (form constant character) is also similar to FDB, but ASCII values are inserted. The END pseudo-op informs the assembler that no more assembly statements follow.

Figure 9.5 is the assembly language program for the flowchart of Figure 9.3 and the machine code of Figure 9.4. The appearance of this program is much neater. The symbolic labels and operands are functional in nature and make the program easier to follow. In this program the programmer doesn't have to worry about selecting the proper hex opcode for BCS or SUB A or about the address of COUNT or the relative values for the branches. The comments serve to explain the flow of the program. The overall statement that can be made is that the assembler relieves the programmer of many menial tasks, thereby allowing the programmer to concentrate on solving the problem at hand.

Figure 9.6 shows another example of an assembly language program. This short program demonstrates the operation of some of the pseudo-ops. The FCB and FCC pseudo-ops are used to construct a message to be printed by the MIKBUG subroutine PDATA1. The message begins and ends with a carriage return and line feed. The entire message ends with a hexadecimal 4. This informs PDATA1 that all characters have been printed. Note the LDX instruction in the example. It loads the immediate value of the start of the message. This is an excellent example of how symbols are used to represent values.

Now that two sample assembly language programs have been shown, it might appear that they are simple to write and easy to handle. This is not always the case, however, since errors are possible in the writing of programs. Figure 9.7 shows such a program with several assembly errors. Common assembly errors are duplicate labels, undefined operands (specifying a symbolic operand for which there is no corresponding label), incorrect opcodes, and incorrect constants.

The assembler shown in the example is a two-pass assembler, that is, it must read the source data twice before it is able to produce the hex machine code. This feature allows, for example, an instruction to reference a label before the label actually appears. During the first pass, the assembler records all the labels, checks for duplicates and illegal labels, and assigns to each label an address. It also checks all opcodes for validity. The assembler is able to assign addresses to labels because of the ORG pseudo-ops and because it knows how many bytes are occupied by each opcode and pseudo-op (i.e., RMB, FDB). The second pass begins when the END pseudo-op is encountered. On the second pass, the assembler actually builds the object code. It does so by inserting the hex values for the opcodes and by inserting the hex addresses for the labels which appear as operands. It is on the second pass that undefined labels are detected. In addition to

*FIGURE 9.5: Assembly Language Program for Decimal Output*

```
                               04/06/78      MPCASM V2.2     13.13.24     PAGE    1
PASS 1 BEGUN
PASS 2 BEGUN
                               NAM    SAMPLE
      0200                     ORG    $200
                        *      ASSUME VALUE TO BE PRINTED IS IN A-ACCUM
      0200  7F 0238 DECOUT     CLR    COUNT     CLEAR COUNT INITIALLY
      0203  80 64   SUB1       SUB A  #100      SUBTRACT 100
      0205  25 05              BCS    ADD1      IF RESULT NEGATIVE, JUMP
      0207  7C 0238            INC    COUNT     INCREMENT QUOTIENT,
      020A  20 F7              BRA    SUB1      TRY AGAIN
      020C  8B 64   ADD1       ADD A  #100      MAKE POSITIVE
      020E  B7 0239            STA A  VALUE     STORE TEMPORARILY
      0211  B6 0238            LDA A  COUNT     LOAD COUNT FOR PRINTING
      0214  BD 0250            JSR    PRINT     PRINT HUNDREDS DIGIT
      0217  7F 0238            CLR    COUNT     INITIALIZE COUNT AGAIN
      021A  B6 0239            LDA A  VALUE     GET REMAINDER
      021D  80 0A   SUB2       SUB A  #10       NOW DIVIDE BY 10
      021F  25 05              BCS    ADD2
      0221  7C 0238            INC    COUNT
      0224  20 F7              BRA    SUB2
      0226  8B 0A   ADD2       ADD A  #10       MAKE POSITIVE
      0228  B7 0239            STA A  VALUE     STORE REMAINDER
      022B  B6 0238            LDA A  COUNT     LOAD QUOTIENT
      022E  BD 0250            JSR    PRINT     PRINT TENS DIGIT
      0231  B6 0239            LDA A  VALUE     LOAD
      0234  BD 0250            JSR    PRINT     AND PRINT UNITS DIGIT
      0237  39                 RTS              RETURN TO CALLER
      0238  0001    COUNT      RMB    1
      0239  0001    VALUE      RMB    1
            0250    PRINT      EQU    $250
                               END
    STOP
```

building the object code on the second pass, the assembler prints a copy of the input, thus producing the assembly listing.

## *Source Code and Text Editing*

The discussion of assemblers so far has dealt only with the features of the assembler and its handling of assembly language statements. The method of communicating with the assembler has not yet been covered. This section will discuss preparation of data for use by the assembler.

Each assembly language statement is a source code record. Each statement is a series of ASCII characters ending with a carriage return. The carriage return signals the end of one statement and the beginning of another. When using an assembler, it is possible to sit down at a teletype and type in each line for the assembler. This, however, would be very time consuming and error prone, especially since a two-pass assembler requires the source data to be input twice. There is a much more efficient method of preparing data for an assembler which involves the use of a text editor program.

*FIGURE 9.6: Example Assembly Language Program*

```
                                04/06/78      MPCASM V2.2    12.54.34    PAGE   1
PASS 1 BEGUN
PASS 2 BEGUN
00100                           NAM     SAMPL2
00110 0050                      ORG     $50
00120 0050 CE 0100 BEGIN        LDX     #MESG      LOAD INDEX W/ADDR OF MESSAGE
00130 0053 BD E07E              JSR     PDATA1     PRINT MESSAGE
00140 0056 3F                   SWI                RETURN TO MIKBUG
00150 0100                      ORG     $100
00160 0100 0D         MESG      FCB     $0D,$0A,0,0
      0101 0A
      0102 00
      0103 00
00170 0104 47                   FCC     /GOOD MORNING/
      0105 4F
      0106 4F
      0107 44
      0108 20
      0109 4D
      010A 4F
      010B 52
      010C 4E
      010D 49
      010E 4E
      010F 47
00180 0110 0D                   FCB     $D,$A,4
      0111 0A
      0112 04
00190      E07E       PDATA1 EQU     $E07E
00200                           END
     STOP
```

*FIGURE 9.7: Assembly Language Program with Errors*

```
                                04/06/78      MPCASM V2.2    13.45.06    PAGE   1
PASS 1 BEGUN
***** ERROR 204      #10J
00140                SUB1     SUB A    #10J        SUBTRACT 100
***** ERROR 206      #10
00280                ADD1     ADD A    #10         MAKE POSITIVE
***** ERROR 207   P     P
00330                         JSP      PRINT          AND PRINT UNITS DIGIT

  ASSEMBLY ABORTED AFTER PASS 1
     3 ERRORS
     STOP
```

A *text editor*, or simply editor, is a program which aids in creating and maintaining source data. The editor has a series of commands which the programmer can use to manipulate data. The most basic of these commands is the CREATE command. With this command, an initial version of a program is created. When the CREATE command is used, the editor first issues a line number which will identify that particular source statement through all subsequent editing activity. When the line number is printed, the programmer types in the source statement. As soon as the programmer enters the carriage return, the editor prints a higher line number for the next source statement. Entry of all the source statements of a program continues in this manner. The editor provides a method of terminating the entry of source input (for example, entering only a carriage return after a line number has been printed). In this method, an entire program can be created via a text editor.

The real power of a text editor, however, lies in the other commands. There are several commands which aid in the modification of previously created source data. An extension of the CREATE command can add new lines of source data to the end of the existing data. An ADD or INSERT command can add new lines of source data between existing lines. The DELETE command can delete one or more existing lines of source data. The EDIT or CHANGE command can modify existing lines of source code. The MOVE command can move existing lines of source code from one place in the program to another. The FIND command can find and/or print all occurrences of a specific text item. All of these commands are used for modification of existing programs. The modification may be necessary because of errors in the program, or simply because design changes require that the program be altered.

There are a few commands which are used only to aid in the process of creating and modifying source data. The two most common of these are the LIST and RESEQUENCE commands. The LIST command displays all or selected parts of the program. This gives the programmer the opportunity to spot check the program before submitting it to an assembler. The RESEQUENCE command adjusts all the line numbers so that they begin with a certain value and have a constant increment between lines. Another valuable feature of text editors is the TAB feature which provides automatic insertion of spaces up to a predetermined column. This saves manually typing in many spaces (e.g., the spaces between the beginning of the line and the opcode when no label is present).

It would be futile to show examples of text editing because different text editor programs have radically different formats. While many of the functions listed in this chapter are identical to the functions of many text editors, the formats and keywords for implementing these functions are quite different. Basically, however, there are two types of editors, line-number driven and pointer driven.

In a *line-number driven* text editor, virtually all functions are performed with respect to line numbers. Each numbered line terminates with a carriage return. Specifically numbered lines can be added, deleted, or changed. All typed output by the text editor inserts the line number before each line of text. The sample programs of figures 9.5 and 9.6 were created by a line-number driven text editor. The leftmost column in each example contains the editor line numbers. A *pointer driven* text editor relies on a transparent pointer which always points between two characters. Each line terminates with a carriage return, but there is no other identification of the line. All editor functions are performed with respect to the position of the pointer and the line in which the pointer is. Text can be inserted, changed, or deleted beginning with the pointer, or lines can be deleted beginning with the current line.

Either type of editor is sufficient to create and maintain source code. In general, line-number driven editors are easier to use. Also, they occupy more memory than pointer driven editors; for this reason, computer systems with smaller amounts of memory (e.g., microcomputer systems as opposed to minicomputer systems) are more apt to have pointer driven editors. In any event, familiarity is the key. Once one becomes familiar with either type of editor, the user will be able to do all that is necessary, and will be reluctant to switch to the other editor.

In addition to their source data manipulation capabilities, most editors also possess file maintenance capabilities. Whenever a program is to be initially created, the programmer types in single lines of the program. The editor stores the lines in the main memory of the computer system. Changes can be made to this memory copy of the program. When the editing process is complete, the programmer often has the ability to take the memory-resident copy of the program and copy it to an off-line storage device. This makes a permanent copy of the program and frees main memory for other purposes. The program can be written to paper tape, magnetic tape cassettes, large magnetic tapes, or disk storage units. If and when modifications are required, the program can be read from the mass storage device into main memory, modified by the editor, and rewritten to the storage device.

Each quantity of memory written to mass storage is called a *file*. Files can be written to or read from a storage device. Each file can be named by the program that creates it. They can be deleted, renamed, and combined. These capabilities are sometimes provided with editors. When a file is created by an editor, it is called a source file because it is source code.

When files are created, they can be read both by editors and by assemblers. After a source file is created by the editor, it can be read and assembled by the assembler. If there are any assembly errors, or if the program must be modified for any reason, the source code can be fetched by the editor, modified and rewritten. The program can then be reassembled.

As the assembler program runs, it translates the source code into object code. This object code can also be stored on an off-line storage device for subsequent retrieval. In this case, the file is called an object file because it is object code rather than source code. Figure 9.8 shows an assembly listing with the initial prompts for file names. The first prompt asks for the *source input* (SI) file name. The next prompt asks for the object or *machine file* (MF) file name. The third and fourth prompts are for control of the assembly listing. It is possible to get only a listing of assembly

*FIGURE 9.8: Assembly Listing with Options and Object Output*

```
      MOTOROLA M6800 CROSS ASSEMBLER, BCL VERSION 2.2


ENTER SI FILENAME---> SAMPLE
ENTER MF FILENAME---> SMPLOBJ
FULL LISTING ? ------> Y
LISTING ON TTY? -----> Y
---


                               04/06/78      MPCASM V2.2    13.35.04    PAGE    1
PASS 1 BEGUN
PASS 2 BEGUN
                               NAM     SAMPLE
      0200                     ORG     $200
                        *      ASSUME  VALUE  TO  BE PRINTED IS IN A-ACCUM
      0200  7F 0238  DECOUT    CLR     COUNT       CLEAR COUNT INITIALLY
      0203  80 64    SUB1      SUB A   #100        SUBTRACT 100
      0205  25 05              BCS     ADD1        IF RESULT NEGATIVE, JUMP
      0207  7C 0238            INC     COUNT       INCREMENT QUOTIENT,
      020A  20 F7              BRA     SUB1        TRY AGAIN
      020C  8B 64    ADD1      ADD A   #100        MAKE POSITIVE
      020E  B7 0239            STA A   VALUE       STORE TEMPORARILY
      0211  B6 0238            LDA A   COUNT       LOAD COUNT FOR PRINTING
      0214  BD 0250            JSR     PRINT       PRINT HUNDREDS DIGIT
      0217  7F 0238            CLR     COUNT       INITIALIZE COUNT AGAIN
      021A  B6 0239            LDA A   VALUE       GET REMAINDER
      021D  80 0A    SUB2      SUB A   #10         NOW DIVIDE BY 10
      021F  25 05              BCS     ADD2
      0221  7C 0238            INC     COUNT
      0224  20 F7              BRA     SUB2
      0226  8B 0A    ADD2      ADD A   #10         MAKE POSITIVE
      0228  B7 0239            STA A   VALUE       STORE REMAINDER
      022B  B6 0238            LDA A   COUNT       LOAD QUOTIENT
      022E  BD 0250            JSR     PRINT       PRINT TENS DIGIT
      0231  B6 0239            LDA A   VALUE       LOAD
      0234  BD 0250            JSR     PRINT       AND PRINT UNITS DIGIT
      0237  39                 RTS                 RETURN TO CALLER
      0238  0001     COUNT     RMB     1
      0239  0001     VALUE     RMB     1
            0250     PRINT     EQU     $250
                               END
     STOP
      1.009 CP SECONDS EXECUTION TIME
..CONNECT,OUTPT
..COPY,SMPLOBJ,OUTPT
 S00600004844521B
 S11302007F0238806425057C023820F78B64B702AE
 S113021039B60238BD02507F0238B60239800A2549
 S1130220057C023820F78B0AB70239B60238BD02C2
 S10B023050B60239BD02503939
 S9030000FC
```

errors. Following the last prompt is the actual assembly listing. When the assembly is complete, the object output will have been written to file SMPLOB. One of the features of this particular assembler is that object files can be punched on paper tape if a teletype is being used for keyboard entry. The last two commands to the assembler request that the object file be copied to the output device, namely, the teletype. The paper tape punch must be turned on before hitting the carriage-return key. When the return key is struck, the object file is copied to both the teletype and the paper tape punch. The paper tape is punched in the MIKBUG format, and can be loaded by the L command.

At this point, the full software development process has been covered. The process involves specifying the requirements of the program, designing the program with flowcharts, preparing the program with a text editor, assembling the program, and copying the output to paper tape for eventual loading into the computer which will execute the program. It must be emphasized that rarely, if ever, is the process a straight-line process that begins with conception and ends with a working program. The most common problem is assembly errors, but requirements and design also change. Software design is a repetitive process with many iterations of certain steps. A gross-level flowchart of the process is shown in Figure 9.9.

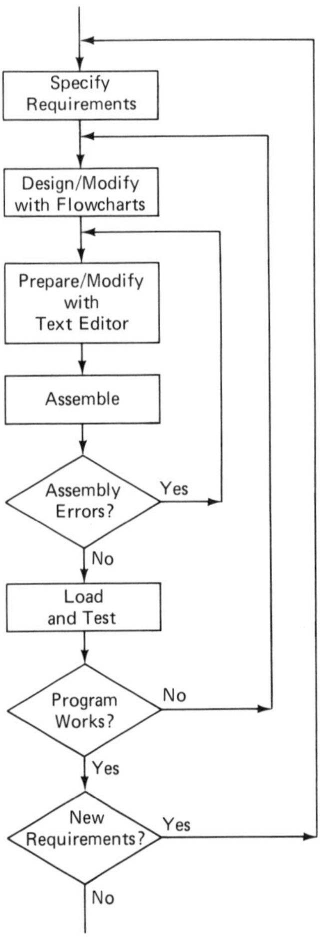


*FIGURE 9.9:*
*Software Development Process*

## *A Development System*

Now that the software development process has been covered, it is appropriate to consider a means for implementing the process. A development system is a computer system which contains all the tools for designing and developing software. These tools include the software tools such as editors and assemblers, as well as hardware tools such as main memory and I/O devices. Most systems involved in development of software for microprocessor systems are themselves based on microprocessors. Many of the currently popular hobby and personal computer systems can be considered development systems because they possess most of the hardware and software tools.

One of the most important features of the software development system is memory. There must be sufficient memory for loading programs and data. This means there must be at least 8K bytes (K is used interchangeably for 1000 or 1024) of read/write memory, but development systems typically include 16K or more bytes of memory. In many cases, some of the necessary programs permanently reside in ROMs, but the requirement still exists for large amounts of read/write memory.

### *Hardware Subsystems*

An important hardware feature of development systems is I/O capability. Several I/O devices are required. The most important of these is a *system control device*. From this device, the operator may request the loading of programs. Each of the programs involved, e.g., the editor and assembler, may use this device for data entry and for outputting short messages. The system control device is generally a teletype or CRT terminal.

Another essential I/O device is a device (or devices) for mass off-line storage. It is used for storage of large volumes of data, source code, and programs for subsequent loading and testing. Typical mass storage devices are paper tape, magnetic tape cassettes, magnetic tape reels and floppy discs or diskettes.

Paper tape is probably the cheapest and most primitive mass storage device. They are very bulky because normally only 8 or 10 bytes are stored per inch of tape. The paper tape readers and punches on teletypes operate at only 10 characters per second, making this device a very slow mass storage method. Although high-speed (300–600 characters per second) paper tape readers and punches are available, they tend to be as expensive as other storage peripherals. Paper tape is very unwieldy because it must always be rolled up when not in use; rolling can be time consuming, and if the operator is not careful, the tapes can be creased, torn, or otherwise rendered unusable. Also, paper tape is not reusable.

The magnetic media are currently the most popular mass storage devices. Magnetic tape cassettes are functionally very similar to paper tape but possess many advantages. Audio quality cassettes are often used in this method. The cassettes tend to be slow, typically 30–60 characters per second. Data is transferred to and from the cassette serially in the RS-232 standard. Because of their small size, they are easily handled. Storage capacity of the cassettes is typically 50,000–100,000 bytes. Audio quality cassette recorders can be used for writing and reading data. With only a few additional electronic components, most commercially available cassette recorders can be interfaced to a microprocessor system. Of course, the magnetic media are totally reusable; if the information on a tape is no longer needed, then new data is simply rewritten on top of the old data. One of the problems with cassette tape storage is reliability: audio grade cassettes can be of dubious quality, and small variations in circuit parameters in the interface can cause data to be erroneously written or read.

The larger tape reels offer a far superior storage device. These tapes can store 800 or 1600 bits per inch (bpi), and operating speeds are on the order of 30–60 inches per second. The storage capacity of these tapes is many millions of bytes. The major disadvantage of magnetic tapes is cost. A tape controller unit is required for every one to four tape drives, and the cost of a drive and a controller is on the order of $10,000.

One of the problems associated with tape storage media is the fact that tape is a sequential access medium, that is, one record of data is written at a time, one after the other. If the tape is positioned at the last data item in a file and the first item is desired, then the tape must rewind until the beginning is reached; this can take several seconds to a minute. Floppy discs and hard discs offer random access to data. A floppy disc is a small device which resembles a 45rpm record. Data is stored in concentric circles (called tracks) on the disc. The read/write head of the floppy disc can move from the outside circle to the inside circle, allowing relatively quick access to data anywhere on the disc. Typical time for the floppy disc read/write head to travel between the extreme outside and the extreme inside tracks is 100–300 milliseconds. Storage capacity of floppy discs is typically one half to a million bytes. Floppy disc systems, though more expensive than tape cassette systems, are not prohibitively expensive.

Another highly desirable I/O device is a high-speed output device, specifically a line printer. A teletype can provide a hard copy for assembly listings and other important documents, but it is very slow. While the speed of teletypes and other terminals is usually stated in characters per second, the speed of line printers is measured in lines per minute, usually one hundred to several hundred. Although line printers can be expensive, they are indispensable to the development of software for any nontrivial application.

In addition to peripheral I/O devices, there are two additional hardware modules which are sometimes included in development systems. These devices are the PROM programmer and the user system evaluator. Recall that a programmable read-only memory (PROM) is one in which the contents are not alterable under normal operating conditions. The contents are alterable, however, when special voltages are applied. These devices, which apply voltages and insert programs into the PROMs, are available as I/O peripherals with which data from main memory can be transferred into PROM addresses. The process of fixing the contents of PROMs is sometimes called "burning." Many different varieties of PROMs exist, each with different data capacity, pin configurations, and burning requirements. The PROM programmer must be able to accommodate all the PROM types required by the purchaser. This is often done with "personality cards," printed circuit boards which may be inserted in the programmer and which provide the environment necessary for the PROM type. If a PROM programmer is used, an eraser may also be necessary. Many ultraviolet (UV) PROMs lose their data when exposed to the light for a period of time. These erasers, while not connected directly to the development system, can be very handy. The PROM altering capability is desirable when a significant amount of prototype testing is required.

The other device valuable in prototype testing is the user system evaluator (USE). The USE consists basically of a cable which connects a system under test to the development system. On one end of the cable are all the signal pins of the development system MPU; these include the address bus, the data bus, the control signals, and, optionally, the two clock signals and the nonmaskable interrupt. On the other end of the cable is a male connector, the signal pins of which are identical to those of an MC6800. If this connector is inserted into the MPU socket of a small computer system, then all the debugging hardware and software in the development system is available for testing the smaller system. The USE can be applied to both hardware and software debugging, and also to production level testing.

A block design representation of a complete development system is shown in Figure 9.10.

### *Software Subsystems*

Just as several hardware subsystems are required in a development system, so are several software modules. The most important of these is the operating system program. It is the operating system which initializes the system at start-up (or after a program crash), interfaces the system control device, and facilitates the loading, execution, and orderly exit from all programs. In most microprocessor-based development systems, the oper-

*FIGURE 9.10: Complete Development System*

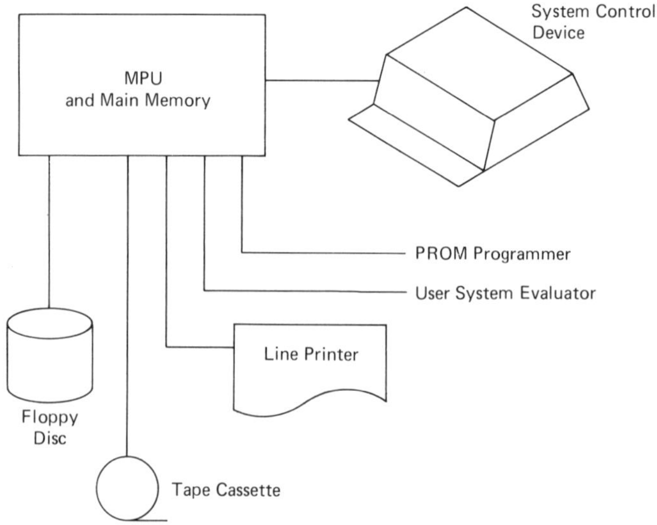


ating system is contained in ROM so it cannot be destroyed by loss of power or by programmer error.

Other programs necessary in a development system are a text editor, one or more language translators, a debugging program, and several utility programs. Included in the language translators is an assembler, but several more translators may be desirable. The BASIC language is becoming very popular in microcomputer systems, as is PL/1 and its derivatives. A few FORTRAN compilers are becoming available. Debugging programs, like MIKBUG, are also desirable. These programs must allow memory and register examination, ability to execute programs and portions of programs, and the ability to insert breakpoint in programs. Utility programs are those which provide general file maintenance and display capabilities. Utilities are not directly related to design, but generally perform useful functions within a system. Examples of utility programs are those which transfer files from one I/O device to another, those which list the name of files on a specific device, and those which examine and display files.

While an individual or industrial concern may not be able to afford the cost of a development system, development capabilities are nevertheless available. Time-sharing services exist which provide most of the resources of a development system. This service is a large-scale computer which is available to many users on a time-shared basis; that is, several users with terminals may use the computer at a given time, but only one user is able to use the CPU for a given period of time. If those periods are small enough, then several users appear to be using the system simultaneously. This is easily implemented since user activity at a terminal is extremely slow compared to the operating speed of the CPU.

Time-sharing services typically provide mass storage facilities and editing and translation programs. High-speed output devices are optional. PROM programmers, hardware debugging features, and other devices intimately related to the microprocessor are rarely, if ever, provided in time-sharing services. The greatest usefulness of time-sharing facilities is quick access to software development tools. A time-sharing service is paid for as it is used; if a need for software development arises, the service may be used for a short period of time. This is often far less expensive than purchasing a full or even somewhat limited development system.

The assemblers available on time-sharing services are called cross assemblers. These are programs written for execution on a given machine which translate assembly code for another machine. They are the opposite of a resident assembler which executes on the machine for which the object code is produced.

## *Summary*

Software development is not a trivial process. As the complexity of the software grows, so does the complexity of the tools necessary to generate software growth. While extensive programs and hardware devices are the mechanics of software development, the keys are specification and program design. Implementation in code should be the last step of any software project.

### *EXERCISES*

1. Develop the flowchart for inputting of a hex character.
2. Develop the flowchart for outputting an 8-bit signed 2's complement binary number. Precede the number with a minus sign if applicable, and don't print leading zeros.
3. Explain briefly the functions of the ORG, EQU, and FDB pseudo-ops.
4. Write the assembly language program for the decimal input subroutine of Figure 9.2. Any errors should cause a jump to the external routine IWERR.
5. List three mass storage devices in ascending order of access speed.
6. Explain briefly the difference between a line number driven text editor and a pointer driven text editor.
7. In typical text editors, what ASCII character separates lines of text?

# 10 Extensions

All discussions so far of the computer have been within the computer itself. In terms of electronic hardware, only digital electronics has been discussed. Voltages of only +5 and ground have been considered, while the vast majority of electronics actually deals with an infinite number of voltage values. Similarly, while we have discussed number representations in the computer, only integers have been considered. This chapter deals with extending the realm of the computer beyond binary voltages and integral numbers. Methods of dealing with analog voltages and with real numbers will now be considered. In addition, an extension of input and output capability will also be covered.

## Digital-to-Analog and Analog-to-Digital Conversion

The computer can only work with logic-level voltages and binary integers even though the vast majority of electronics deals with analog voltages (and currents). All computer handling of analog voltages involves recognition of voltage values for measurement and monitoring, and generation of voltage values for control. There must be a conversion process between the binary values in the computer and the analog voltages on the outside.

An example analog voltage value as a function of time is shown in Figure 10.1. At any given time, the actual voltage value can be approximated by an integral number of voltage increments. In the figure, the highest voltage is represented by eight increments of a fixed voltage value. The actual voltage V is approximately equal to six increments. The approximation will be better if there are a larger number of increments to work with. Each voltage value then can be represented by a number of fixed increments. The computer can either generate these values or measure these values. The first process is called digital-to-analog conversion (D/A) and the second is analog-to-digital (A/D) conversion.

The D/A conversion process is by far simpler and will be discussed

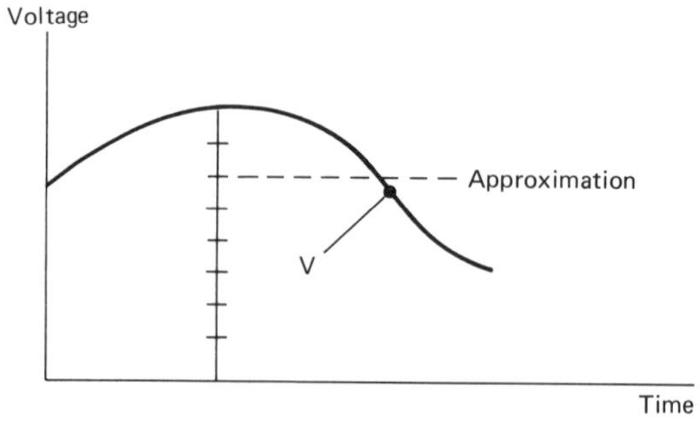


*FIGURE 10.1:*
*Analog Voltage and Approximation*

first. Consider the resistor network of Figure 10.2. Assume that $A$, $B$, and $C$ are logic voltages, either 0 or +5 volts. If $A$ is 0 volts, then no current will flow through R1. If $A$ is +5 volts, then a current of $5/x$ will be generated. $B$ can generate a current of 0 or $5/2x$, and $C$ can generate either 0 or $5/4x$. The current $i$ is the sum of the currents generated by $A$, $B$, and $C$. There are actually 8 different currents which can be generated. The range is 0 to 5 $(1/x + 1/2x + 1/4x)$. The number of voltage sources can be increased to any manageable number. The resistance is halved for each successive voltage source.

D/A converters like these are available as integrated circuit packages. They are classified by the number of digital inputs, $n$, and they are referred to as $n$-bit D/A converters. Each such converter can generate $2^n$ different current values. The most common D/A converters are 6, 7, 8, 10, 12, and 14 bits.

With the addition of a current-to-voltage converter, a digital-value-to-analog-voltage converter is available. Such a converter provides the function of Figure 10.1. Figure 10.3 shows a rough schematic of a D/A converter. The biasing circuitry of the current-to-voltage converter can be selected to adjust the final voltage range of the circuit. The digital inputs of this figure can be connected to one of the output ports of a parallel interface device such as a PIA. In this way, voltages can easily be generated by the microcomputer.

The process of converting an analog voltage value is not nearly so

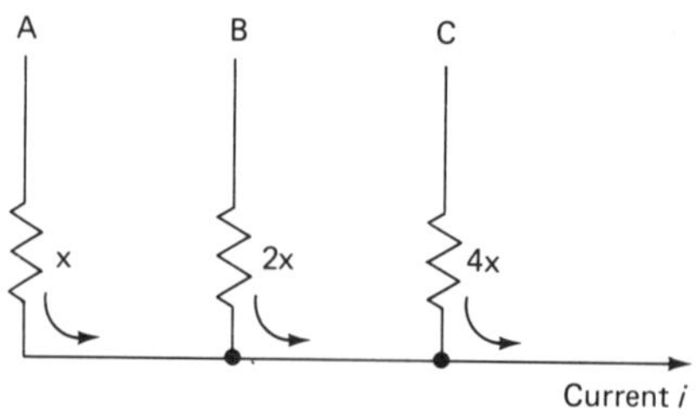


*FIGURE 10.2:*
*Logic Levels to Analog Current*

*FIGURE 10.3: Typical Digital-to-Analog Voltage Conversion Circuit*

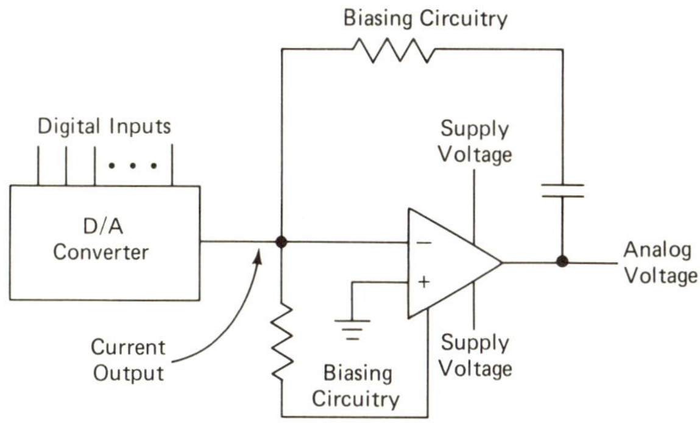


simple. One of the cheapest ways to convert an analog voltage to a digital value is to employ a D/A converter and a comparator. This method is shown in Figure 10.4. An unknown analog voltage is connected to the positive input of the comparator, and a D/A-generated voltage is connected to the negative input. The output of the comparator will be a logic 1 if the unknown voltage is greater than the D/A voltage. The comparator output will be a logic 0 otherwise. By applying known digital values to the D/A converter and evaluating the output of the comparator, the unknown analog value can be determined. This is a repetitive procedure in which many digital values are applied.

There are two popular methods for evaluating the unknown analog voltage. These methods are known as the *ramp* method and the *successive approximation* method. The ramp method proceeds by first applying a value of 1 to the D/A converter and checking the comparator. If the comparator is one, then the analog value is determined. Otherwise, the binary value is incremented and the process is repeated. The method is called ramp because the known value increases at a fixed rate. This method is conceptually simple, but it is very time consuming. For an $n$-bit D/A

*FIGURE 10.4: Typical Analog-Voltage-to-Digital-Value Circuit*

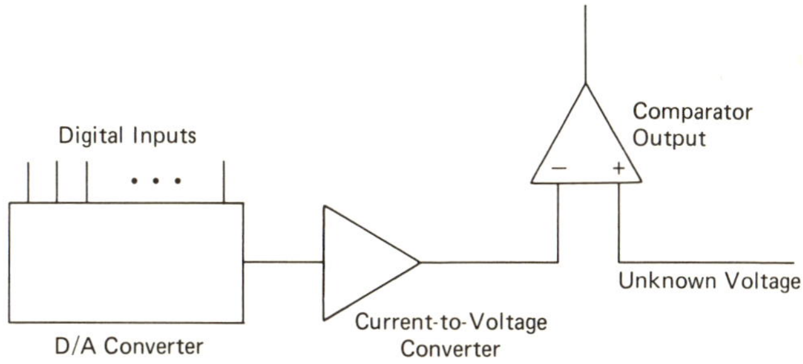

converter, the unknown voltage will be determined in $2^n/2$ repetitions of the process, on the average.

The successive approximation method is conceptually more difficult but much faster. The voltage range is repeatedly divided in half. At the first approximation, the middle voltage value is attempted, thus cutting the entire range in half. By evaluating the comparator it can be determined whether the unknown value is in the upper or lower half. Once this is determined, the second approximation attempts a value which is half of the remaining half. The approximation continues for as many bits as there are in the D/A converter. The final approximation is the binary value of the analog voltage. The concept is shown in Figure 10.5; part (a) shows the voltage range divided into eighths by the first three approximations; part (b) shows the first three attempts for a specific unknown analog value. Figure 10.6 illustrates a procedure for approximating the unknown. The procedure is listed in part (a), and the binary values for the first three attempts are shown in part (b). This procedure is easily converted to a program: the entire range is divided in half by setting the most significant bit and resetting all the others. Each successive half is again halved by setting the next least-significant bits in succession.

The successive approximation method is a much cleaner and quicker method of A/D conversion than the ramp method. For an $n$-bit D/A converter, $n$ and only $n$ approximations must be attempted. The accuracy for conversion by this method is $\pm 1/2$ bit.

Analog-to-digital packages can be purchased which convert an analog signal directly to a digital value without any programming activity. These devices, which provide high performance, tend to be very expensive. The procedures described above are valid and inexpensive methods of analog-to-digital conversion.

*FIGURE 10.5: Successive Approximation Concept*

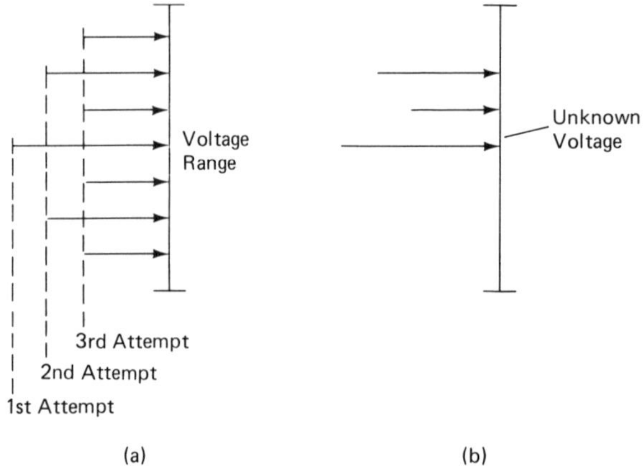

*FIGURE 10.6: Analog-to-Digital Conversion Flowchart and Sample Values*

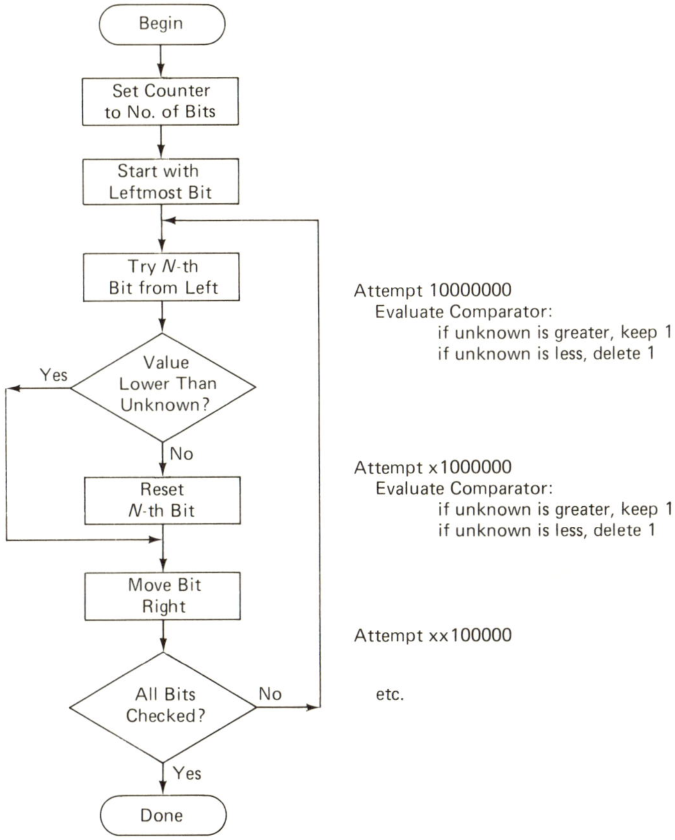


(a) Successive approximation flowchart (b) Samples

## Binary Multiplication

So far, only two arithmetic processes, addition and subtraction, have been covered. Although virtually all arithmetic processes can be accomplished with addition and subtraction, the processes can be done much more efficiently with higher-level operations, one of the most straightforward of which is multiplication. The example of this chapter covers only a very simple multiplication: the multiplication of two unsigned binary integers.

The two components of the multiplication process are the multiplier and the multiplicand, and the result is the product. For an $n$-bit multiplier and an $m$-bit multiplicand, the product will be up to $n + m$ bits. The basic process is shown in Figure 10.7. The process in binary is the same as in decimal. The multiplicand is multiplied by each digit of the multiplier, and

*FIGURE 10.7: Multiplication Process*

| Binary | | Decimal |
|---|---|---|
| 1001 | multiplier | 9 |
| 1101 | multiplicand | 13 |
| 1001 | | 27 |
| 0000 | | 9 |
| 1001 | | |
| 1001 | | |
| 1110101 | product | 117 |

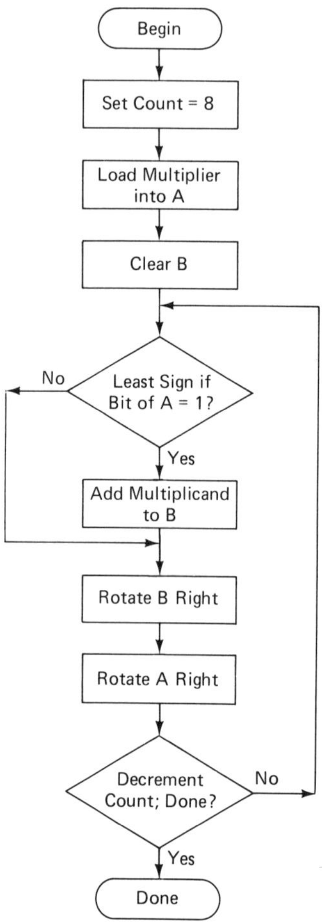


*FIGURE 10.8: Flowchart for Binary Multiplication*

the least significant digit of the partial product begins in the same column as the multiplier digit. In binary, the multiplicand is multiplied by either a one or a zero, so the partial products can be determined by simple addition. The final product is the addition of each of the partial products.

On paper, the process is quite simple, and in the computer it is not that much more difficult. For convenience, an 8-bit multiplier and an 8-bit multiplicand will be used. In the computer the product will be cumulative as the multiplicand is added or not added, depending on each bit of the multiplier. If two accumulators are available, as they are in the MC6800, the 8-bit multiplication can be accomplished in a very small number of steps. The flowchart of the multiplication process is shown in Figure 10.8. The first step is to load the multiplier into accumulator A. The product, accumulator B, is then cleared. A check is made of the least significant bit of the multiplier; if it is 1, the multiplicand is added to the product. In either event, the product is rotated 1 bit right, then the multiplier is rotated 1 bit right. The rotate instruction moves the least significant bit of B through the carry to A. This has the effect of extending the product and eliminating one bit of the multiplier. The least significant bit of accumulator A, which is actually the second multiplier bit, is checked. If it's 1, the multiplicand is added to the already shifted product. The product is again rotated, followed by the multiplier. After 8 iterations, the multiplier will be completely lost, and the product will occupy both accumulators.

It seems that, with two accumulators, the MC6800 was tailor-made for binary multiplication. The same process can readily be performed in other microprocessors, and multiplication of numbers of any bit length can also be multiplied in most microprocessors. Signed 2's complement multiplication can also be performed, but the process is not quite so simple. Also, division, while similar in theory, is quite difficult in practice.

## *Floating-Point Numbers*

One of the most severe restrictions associated with microprocessors is the range of numbers which can be represented. So far, only integers have been considered. With an 8-bit microprocessor, only 256 values can be represented. The restriction can be alleviated somewhat by using 2 bytes to represent numbers. This extends the range of integers, but still excludes all real numbers. An artificial solution to this problem is available using BCD numbers. If 6-digit BCD numbers are used (occupying 3 bytes), then two of them may be assumed to be fractional digits. This may be sufficient for representation of dollars and cents, but the general problem of real numbers still exists. The only acceptable solution is floating-point representation.

In high school physics and chemistry, scientific notation is used to represent real numbers. The primary advantage is that it can easily represent very large and very small numbers. In scientific notation, any number can be represented as $a \times 10^b$ where $a$ is any real number between 1.00 and 9.999, and $b$ is an integer exponent. Examples of scientific notation are $-6.23 \times 10^{21}$ and $7.07 \times 10^{-12}$.

Floating point is a similar method of representing real numbers, but it lends itself more easily to computer representation. There are a few popular representations of floating numbers, but only one will be considered. Numbers can be represented as $m \times 16^e$, where $m$, called the mantissa, is a number between 0 and 1 (exclusive), and $e$ is the integer exponent of 16. The mantissa is always a hexadecimal fraction between .000001 and .FFFFFF. The point at the left of the numbers is the hexadecimal point (not the decimal point), or, in general, the radix point. Typical floating-point numbers are:

$$.8 \times 16^0 = \frac{8}{16} \times 16^0 = .5_{10}$$

$$-.C \times 16^2 = -\frac{12}{16} \times 16^2 = -12 \times 16 = -192_{10}$$

$$-.1 \times 16^1 = -\frac{1}{16} \times 16 = -1$$

$$.64 \times 16^2 = \frac{100}{256} \times 16^2 = 100_{10}$$

Note that the floating-point numbers have been written in hexadecimal and have subsequently been converted to decimal.

The reason why floating-point numbers lend themselves to computer representation is that both the mantissa and exponent can be stored as integers, even if they are used otherwise. Typical floating-point representations in microprocessors occupy 32 bits as shown in Figure 10.9. The leftmost bit is the sign of the number, 1 for negative, 0 for positive. The next seven bits are the exponent of the number. The exponent is expressed in excess $-64$ notation, that is, 64 must be subtracted from the actual binary value in order to determine the true exponent. The mantissa occupies the

*FIGURE 10.9: Floating-point Representation in Microprocessors*

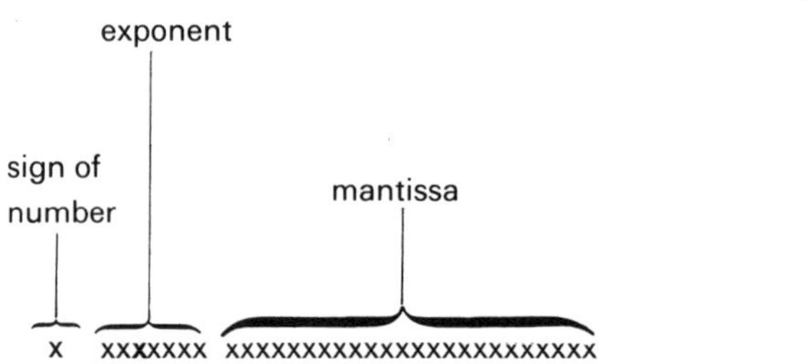

remainder, 6 hex characters. In this representation, the most significant digit of the mantissa is always nonzero, and numbers from $1 \times 16^{-70}$ to almost $1 \times 16^{64}$ can be represented.

In computer representation, the four preceding examples are as follows:

$$
\begin{aligned}
&40800000 = .8 \times 16^{(64-64)} = .5_{10} \\
&\text{C2C00000} \qquad\qquad\quad = -192_{10} \\
&\text{C1100000} \qquad\qquad\quad = -1 \\
&42640000 \qquad\qquad\quad\; = 100_{10}
\end{aligned}
$$

It is not enough to simply represent real numbers in a computer system. The arithmetic operations must also be possible. The processes will be described here but not explored in detail. Addition and subtraction of floating-point numbers is similar to that of binary integers. The only problem is that the exponents of the two numbers must be equal. The process of adjusting exponents for addition or subtraction is called *normalization.* In floating-point multiplication, multiplication of the mantissas proceeds as in binary multiplication, and the two exponents are added. Similarly, in floating-point division, the mantissas are divided as in binary division, and the exponent of the divisor is subtracted from the exponent of the dividend.

Throughout many floating-point operations, a *guard byte* is employed. The guard byte is an extra pair of hexadecimal digits appended to the least significant end of the mantissa. Arithmetic operations are then performed with 8 digits, rather than 6. Following the operations, the result is rounded to 6 digits. The guard byte is used to preserve accuracy.

In many minicomputers and most large-scale computers, floating-point numbers and operations are handled by hardware. Registers of 32 bits are used as floating-point accumulators. Special arithmetic units have been designed which can perform floating-point arithmetic by hardware. Unfortunately, this technology is not yet available to microprocessors; numbers must be converted to floating point by software, the operations must be performed by software (usually 8 bits at a time), and conversions from floating point must be done by software. This means that large amounts of memory must be committed to programs which handle floating-point numbers. For those applications requiring the range and accuracy of floating-point numbers, substantial program design time and memory must be committed.

## *Direct Memory Access I/O*

The input/output process is the transferring of data between the computer system and peripheral devices via an interface. In normal operation, the microprocessor initializes the interface, then begins the transfer process. In an output operation, the microprocessor loads a byte from memory, stores it out to the device, then resumes its other tasks until the device is ready for another byte. The input process is similar. The microprocessor determines the readiness of the device by testing the device (a process known as polling), or the device may generate an interrupt. In addition, the microprocessor must keep track of what address in memory is involved in the transfer and how many bytes must be transferred.

For low-speed devices, such as teletypes or 30-character-per-second cassette tapes, this is an acceptable practice. But many I/O devices operate at speeds of thousands of bytes per second, and hundreds of bytes are often involved in a transfer operation. In these latter cases, much of the microprocessor's time would be spent tending to I/O activity, with little left for other program execution. There are applications in which the microprocessor's availability is a key resource.

The direct memory access (DMA) technique offers an alternative method in which data can be transferred directly between system memory and an I/O device without processor intervention. In this technique a special device known as DMA controller is required to coordinate the activity. The DMA controller must have access to both system memory and the particular I/O device or device controller. Figure 10.10 shows a typical system using DMA. Note that the DMA controller responds to addresses generated by the microprocessor and also generates addresses to which system memory responds.

In order to control the transfer of data, the DMA controller must know three things: (1) whether the data is to be input to or output from system memory; (2) the total number of bytes to be transferred; (3) the memory address to which or from which data must be transferred. The logical structure of a typical DMA controller is shown in Figure 10.11. The

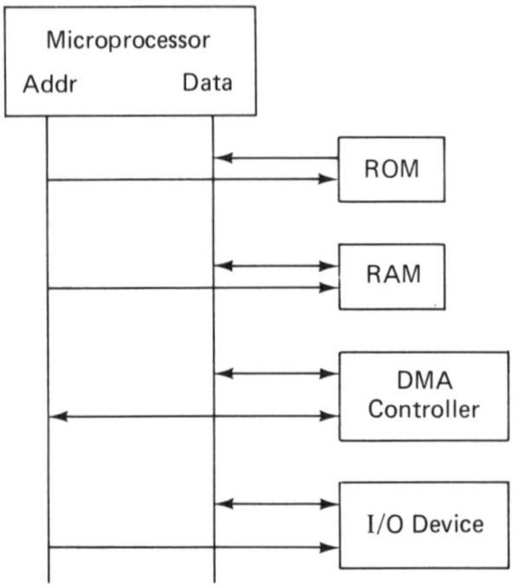


*FIGURE 10.10:*
*Typical System Using DMA Controller*

*FIGURE 10.11: Typical DMA Controller*

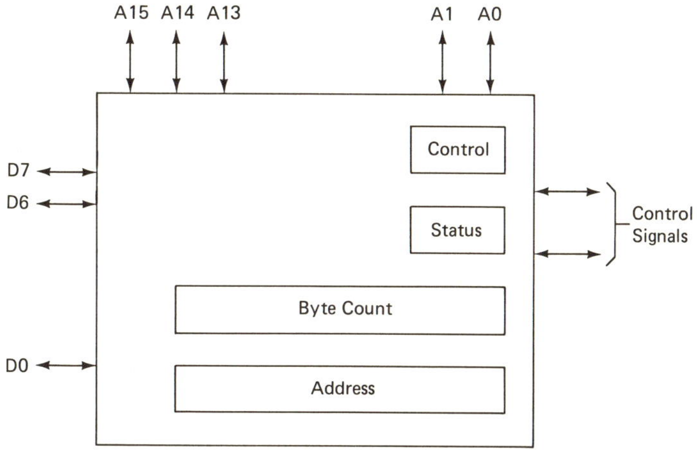


control register will contain information such as the direction of transfer and possibly some information concerning the nature of the I/O device. The status register may contain information such as error indications received from the I/O device and whether or not the controller is busy or idle. The byte count register, a down counter which initially contains the number of bytes to be transferred, holds the remaining number of bytes to be transferred. The address register is an up counter containing the address of the byte to be transferred next. All of these registers must be available to the microprocessor for loading and storing, as are the registers of, for example, the PIA.

Using the DMA controller, the I/O data transfer process is now radically different. The microprocessor first stores all the necessary information in the DMA controller. The microprocessor then initiates the I/O device for data transfer, leaving itself free for other activity until all the data has been transferred. As the I/O device is ready for another byte to be transferred, it will inform the DMA controller. The DMA controller then outputs the appropriate address for transfer of another byte. Note that the DMA controller supplies the address, and the peripheral device either receives data from or issues data to the system data bus. After a byte is transferred, the address register is incremented and the byte count register is decremented. Bytes are transferred in this manner until the byte count register reaches zero. At this time, there is an indication that the total transfer is complete. This indication may be the setting of a bit in the status register or the generation of an interrupt. The microprocessor can be sure that the I/O transfer has taken place, and it is free to initiate another I/O operation.

There is only one problem remaining in the DMA transfer process.

During the time in which I/O data is transferred, the microprocessor is using the address and data busses for fetching instructions and for loading and storing data. Recall that in normal operation, the microprocessor transfers data when the $\phi 2$ clock is high, and internal operations occur when the $\phi 1$ clock is high. It is the responsibility of the DMA controller to make sure that the address and data busses are available for the transfer of data. This may be done by temporarily stopping the clocks (after the negative-going edge of $\phi 2$) by stretching the $\phi 1$ clock, or by applying a logic 0 to the halt input of the microprocessor. In either of the first two events, the DMA controller must set the appropriate levels on TSC and DBE in order to ensure that all busses are in the tristate level. Recall also that the clocks must not be stopped too long because the microprocessor is a dynamic device.

A microcomputer system must be altered substantially in order to allow DMA transfer of I/O data. In return for this high cost, there must be an application characterized by high speed, high volume I/O, and also by a high level of microprocessor activity. DMA is essentially a high-performance computer technique.

## Summary

Chapter 10 has presented three techniques which extend the capability of microprocessor systems. The first of these extends the primarily digital microprocessor into the world of analog electronics; the second expands the primarily integer-oriented computer into the world of real numbers; and the third extends a computer system into a high-performance environment. Each of these techniques requires additional cost for hardware and software, but if the system requirements are there, the techniques are available.

### EXERCISES

1. How many distinct voltages can be generated with a 7-bit D/A converter? With a 12-bit D/A converter?

2. In an A/D application using an 8-bit D/A converter in which the voltage range is $-4$ to $+6$, what is the voltage value represented by each binary value? What voltage values do the binary values 00010110 and 11011001 represent? Approximately what binary value would correspond to a voltage of 2.62 volts?

3. Perform the following multiplications in binary:

| a) 0110 | b) 1111 | c) 01001110 |
|---|---|---|
| 1100 | 1111 | 11000111 |

4. What decimal values do the following floating-point quantities represent?

   a) 41340000  b) BF200000  c) 40C00000

5. Represent the following decimal values in floating-point notation:

   a) 16  b) $1/16$  c) 3.75  d) 256.5

6. In order to transfer I/O data into memory, what three items does the DMA controller need to know from the microprocessor?
7. What is the importance of the $\phi 1$ and $\phi 2$ clocks in DMA transfer?

# 11 Trends

The microprocessor itself is an astounding technical development. Computer power is now available to thousands of applications in which it was unthinkable to apply a computer. But these very applications are putting new demands on microprocessor manufacturers for developments which are even more outstanding. The technology which miniaturized electronic circuitry has progressed, and even smaller circuits are being developed. Within the framework of more miniaturization, there are two distinct trends.

The first major trend is to put more raw computing power into the microprocessor itself. This increased power may take the form of more bits on which to operate. At the time of writing, several manufacturers have announced plans to market 16-bit microprocessors. Basically the same operations will be available, but they will be available with the larger data word. Since many real-world applications must be represented by more than 8 bits, the 16-bit functions mean an increase in processing speed and power. The second tendency toward power takes the form of more complex and more varied operations on 8-bit data. This increased power is manifested in more internal registers, instructions, addressing modes, and more powerful instructions. The intent of this type of development is to provide a smaller and cheaper replacement for minicomputers.

At the time of writing, Motorola announced plans for the MC6809 microprocessor. The MC6809 is essentially an 8-bit microprocessor with 16-bit capabilities. It is a 40-pin device with only an 8-bit data bus, however, many 16-bit operations are possible. Loads, stores, adds, and subtracts with memory operands are accomplished by consecutive 8-bit operations. Internally, 16-bit shifts and rotates are possible.

The real power of the MC6809 lies in the greatly enhanced instruction set. The following is a description of some of its new features. There are two index registers and two stack pointers, any of which may be used with indexed instructions. The branch instructions may have 8- or 16-bit relative values, and the indexed instructions may have 8- or 16-bit offsets. There are register transfer and register exchange instructions. There are multiple

*FIGURE 11.1: MC6809 Product Specification Sheet* (Courtesy of Motorola Semiconductor Products Inc.)

## HIGH-PERFORMANCE MICROPROCESSOR

- **MC6800 COMPATIBLE**
  - Hardware — Interfaces With All M6800 Peripherals
  - Software — Upward Compatible Instruction Set and Addressing Modes
- **HARDWARE FEATURES**
  - On-Chip Oscillator (MC6809)
  - Optional ÷1 External Clock Inputs (MC6809E)
  - MRDY Input Extends Data Access Times for Use With Slow Memory
  - $\overline{\text{BREQ}}$/TSC Allows Quick Access to Bus for DMA and Memory Refresh
  - Last Instruction Cycle Output for Identification of Opcode Fetch (MC6809E)
  - Fast Interrupt Request Input Stacks Only Program Counter and Condition Code
  - Interrupt Acknowledge Output Allows Vectoring by Device
  - Busy Output Eases Multiprocessor Design (MC6809E)
- **ARCHITECTURAL FEATURES**
  - Two 8-Bit Accumulators Can Be Concatenated to Form One 16-Bit Accumulator
  - Two 16-Bit Index Registers
  - Two 16-Bit Indexable Stack Pointers
  - Direct Page Register Allows Direct Addressing Throughout Memory Space
- **INSTRUCTION SET**
  - Extended Range Branches
  - 16-Bit Arithmetic
  - Push/Pull Any Register or Set of Registers To/From Either Stack
  - 8 × 8 Unsigned Multiply
  - Transfer/Exchange Any Two Registers of Equal Size
  - Enhanced Pointer Register Manipulation
- **ADDRESSING MODES**
  - All MC6800 Modes, Plus PC Relative, Extended Indirect, Indexed Indirect, and PC Relative Indirect
  - Direct Addressing Available for All Memory Access Instructions
  - Index Mode Options Include Accumulator or Up to 16-Bit Constant Offset, and Auto-Increment/Decrement (by 1 or 2) With Any of the Four Pointer Registers

# MOS

**(N-CHANNEL, SILICON-GATE, DEPLETION LOAD)**

## HIGH-PERFORMANCE MICROPROCESSOR

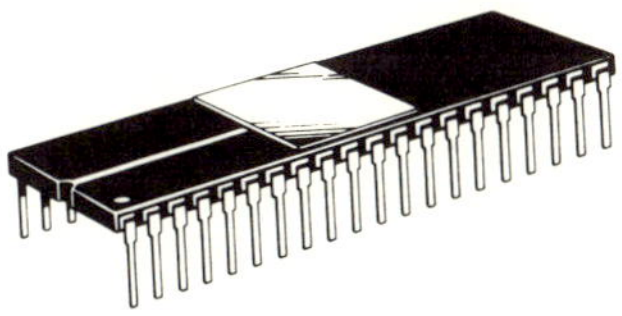

**L SUFFIX**
CERAMIC PACKAGE
CASE 715

NOT SHOWN:
**P SUFFIX**
PLASTIC PACKAGE
CASE 711

**FIGURE 1 – BLOCK DIAGRAMS**

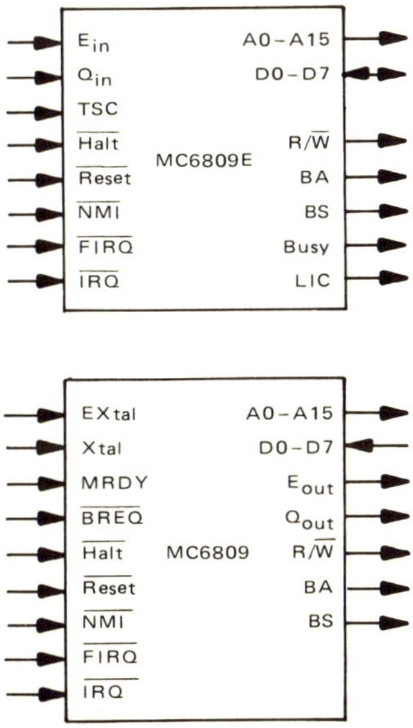

register PSHs and PULs. Index registers may be automatically incremented or decremented on indexed instructions. There is an 8-bit by 8-bit unsigned binary multiply. Immediate operands may be added to any of the index registers or stack pointers. Many of these new instructions have multiple-byte opcodes. A product specification sheet is shown in Figure 11.1. The MC6809 is hardware- and bus-compatible with the entire Motorola family of peripheral devices.

The second major trend in microprocessor development is the incorporation of more computer functions in one package. The ultimate goal is to provide a complete computer system in a single integrated circuit package. Such an integrated circuit will require only a power supply and a clock pulse to provide complete computer capability. Computers of this type will find application in industrial areas where sophisticated control is required. This development will allow microcomputers to function where current microprocessor-based systems are inadequate. Motorola has announced two products along these lines. The first is the MC6802, which requires a minimum of two chips for a complete system, and the MC6801, which can be a 1-chip computer.

The MC6802 is simply an MC6800 CPU with 128 bytes of RAM packaged in one chip. Its instruction set is identical to that of the MC6800. The MC6802 contains an on-chip clock circuit which requires only a crystal input rather than a full two-phase clock. Thirty-two bytes of the on-board RAM may be retained via a low power Vcc input. The 128 bytes of RAM may be used, or they may be disabled so external RAM can be used.

The MC6802, together with the Motorola MC6846 ROM, I/O, and TIMER chip, provide a complete computer system in two chips. The MC6802, however, retains the complete flexibility and expandability of the MC6800: it can address up to 64K bytes of memory. The product specification sheets for the MC6802 and the MC6846 are shown in figures 11.2 and 11.3.

The Motorola MC6801 is a complete computer on a single chip. It requires only a +5 volt power supply and a crystal for operation. The MC6801 contains 2K bytes of ROM, 128 bytes of RAM, and a complete MC6800 in a single 40-pin chip. The instruction set of the MC6801 is identical to that of the MC6800, except that the MC6801 has nine new instructions, one of which is an 8-bit by 8-bit unsigned integer multiply. In addition, the MC6801 has 31 I/O lines. Twenty-four of these I/O lines, divided into three 8-bit ports, are parallel and are almost identical to the lines of an MC6820 PIA. Each of the 24 lines may be input or output, depending on the contents of the associated data direction registers. There is also an on-board timer-counter, and there is an on-board serial I/O line. In addition to the reset interrupt, nonmaskable interrupt, and software interrupt, five other interrupt vectors are reserved.

*FIGURE 11.2: MC6802 Microprocessor Product Specification Sheet* (Courtesy of Motorola Semiconductor Products Inc.)

## MICROPROCESSOR WITH CLOCK AND RAM

The MC6802 is a monolithic 8-bit microprocessor that contains all the registers and accumulators of the present MC6800 plus an internal clock oscillator and driver on the same chip. In addition, the MC6802 has 128 bytes of RAM on board located at hex addresses 0000 to 007F. The first 32 bytes of RAM, at hex addresses 0000 to 001F, may be retained in a low power mode by utilizing $V_{CC}$ standby, thus facilitating memory retention during a power-down situation.

The MC6802 is completely software compatible with the MC6800 as well as the entire M6800 family of parts. Hence, the MC6802 is expandable to 65K words.

- On-Chip Clock Circuit
- 128 x 8 Bit On-Chip RAM
- 32 Bytes of RAM Are Retainable
- Software-Compatible with the MC6800
- Expandable to 65K words
- Standard TTL-Compatible Inputs and Outputs
- 8 Bit Word Size
- 16 Bit Memory Addressing
- Interrupt Capability

**MOS**

**(N-CHANNEL, SILICON-GATE, DEPLETION LOAD)**

**MICROPROCESSOR WITH CLOCK AND RAM**

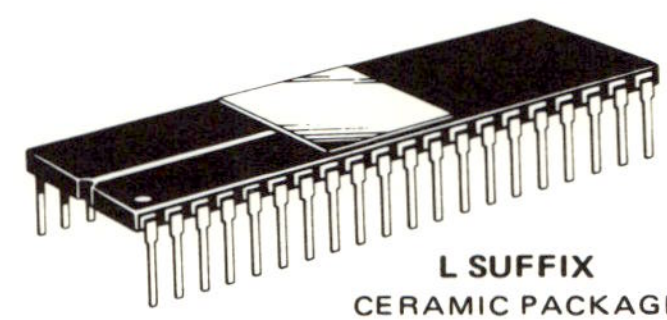

**L SUFFIX**
CERAMIC PACKAGE
CASE 715

**P SUFFIX**
PLASTIC PACKAGE
CASE 711

*FIGURE 11.3: MC6846 ROM, I/O, Timer Chip Product Specification Sheet*
(Courtesy of Motorola Semiconductor Products Inc.)

## ROM–I/O–TIMER

The MC6846 combination chip provides the means, in conjunction with the MC6802, to develop a basic 2-chip microcomputer system. The MC6846 consists of 2048 bytes of mask-programmable ROM, an 8-bit bidirectional data port with control lines, and a 16-bit programmable timer-counter.

This device is capable of interfacing with the MC6802 (basic MC6800, clock and 128 bytes of RAM) as well as the MC6800 if desired. No external logic is required to interface with most peripheral devices.

- 2048 8-Bit Bytes of Mask-Programmable ROM
- 8-Bit Bidirectional Data Port for Parallel Interface plus Two Control Lines
- Programmable Interval Timer-Counter Functions
- Programmable I/O Peripheral Data, Control and Direction Registers
- Compatible with the Complete M6800 Microcomputer Product Family
- TTL-Compatible Data and Peripheral Lines
- Single 5-Volt Power Supply

**FIGURE 1 – TYPICAL MICROCOMPUTER**

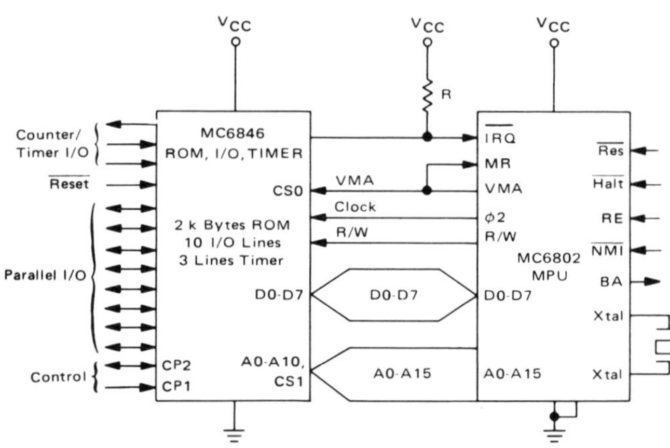


Figure 1 is a block diagram of a typical cost effective microcomputer. The MPU is the center of the microcomputer system and is shown in a minimum system interfacing with a ROM combination chip. It is not intended that this system be limited to this function but that it be expandable with other parts in the M6800 Microcomputer family.

# MOS

**(N-CHANNEL, SILICON-GATE, DEPLETION LOAD)**

## ROM–I/O–TIMER

**L SUFFIX**
CERAMIC PACKAGE
CASE 715

NOT SHOWN:
**P SUFFIX**
PLASTIC PACKAGE
CASE 711

**FIGURE 2 – ROM–I/O–TIMER**

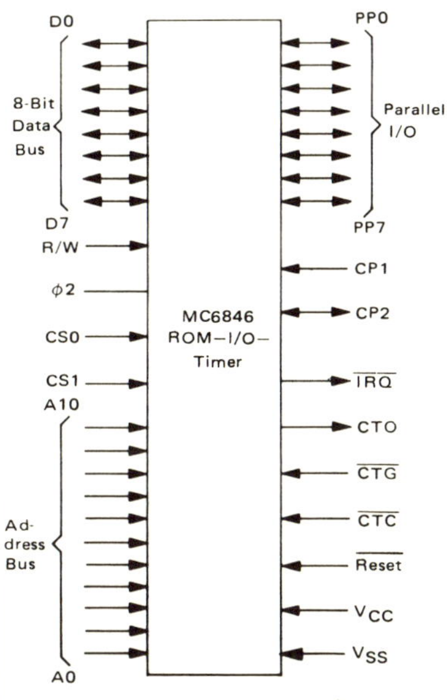

*FIGURE 11.4: MC6801 Product Specification Sheet* (Courtesy of Motorola Semiconductor Products Inc.)

## MICROCOMPUTER UNIT (MCU)

The MC6801 MCU is an 8-bit microcomputer system which is expandable, using the M6800 microprocessor family. The MC6801 MCU is object code compatible with the M6800 instruction set with improved execution times of key instructions plus, several new 16-bit and 8-bit instructions. The MC6801 MCU can operate single chip or be expanded to 65K words. The MC6801 MCU is TTL compatible and requires one +5.0 volt power supply. The MC6801 MCU has 2K bytes of ROM and 128 bytes of RAM on board UART and parallel I/O and three 16-bit timer functions.

- Expanded M6800 instruction set
- On-Board UART
- Object code compatible
- 16-Bit Timer
- Single chip or expandable to 65K words
- 2K bytes of ROM
- 128 bytes of RAM (64 bytes retainable)
- 31 parallel I/O lines
- Internal Clock/Divided-by-Four mask option (MC6801)
- External Clock/Divide-by-One mask option (MC6801E)
- TTL compatible inputs and outputs
- Interrupt capability

FIGURE 1 – SINGLE-CHIP MICROCOMPUTER BLOCK DIAGRAM

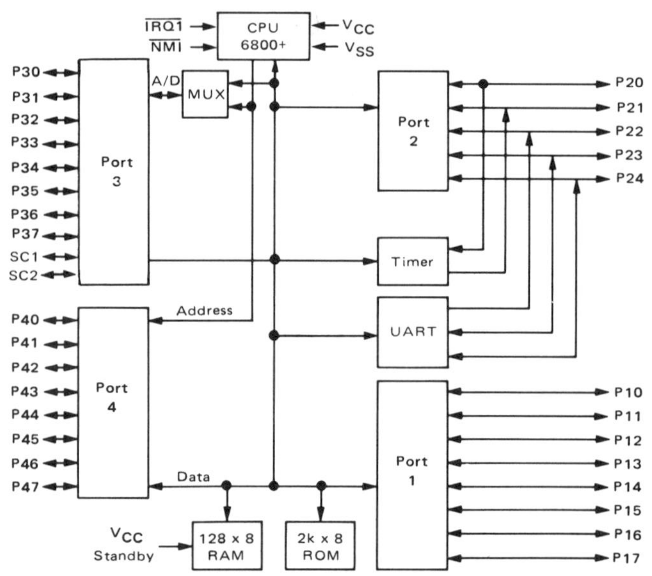

# MOS

**(N-CHANNEL, SILICON-GATE DEPLETION LOAD)**

**MICROCOMPUTER**

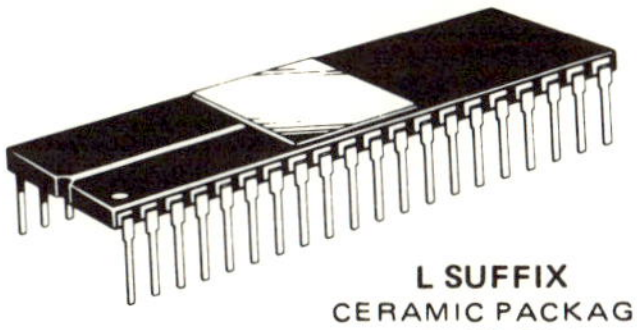

**L SUFFIX**
CERAMIC PACKAGE
CASE 715

**P SUFFIX**
PLASTIC PACKAGE
CASE 711

**FIGURE 2 – MC6801**

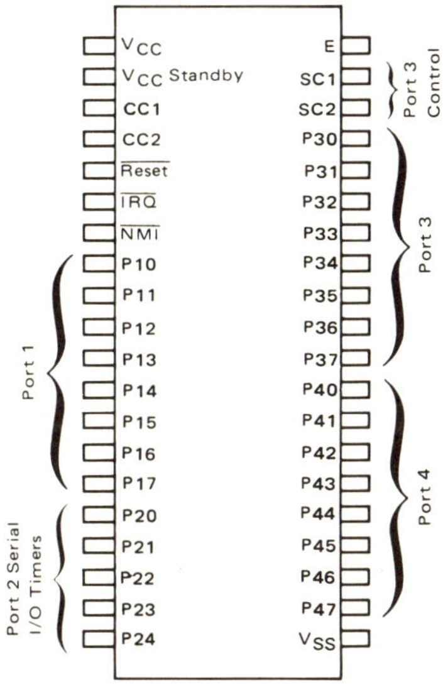

The MC6801 has three different modes of operation, selectable at the time of purchase. In the first mode, all I/O lines are used for I/O, and the only memory possible in the system is the internal memory. In the second mode, up to 8 of the I/O lines may be used as address bits for addressing external memory. In the third mode, all 8 bits of one port are address bits, and up to 8 bits of a second port may be used as address bits. In the second and third modes, the bits of the I/O ports not designated as address bits may be used as parallel input data lines. Also, in the second and third modes, one of the ports is reserved as a system data bus.

The product specification sheet for the MC6801 microcomputer is shown in Figure 11.4. While the MC6801 is a flexible and expandable device, its power lies primarily in single-chip industrial applications. The 2K bytes of ROM and 128 bytes of RAM can accommodate substantial programs.

Looking beyond the announced devices at this time, even more complex ones are on the horizon. Floating-point and D/A capabilities will eventually be incorporated in the computer system on a chip. The chip will contain more and more internal memory. In the long run, the limiting item will not be the complexity or number of functions on the chip, but will, in fact, be the interface between the chip and the outside world. The number of signal pins will turn out to be a formidable constraint. Increasing development of the technology will mean higher and higher operating speeds.

Regardless of how expansive are the increases in the technology, an understanding of the fundamental properties of microprocessors will be essential. Familiarity with binary numbers, operation of logic gates, the basic architecture of computers, instructions, and design of programs will still be the keys to applying microcomputers to gainful applications. It has been the intention here to provide that necessary familiarity. Also, while the Motorola product family has been shown extensively, most microprocessors have a variety of products and intend to expand with the technology. It is hoped that this book has provided a point of reference in the study of other microprocessor families.

# Index